THE GREATEST FAILURE IN ALL HISTORY

John Spargo

1920

***
Mauro Liistro Editore
© 2016 Some Righits Reserved

***

ISBN-13: 978-1530806492

Table of Contents

TABLE OF CONTENTS	3
"THE GREATEST FAILURE IN ALL HISTORY"	4
I WHY HAVE THE BOLSHEVIKI RETAINED POWER?	15
II THE SOVIETS	20
III THE SOVIETS UNDER THE BOLSHEVIKI	29
IV THE UNDEMOCRATIC SOVIET STATE	44
V THE PEASANTS AND THE LAND	68
VI THE BOLSHEVIKI AND THE PEASANTS	86
VII THE RED TERROR	127
VIII INDUSTRY UNDER SOVIET CONTROL	171
IX THE NATIONALIZATION OF INDUSTRY—I	211
X THE NATIONALIZATION OF INDUSTRY—II	243
XI FREEDOM OF PRESS AND ASSEMBLY	267
XII "THE DICTATORSHIP OF THE PROLETARIAT"	302
XIII STATE COMMUNISM AND LABOR CONSCRIPTION	316
XIV LET THE VERDICT BE RENDERED	351
II Regulation Concerning the Administration of National Undertakings	390

"THE GREATEST FAILURE IN ALL HISTORY"

Books by

JOHN SPARGO

RUSSIA AS AN AMERICAN PROBLEM
THE PSYCHOLOGY OF BOLSHEVISM
BOLSHEVISM
AMERICANISM AND SOCIAL DEMOCRACY
SOCIAL DEMOCRACY EXPLAINED

"BOLSHEVISM" "THE PSYCHOLOGY OF BOLSHEVISM"

"RUSSIA AS AN AMERICAN PROBLEM"

"SOCIAL DEMOCRACY EXPLAINED"

THE GREATEST FAILURE IN ALL HISTORY

Original Copyright, 1920, by Harper & Brothers
Printed in the United States of America
Published August, 1920

***

2016 Mauro Liistro Editore
Some rights reserved

***

To The
MISGUIDED, THE MISTAKEN, AND THE MISINFORMED

Who Have Hailed Bolshevism in Russia as the Advent of
A NEW FREEDOM

I Submit a Part of the Indisputable Evidence Upon Which, as a Socialist, Who Believes in Democracy in Government and Industry—and in the Generous Individualism Which Communism of Opportunity Alone Can Give—I Base My Condemnation of Bolshevism as a Mad Attempt, by a Brutal and Degrading Tyranny, to Carry Out an Impossible Program

NOTE

My thanks are due to many friends, in this country and in Europe, for their kindly co-operation, assistance, and advice. I do not name them all—partly because many of them have requested me not to do so. I must, however, express my thanks to Mr. Henry L. Slobodin of New York, for kindly placing his materials at my disposal; Dr. S. Ingerman of New York, for his valuable assistance; Mr. Jerome Landfield of New York, for most valuable suggestions; Prof. V. I. Issaiev of London, for personal courtesies and for the assistance derived from his valuable collection of data; Dr. Joseph M. Goldstein, author of *Russia, Her Economic Past and Future*; Mr. Gregor Alexinsky; Mr. Alexander Kerensky, former Premier of Russia; Madame Catherine Breshkovsky; Dr. J. O. Gavronsky of London; the editors of *Pour la Russie*, Paris; Gen. C. M. Oberoucheff, military commander of the Kiev District under the Provisional Government; Mr. J. Strumillo, of the Russian Social Democratic Party; Mr. G. Soloveytchik of Queen's College, Oxford; to the Institute for Public Service for the diagram used on page 65; and, finally, my old friend and colleague of twenty-five years ago, Col. John Ward, C.B., C.M.G., member of the British House of Commons, founder of the Navvies' Union, whose courageous struggle against Bolshevism has won for him the respect and gratitude of all friends of Russian freedom.

J. S.

PREFACE

LIKE the immortal Topsy, this book may be said to have "just growed." In it I have simply assembled in something like an orderly arrangement a vast amount of carefully investigated evidence concerning the Bolshevist system and its workings — evidence which, in my judgment, must compel every honest believer in freedom and democracy to condemn Bolshevism as a vicious and dangerous form of reaction, subversive of every form of progress and every agency of civilization and enlightenment.

I do not discuss theories in this book, except in a very incidental way. In two earlier volumes my views upon the theories of Bolshevism have been set forth, clearly and with emphasis. On its theoretical side, despite the labored pretentiousness of Lenin and his interminable "Theses," so suggestive of medieval theology, Bolshevism is the sorriest medley of antiquated philosophical rubbish and fantastic speculation to command attention among civilized peoples since Millerism stirred so many of the American people to a mental process they mistook for and miscalled thinking.

No one who is capable of honest and straight-forward thinking upon political and economic questions can read the books of such Bolshevist writers as Lenin, Trotsky, and Bucharin, and the numerous proclamations, manifestoes, and decrees issued by the Soviet Government and the Communist Party, and retain any respect for the Bolsheviki as thinkers. Neither can any one who is capable of understanding the essential difference between freedom and despotism read even those official decrees, programs, and legal codes which they themselves have caused to be published and doubt that the régime of the Bolsheviki in Russia is despotic in the extreme. The cretinous-minded admirers and defenders of Bolshevism, whether they call themselves Liberals, Radicals, or Socialists—dishonoring thereby words of great and honorable antecedents—"bawl for freedom in their senseless mood" and, at the same time, give their hearts' homage to a monstrous and arrogant tyranny.

In these pages will be found, I venture to assert, ample and conclusive evidence to justify to any healthy and rational mind the description of Bolshevism as "a monstrous and arrogant tyranny." That is the purpose of the volume. It is an indictment and arraignment of Bolshevism and the Bolsheviki at the bar of enlightened public opinion. The evidence upon which the indictment rests is so largely drawn from official publications of the Soviet Government and of the Communist Party, and from the authorized writings of the foremost spokesmen of Russian Bolshevism, that the book might almost be termed a self-revelation of Bolshevism and the Bolsheviki. Such evidence as I have cited from non-Bolshevist sources is of minor importance, slight in quantity and merely corroborative of, or supplementary to, the evidence drawn from the Bolshevist sources already indicated. Much of the evidence has been published from time to time in numerous articles, state reports, and pamphlets, both here and in England, but this is the first volume, I believe, to bring the material together in a systematic arrangement.

Following the publication of my *Bolshevism* I found myself called upon to deliver many addresses upon the subject. Some of these were given before college and university audiences— at Dartmouth, Princeton, Columbia, Barnard, and elsewhere— while others were given before a wide variety of public audiences. The circulation of my book and many magazine and newspaper articles on the subject, together with the lectures and addresses, had the result of bringing me a veritable multitude of questions from all parts of the country. The questions came from men and women of high estate and of low, ranging from United States Senators to a group of imprisoned Communists awaiting deportation. Some of the questions were asked in good faith, to elicit information; others were obviously asked for quite another purpose. For a long time it seemed that every statement made in the press about Bolshevism or the Bolsheviki reached me with questions or challenges concerning it.

To every question which was asked in apparent good faith I did my best to reply. When—as often happened—the information was not in my possession, I invoked the assistance of those of my Russian friends in Europe and this country who have made it their special task to keep well informed concerning developments in Russia. These friends not only replied to my specific questions, but sent me from time to time practically every item of interest concerning developments in Russia. As a result, I found myself in the possession of an immense mass of testimony and evidence of varying value. Fully aware of the unreliability of much of the material thus placed in my hands, for my own satisfaction I weeded out all stories based upon hearsay, all stories told by unknown persons, all rumors and indefinite statements, and, finally, all stories, no matter by whom told, which were not confirmed by dependable witnesses. This winnowing process left the following classes of evidence and testimony: (1) Statements by leading Bolsheviki, contained in their official press or in publications authorized by them; (2) reports of activities by the Soviet Government or its officials, published in the official organs of the government; (3) formal documents—decrees, proclamations, and the like—issued by the Soviet Government and its responsible officials; (4)

statements made by well-known Russian Socialists and trades-unionists of high standing upon facts within their own knowledge, where there was confirmatory evidence; (5) the testimony of well-known Socialists from other countries, upon matters of which they had personal knowledge and concerning which there was confirmatory evidence.

Every scrap of evidence adduced in the following pages belongs to one or other of the five classes above described. Moreover, the reader can rest assured that every possible care has been taken to guard against misquotation and against quotation which, while literally accurate, nevertheless misrepresents the truth. This is often done by unfairly separating text from context, for example, and in other ways. I believe that I can assure the reader of the freedom of this book from that evil; certainly nothing of the sort has been intentionally included. While I have accepted as correct and authentic certain translations, such as the translations of Lenin's *Soviets at Work* and his *State and Revolution*, both of which are largely circulated by pro-Bolshevist propagandists, and such collections of documents as have been published in this country by the *Nation*—the Soviet Constitution and certain Decrees—and by *Soviet Russia*, the official organ of the Soviet Government in this country, I have had almost every other line of translated quotation examined and verified by some competent and trustworthy Russian scholar.

The book does not contain all or nearly all the evidence which has come into my possession in the manner described. I have purposely omitted much that was merely harrowing and brutal, as well as sensational incidents which have no direct bearing upon the struggle in Russia, but properly belong to the category of crimes arising out of the elemental passions, which are to be found in every country. Crimes and atrocities by irresponsible individuals I have passed over in silence, confining myself to those things which reflect the actual purposes, methods, and results of the régime itself.

I have not tried to make a sensational book, yet now that it is finished I feel that it is even worse than that. It seems to me to be a terrible book. The cumulative effect of the evidence of brutal oppression and savagery, of political trickery and chicane, of reckless experimentation, of administrative inefficiency, of corrupt bureaucratism, of outraged idealism and ambitious despotism, seems to me as terrible as anything I know—more terrible than the descriptions of czarism which formerly harrowed our feelings. When I remember the monstrous evils that have been wrought in the name of Socialism, my soul is torn by an indescribable agony.

Yet more agonizing still is the consciousness that here in the United States there are men and women of splendid character and apparent intelligence whose vision has been so warped by hatred of the evils of the present system, and by a cunning propaganda, that they are ready to hail this loathsome thing of hatred, this monstrous tyranny, as an evangel of fraternalism and freedom; ready to bring upon this nation—where, despite every shortcoming, we are at least two centuries ahead of Bolshevized Russia, politically, economically, morally—the curse which during less than thirty months has afflicted unhappy Russia with greater ills than fifty years of czarism.

They will not succeed. They shall strive in vain to replace the generous spirit of Lincoln with the brutal spirit of Lenin. For us there shall be no dictatorship other than that of our own ever-growing conscience as a nation, seeking freedom and righteousness in our own way.

We shall defeat and destroy Bolshevism by keeping the light shining upon it, revealing its ugliness, its brutality, its despotism. We do not need to adopt the measures which czarism found so unavailing. Oppression cannot help us in this fight, or offer us any protection whatsoever. If we would destroy Bolshevism we must destroy the illusions which surround it. Once its real character is made known, once men can see it as it is, we shall not need to fear its spread among our fellow-citizens. Light, abundant light, is the best agent to fight Bolshevism.

JOHN SPARGO.

"NESTLEDOWN,"

OLD BENNINGTON, VERMONT,

May 1920.

"THE GREATEST FAILURE IN ALL HISTORY"

"THE GREATEST FAILURE IN ALL HISTORY"

I

WHY HAVE THE BOLSHEVIKI RETAINED POWER?

THE Bolsheviki are in control of Russia. Never, at any time since their usurpation of power in November, 1917, have Lenin and Trotsky and their associates been so free from organized internal opposition as they are now, after a lapse of more than two and a quarter years. This is the central fact in the Russian problem. While it is true that Bolshevist rule is obviously tottering toward its fall, it is equally true that the anti-Bolshevist forces of Russia have been scattered like chaff before the wind. While there is plenty of evidence that the overwhelming mass of the Russian people have been and are opposed to them, the Bolsheviki rule, nevertheless. This is what many very thoughtful people who are earnestly seeking to arrive at just and helpful conclusions concerning Russia find it hard and well-nigh impossible to understand. Upon every hand one hears the question, "How is it possible to believe that the Bolsheviki have been able for so long to maintain and even increase their power against the opposition of the great mass of the Russian people?"

The complete answer to this question will be developed later, but a partial and provisional answer may, perhaps, do much to clear the way for an intelligent and dispassionate study of the manner in which Bolshevism in Russia has been affected by the acid test of practice. In the first place, it would be interesting to discuss the naïveté of the question. Is it a new and unheard-of phenomenon that a despotic and tyrannical government should increase its strength in spite of the resentment of the masses? Czarism maintained itself in power for centuries against the will of the people. If it be objected that only a minority of the people of Russia actively opposed czarism, and that the masses as a whole were passive for centuries, no such contention can be made concerning the period from 1901 to 1906. At that time the country was aflame with passionate discontent; the people as a whole were opposed to czarism, yet they lacked the organized physical power to overthrow it. Czarism ruled by brute force, and the methods which it developed and used with success have been adopted by the Bolsheviki and perfected by them.

However, let a veteran Russian revolutionist answer the question: Gen. C. M. Oberoucheff is an old and honored member of the Party of Socialists-Revolutionists of Russia and under the old régime suffered imprisonment and exile on account of his activities in the revolutionary movement. Under the Provisional Government, while Kerensky was Premier, he was made Military Commissary of Kiev, at the request of the local Soviet. General Oberoucheff says:

"Americans often ask the question: 'How can it be explained that the Bolsheviki hold power?... Does this not prove that they are supported by the majority of the people?' For us Russians the reply to this question is very simple. The Czars held power for centuries. Is that proof that their rule was supported by the will of the people? Of course not. They held power by the rule of blood and iron and did not rest at all upon the sympathies of the great masses of the people. The Bolsheviki are retaining their power to-day by the same identical means.... Russia of the Czars' time was governed by

Blue gendarmes. Great Russia of to-day is ruled by Red gendarmes. The distinction is only in color and perhaps somewhat in methods. The methods of the Red gendarmes are more ruthless and cruel than those of the old Blue gendarmes."

The greater part of a year has elapsed since these words were written by General Oberoucheff. Since that time there have been many significant changes in Russia, including recently some relaxation of the brutal oppression. Czarism likewise had its periods of comparative decency. It still remains true, however, that the rule of the Bolsheviki rests upon the same basis as that of the old régime. It is, in fact, only an inverted form of czarism.

As we shall presently see, the precise methods by which monarchism was so long maintained have been used by the Bolsheviki. The main support of the old régime was an armed force, consisting of the corps of gendarmes and special regiments of guards. Under Bolshevism, corresponding to these, we have the famous Red Guards, certain divisions of which have been maintained for the express purpose of dealing with internal disorder and suppressing uprisings. Just as, under czarism, the guard regiments were specially well paid and accorded privileges which made them a class apart, so have these Red Guards of the Bolsheviki enjoyed special privileges, including superior pay and rations.

Under czarism the *Okhrana* and the Black Hundreds, together with the Blue gendarmes, imposed a reign of terror upon the nation. They were as corrupt as they were cruel. Under the Bolsheviki the Extraordinary Committees and Revolutionary Tribunals have been just as brutal and as corrupt as their czaristic predecessors. Under the Bolsheviki the system of espionage and the use of provocative agents can be fairly described as a continuance of the methods of the old régime.

Czarism developed an immense bureaucracy; a vast army of petty officials and functionaries was thus attached to the government. This bureaucracy was characterized by the graft and corruption indulged in by its members. They stole from the government and they used their positions to extort blackmail and graft from the helpless and unhappy people. In the same manner Bolshevism has developed a new bureaucracy in Russia, larger than the old, and no less corrupt. As we shall see later on, the sincere and honest idealists among the Bolsheviki have loudly protested against this evil. Moreover, the system has become so burdensome economically that the government itself has become alarmed. By filling the land with spies and making it almost impossible for any man to trust his neighbor, by suppressing practically all non-Bolshevist journals, and by terrorism such as was unknown under the old régime, the Bolsheviki have maintained themselves in power.

There is a still more important reason why the Bolshevist régime continues, namely, its own adaptability. Far from being the unbending and uncompromising devotees of principle they are very generally regarded as being, the Bolshevist leaders are, above all else, opportunists. Notwithstanding their adoption of the repressive and oppressive methods of the old régime, the Bolsheviki could not have continued in power had they remained steadfast to the economic theories and principles with which they began. No amount of force could have continued for so long a system of government based on economic principles so ruinous. As a matter of fact, the Bolsheviki have continued to rule Russia because, without any change of mind or heart, but under pressure of relentless economic necessity, they have abandoned their theories. The crude communism which Lenin and his accomplices set out to impose upon Russia by force has been discarded and flung upon the scrap-pile of politics. That this is true will be abundantly demonstrated by the testimony of the Bolsheviki themselves.

No study of the reasons for the success of the Bolsheviki can be regarded as complete which does not take into account the fact that Russia has been living upon the stored-up resources of the old order. When the Bolsheviki seized the reins of government there were in the country large stores of food, of raw materials, of manufactured and partially manufactured goods. There were also large numbers of industrial establishments in working order. With these things alone, even without any augmentation by new production—except, of course, agricultural production—the nation could for a considerable time escape utter destruction. With these resources completely in the hands of the government, any opposition was necessarily placed at a very great disadvantage. The principal spokesmen of the Bolsheviki have themselves recognized this from time to time. On January 3, 1920, *Pravda*, the official organ of the Communist Party—that is, of the Bolsheviki—said:

> We must not forget that hitherto we have been living on the stores and machinery, the means of production, which we inherited from the bourgeoisie. We have been using the old stores of raw material, half-manufactured and manufactured goods. But these stores are getting exhausted and the machinery is wearing out more and more. All our victories in the field will lead to nothing if we do not add to them victories gained by the hammer, pick, and lathe.

It must be confessed that the continued rule of the Bolsheviki has, to a very considerable extent, been due to the political ineptitude and lack of coherence on the part of their opponents. The truth is that on more than one occasion the overthrow of the Bolsheviki might easily have been brought about by the Allies if they had dared do it. The chancelleries of Europe were, at times, positively afraid that the Bolshevist Government would be overthrown and that there would be no sort of government to take its place. In the archives of all the Allied governments there are filed away confidential reports warning the governments that if the Bolsheviki should be overthrown Russia would immediately become a vast welter of anarchy. Many European diplomats and statesmen, upon the strength of such reports, shrugged their shoulders and consoled themselves with the thought that, however bad Bolshevist government might be, it was at least better than no government at all.

Finally, we must not overlook the fact that the mere existence of millions of people who, finding it impossible to overthrow the Bolshevist régime, devote their energies to the task of making it endurable by bribing officials, conspiring to evade oppressive regulations, and by outward conformity, tends to keep the national life going, no matter how bad the government.

//
THE SOVIETS

T

he

first articulate cry of Bolshevism in Russia after the overthrow of the monarchy was the demand "All power to the Soviets!" which the Bolshevist leaders raised in the summer of 1917 when the Provisional Government was bravely struggling to consolidate the democratic gains of the March Revolution. The Bolsheviki were inspired by that anti-statism which one finds in the literature of early Marxian Socialism. It was not the individualistic antagonism to the state of the anarchist, though easily confounded with and mistaken for it. It was not motivated by an exaltation of the individual, but that of a class. The early Marxian Socialists looked upon the modern state, with its highly centralized authority, as a mere instrument of class rule, by means of which the capitalist class maintained itself in power and intensified its exploitation of the wage-earning class. Frederick Engels, Marx's great collaborator, described the modern state as being the managing committee for the capitalist class as a whole.

Naturally, the state being thus identified with capitalist exploitation, the determination to overthrow the capitalist system carried with it a like determination to destroy the political state. Given a victory by the working-class sufficiently comprehensive to enable it to take possession of the ruling power, the state would either become obsolete, and die of its own accord, or be forcibly abolished. This attitude is well and forcibly expressed by Engels in some well-known passages.

Thus, in his Socialism, Utopian and Scientific, *Engels says:*

> The modern state, no matter what its form, is essentially a capitalistic machine, the state of the capitalists, the ideal personification of the total national capital. The more it proceeds to the taking over of productive forces the more does it actually become the national capitalist, the more citizens does it exploit.... Whilst the capitalist mode of production ... forces on more and more

the transformation of the vast means of production, already socialized, into state property, it shows itself the way to accomplish this revolution. The proletariat seizes political power and turns the means of production into state property.

What Engels meant is made clear in a subsequent paragraph in the same work. He argues that as long as society was divided into antagonistic classes the state was a necessity. The ruling class for the time being required an organized force for the purpose of protecting its interest and particularly of forcibly keeping the subject class in order. Under such conditions, the state could only be properly regarded as the representative of society as a whole in the narrow sense that the ruling class itself represented society as a whole. Assuming the extinction of class divisions and antagonisms, the state would immediately become unnecessary:

> The first act by virtue of which the state really constitutes itself the representative of the whole of society—the taking possession of the means of production in the name of society—this is, at the same time, its last independent act as a state. State interference in social relations becomes, in one domain after another, superfluous, and then dies out of itself; the government of persons is replaced by the administration of things and by the conduct of processes of production. The state is not "abolished." *It dies out.*

In another work, The Origin of the Family, Private Property, and the State, *Engels says:*

> We are now rapidly approaching a stage of evolution in production in which the existence of classes has not only ceased to be a necessity, but becomes a positive fetter on production. Hence these classes must fall as inevitably they once rose. The state must irrevocably fall with them. The society that is to reorganize production on the basis of a free and equal association of the producers will transfer the machinery of state where it will then belong: into the museum of antiquities, by the side of the spinning-wheel and the bronze ax.

These passages from the classic literature of Marxian Socialism fairly and clearly express the character of the anti-statism which inspired the Bolsheviki at the outset. They wanted to develop a type of social organization in which there would be practically no "government of persons," but only the "administration of things" and the "conduct of the processes of production." Modern Socialist thinkers have fairly generally recognized the muddled character of the thinking upon which this anti-statism rests. How can there be "administration of things" without "government of persons"? The only meaning that can possibly be attached to the "administration of things" by the government is that human relations established through the medium of things are to be administered or governed. Certainly the "conduct of the processes of production" without some regulation of the conduct of the persons engaged in those processes is unthinkable.

We do not need to discuss the theory farther at this time. It is enough to recognize that the primitive Marxian doctrine which we have outlined required that state interference with the individual and with social relations be reduced to a minimum, if not wholly abolished. It is a far cry from that conception to the system of conscript labor recently introduced, and the Code of Labor Laws of Soviet Russia, which legalizes industrial serfdom and adscription and makes even the proletarian subject to a more rigid and despotic "government of persons" than has existed anywhere since the time when feudalism flourished.

The Bolsheviki believed that they saw in the Soviets of factory-workers, peasants, and Socialists the beginnings of a form of social organization which would supplant the state, lacking its coercive features and better fitted for the administration of the economic life of the nation. The first

Soviet of Workmen's Deputies appeared in October, 1905, in Petrograd, at the time of the abortive revolution. The idea of organizing such a council of workmen's representatives originated with the Mensheviki, the faction of the Social Democratic Party opposed to the Bolsheviki. The sole aim of the Soviet was to organize the revolutionary forces and sentiment. But, during the course of its brief existence, it did much in the way of relieving the distress. The Socialists-Revolutionists joined with the Mensheviki in the creation of this first Soviet, but the Bolsheviki were bitterly opposed to it, denouncing it as "the invention of semi-bourgeois parties to enthrall the proletariat in a non-partizan swamp." When the Soviet was well under way, however, and its success was manifest, the Bolsheviki entered it and became active participants in its work. With the triumph of czarism, this first Soviet was crushed, most of its leaders being banished to Siberia.

Even before the formation of the Provisional Government was completed, in March, 1917, the revolutionary working-class leaders of Petrograd had organized a Soviet, or council, which they called the Council of Workmen's Deputies of Petrograd. Like all the similar Soviets which sprang up in various parts of the country, this was a very loose organization and very far from being a democratic body of representatives. Its members were chosen at casual meetings held in the factories and workshops and sometimes on the streets. No responsible organizations arranged or governed the elections. Anybody could call a mass-meeting, in any manner he pleased, and those who came selected—usually by show of hands—such "deputies" as they pleased. If only a score attended and voted in a factory employing hundreds, the deputies so elected represented that factory in the Soviet. This description equally applies to practically all the other Soviets which sprang up in the industrial centers, the rural villages, and in the army itself.

Among the soldiers at the front company Soviets, and even trench Soviets, were formed. In the cities it was common for groups of soldiers belonging to the same company, meeting on the streets by accident, to hold impromptu street meetings and form Soviets. There was, of course, more order and a better chance to get representative delegates when the meetings were held in barracks.

Not only were the Soviets far from being responsible democratically organized representative bodies; quite as significant is the fact that the deputies selected by the factory-workers were, in many instances, not workmen at all, but lawyers, university professors, lecturers, authors and journalists, professional politicians, and so on. Many of the men who played prominent rôles in the Petrograd Soviet, for example, as delegates of the factory-workers, were Intellectuals of the type described. Any well-known revolutionary leader who happened to be in the public eye at the moment might be selected by a group of admirers in a factory as their delegate. It was thus that Kerensky, the brilliant lawyer, found himself a prominent member of the Petrograd Soviet of Workmen's Deputies, and that, later on, Trotsky, the journalist, and Lenin, the scholar, became equally prominent.

It was to such bodies as these that the Bolsheviki wanted to transfer all the power of the government—political, military, and economic. The leaders of the Provisional Government, when they found their task too heavy, urged the Petrograd Soviet to take up the burden, which it declined to do. That the Soviets were needed in the existing circumstances, and that, as auxiliaries to the Provisional Government and the Municipal Council, they were capable of rendering great service to the democratic cause, can hardly be questioned by any one familiar with the conditions that prevailed. The Provisional

Government, chosen from the Duma, was not, at first, a democratic body in the full sense of that word. It did not represent the working-people. It was essentially representative of the bourgeoisie and it was quite natural, therefore, that in the Soviets there was developed a very critical attitude toward the Provisional Government.

Before very long, however, the Provisional Government became more democratic through the inclusion of a large representation of the working-class parties, men who were chosen by and directly responsible to the Petrograd Soviet. This arrangement meant that the Soviet had definitely entered into co-operation with the Provisional Government; that in the interest of the success of the Revolution the working-class joined hands with the bourgeoisie. This was the condition when, in the summer of 1917, the Bolsheviki raised the cry "All power to the Soviets!" There was not even the shadow of a pretense that the Provisional Government was either undemocratic or unrepresentative. At the same time the new municipal councils were functioning. These admirable bodies had been elected upon the basis of universal, equal, direct, and secret suffrage. Arrangements were far advanced for holding—under the authority of the democratically constituted municipal councils and Zemstvos—elections for a Constituent Assembly, upon the same basis of generous democracy: universal, equal, direct, and secret suffrage, with proportional representation. It will be seen, therefore, that the work of creating a thoroughly democratic government for Russia was far advanced and proceeding with great rapidity. Instead of the power of government being placed in the hands of thoroughly democratic representative bodies, the Bolsheviki wanted it placed in the hands of the hastily improvised and loosely organized Soviets.

At first the Bolsheviki had professed great faith in, and solicitude for, the Constituent Assembly, urging its immediate convocation. In view of their subsequent conduct, this has been regarded as evidence of their hypocrisy and dishonesty. It has been assumed that they never really wanted a Constituent Assembly at all. Of some of the leaders this is certainly true; of others it is only partially true. Trotsky, Lenin, Kamenev, Zinoviev, and others, during the months of June and July, 1917, opposed the policy of the Provisional Government in making elaborate preparations for holding the elections to the Constituent Assembly. They demanded immediate convocation of the Constituent Assembly, upon the basis of "elections" similar to those of the Soviets, knowing well that this would give them an irresponsible mass-meeting, easily swayed and controlled by the demagoguery and political craft of which they were such perfect masters. Had they succeeded in their efforts at that time, the Constituent Assembly would not have been dispersed, in all probability. It would have been as useful an instrument for their purpose as the Soviets. When they realized that the Constituent Assembly was to be a responsible representative body, a deliberative assembly, they began their agitation to have its place taken by the Soviets. They were perfectly well aware that these could be much more easily manipulated and controlled by an aggressive minority than a well-planned, thoroughly representative assembly could be.

The Bolsheviki wanted to use the Soviets as instruments. In this simple statement of fact there is implicit a distinction between Soviet government and Bolshevism, a distinction that is too often lost sight of. Bolshevism may be defined either as an end to be attained—communism—or as a policy, a method of attaining the desired end. Neither the Soviet as an institution nor Soviet government, as such, had any necessary connection with the particular goal of the Bolsheviki or their methods. That the Bolsheviki in Russia and in Hungary have approved Soviet government as the form of government best adapted to the realization of their program, and found the Soviet a desirable instrument, must not be regarded as establishing either the identity of Bolshevism and Soviet government or a necessary relation between the Soviet and the methods of the Bolsheviki. The same instrument is capable of being used by the conservative as well as by the radical.

In this respect the Soviet system of government is like ordinary parliamentary government. This, also, is an instrument which may be used by either the reactionary or the revolutionist. The defender of land monopoly and the Single-taxer can both use it. To reject the Soviet system simply because it is capable of being used to attain the ends of Bolshevism, or even because the advocates of Bolshevism find it better adapted to their purpose than the political systems with which we are familiar, is extremely foolish. Such a conclusion is as irrational as that of the superficial idealists who renounce all faith in organized government and its agencies because they can be used oppressively, and are in fact sometimes so used.

It is at least possible, and, in the judgment of the present writer, not at all improbable, that the Soviet system will prove, in Russia and elsewhere, inclined to conservatism in normal circumstances. Trades-unions are capable of revolutionary action, but under normal conditions they incline to a cautious conservatism. The difference between a trades-union and a factory Soviet is, primarily, that the former groups the workers of a trade and disregards the fact that they work in different places, while the latter groups the workers in a particular factory and disregards the fact that they pursue different trades or grades of labor. What is there in this difference to warrant the conclusion that the factory-unit form of organization is more likely to adopt communist ideals or violent methods than the other form of organization? Surely the fact that the Bolsheviki have found it necessary to restrict and modify the Soviet system, even to the extent of abolishing some of its most important features, disposes of the mistaken notion that Bolshevism and the Soviet system are inseparable.

It is not without significance that the leading theoretician of Bolshevism, Lenin, on the basis of pure theory, opposed the Soviets at first. Nor is the fact that many of the bitterest opponents of Bolshevism in Russia, among the Socialists-Revolutionists, the Mensheviki, the Populists, the leaders of the co-operatives and the trades-unions, are stanch believers in and defenders of the Soviet system of government, and confidently believe that it will be the permanent form of Russian government.

For reasons which will be developed in subsequent chapters, the present writer does not accept this view. The principal objection to the Soviet system, as such, is not that it is inseparable from Bolshevism, that it must of necessity be associated with the aims and methods of the latter, but that—unless greatly modified and limited—it must prove inefficient to the point of vital danger to society. This does not mean that organizations similar in structure to the Soviets can have no place in the government or in industrial management. In some manner the democratization of industry is to be attained in a not far distant future. When that time comes it will be found that the ideas which gave impulse to syndicalism and to Soviet government have found concrete expression in a form wholly beneficent.

III
THE SOVIETS UNDER THE BOLSHEVIKI

After the *coup d'état*, the Soviets continued to be elected in the same haphazard manner as before. Even after the adoption, in July, 1918, of the Constitution, which made the Soviets the basis of the superstructure of governmental power, there was no noticeable improvement in this respect. Never, at any time, since the Bolsheviki came into power, have the Soviets attained anything like a truly representative character. The Constitution of the Russian Socialist Federal Soviet Republic stamps it as the most undemocratic and oligarchic of the great modern nations. The city Soviets are composed of delegates elected by the employees of factories and workshops and by trades and professional unions, including associations of mothers and housewives. The Constitution does not prescribe the methods of election, these being determined by the local Soviets themselves. In the industrial centers most of the elections take place at open meetings in the factories, the voting being done by show of hands. In view of the elaborate system of espionage and the brutal repression of all hostile criticism, it is easy to understand that such a system of voting makes possible and easy every form of corruption and intimidation.

The whole system of government resulting from these methods proved unrepresentative. A single illustration will make this quite plain:

Within four days of the Czar's abdication, the workers of Perm, in the Government of the Urals, organized a Soviet—the Urals Workers' and Soldiers' Soviet. At the head of it, as president, was Jandarmov, a machinist, who had been active in the Revolution of 1905, a Soviet worker and trades-unionist, many times imprisoned under the old régime. This Soviet supplemented and co-operated with the Provisional Government, worked for a democratic Constituent Assembly, and, after the first few days of excitement had passed, greatly increased production in the factories. But when the Bolshevist régime was established, after the adoption of the Constitution, the Government of the Urals, with its four million inhabitants, did not represent, even on the basis of the Soviet figures, more than 72,000 workers. That was the number of workers supposedly represented by the delegates of the Soviet Government. As a matter of fact, in that number was included the anti-Bolshevist strength, the workers who had been outvoted or intimidated, as the case might be. When the peasants elected delegates they were refused seats, because they were known to be, or believed to be, anti-Bolshevists. This is the much-vaunted system of Soviet "elections" concerning which so many of our self-styled Liberals have been lyrically eloquent.

Of course, even under the conditions described, anti-Bolshevists were frequently elected to the Soviets. It was a very general practice, in the early days of the Bolshevist régime, to quite arbitrarily "cleanse" the Soviets of these "undesirable counter-revolutionaries," most of whom were Socialists. In December, 1917, the Soviets in Ufa, Saratov, Samara, Kazan, and Jaroslav were compelled, under severe penalties, *to dismiss their non-Bolshevist members*; in January, 1918, the same thing took place at Perm and at Ekaterinburg; and in February, 1918, the Soviets of Moscow and Petrograd were similarly "cleansed."

It was a very ordinary occurrence for Soviets to be suppressed because their "state of mind" was not pleasing to the Bolsheviki in control of the central authority. In a word, when a local Soviet election resulted in a majority of Socialists-Revolutionists or other non-Bolshevist representatives being chosen, the Council of the People's Commissaries dissolved the Soviet and ordered the election of a new one. Frequently they used troops—generally Lettish or Chinese—to enforce their orders. Numerous examples of this form of despotism might be cited from the Bolshevist official press. For example, in April, 1918, the elections to the Soviet of Jaroslav, a large industrial city north of Moscow, resulted in a large majority of anti-Bolshevist representatives being elected. The Council of the People's Commissaries sent Lettish troops to dissolve the Soviet and hold a new "election." This so enraged the people that they gave a still larger majority for the anti-Bolshevist parties. Then the Council of the People's Commissaries issued a decree stating that as the working-class of Jaroslav had twice proved their unfitness for self-government they would not be permitted to have a Soviet at all! The town was proclaimed to be "a nest of counter-revolutionaries." Again and again the workers of Jaroslav tried to set up local self-government, and each time they were crushed by brutal and bloody violence.[1]

<u>1</u> *The salient facts in this paragraph are condensed from L'Ouvrier Russe, May, 1918. See also Bullard, The Russian Pendulum—Autocracy, Democracy, Bolshevism, p. 92, for an account of the same events.*

L. I. Goldman, member of the Central Committee of the Russian Social Democratic Labor Party, made a report to that body concerning one of these Jaroslav uprisings in which he wrote:

> The population of that city consists mainly of workmen. Having the assistance of a military organization under the leadership of General Alexiev and General Savinkov, the laborers of all the plants and factories took part in the uprising. Before the uprising began the leaders declared that they would not allow it unless they had the sympathy of the laborers and other classes. Trotsky sent a message stating that if the revolt could not be quelled he would go as far as having the city of Jaroslav with its 40,000 inhabitants completely destroyed.... Though surrounded by 17,000 Red Guards, Jaroslav resisted, but was finally captured by the Bolsheviki, due to the superiority of their artillery. The uprising was suppressed by bloody and terrible means. The spirit of destruction swayed over Jaroslav, which is one of the oldest Russian cities.

Bearing in mind that the sole aim of the people of Jaroslav—led by Socialist workmen—was to establish their own local self-government, the inviolability of the Soviet elections, let us examine a few of the many reports concerning the struggle published in the official Bolshevist organs. Under the caption "Official Bulletin," *Izvestia* published, on July 21, 1918, this item:

> At Jaroslav the adversary, gripped in the iron ring of our troops, has tried to enter into negotiations. *The reply has been given under the form of redoubled artillery fire.*

Four days later, on July 25th, *Izvestia* published a military proclamation addressed to the inhabitants of Jaroslav, from which the following passage is taken:

> The General Staff notifies to the population of Jaroslav that all those who desire to live are invited to abandon the town in the course of twenty-four hours and to meet near the America Bridge. Those who remain will be treated as insurgents, *and no quarter will be given to any one*. Heavy artillery fire and gas-bombs will be used against them. *All those who remain will perish in the ruins of the town with the insurrectionists, the traitors, and the enemies of the Workers' and Peasants' Revolution.*

On the day following, July 26th, *Izvestia* published an article to the effect that "after minute questionings and full inquiry" a special commission of inquiry appointed to investigate the Jaroslav insurrection had listed three hundred and fifty persons as having "taken an active part in the insurrection and had relations with the Czechoslovaks," and that the commissioners had ordered the whole three hundred and fifty to be shot.

Throughout the summer the struggle went on, and in the *Severnaya Communa*, September 10, 1918, the following despatch from Jaroslav was published:

> JAROSLAV, *9th September*.—In the whole of the Jaroslav government a strict registration of the bourgeoisie and its partizans has been organized. Manifestly anti-Soviet elements are being shot; suspected persons are interned in concentration camps; non-working sections of the population are subjected to forced labor.

Here is further evidence, from official Bolshevist sources, that when the Soviet elections went against them the Bolshevist Government simply dissolved the offending Soviets. Here are two despatches from *Izvestia*, from the issues of July 28 and August 3, 1918, respectively:

> KAZAN, July 26th.—As the important offices in the Soviet were occupied by Socialists-Revolutionists of the Left, the Extraordinary Commission has

dissolved the Provisional Soviet. The governmental power is now represented by a Revolutionary Committee.

KAZAN, August 1st.—*The state of mind of the workmen is revolutionary.* If the Mensheviki dare to carry on their propaganda death menaces them.

By way of confirmation we have the following, from *Pravda*, August 6, 1918:

KAZAN, *August 4th.*—The Provisional Congress of the Soviets of the Peasants has been dissolved because of the absence from it of poor peasants and *because its state of mind is obviously counter-revolutionary.*

Whenever a city Soviet was thus suppressed a military revolutionary committee, designated by the Bolsheviki, was set up in its place. To these committees the most arbitrary powers were given. Generally composed of young soldiers from distant parts, over whom there was practically no restraint, these committees frequently indulged in frightful acts of violence and spoliation. Not infrequently the Central Government, after disbanding a local Soviet, would send from places hundreds of miles away, under military protection, members of the Communist Party, who were designated as the executive committee of the Soviet for that locality. There was not even a pretense that they had been elected by anybody. Thus it was in Tumen: Protected by a convoy of eight hundred Red Guards, who remained there to enforce their authority, a group of members of the Communist Party arrived from Ekaterinburg and announced that they were the executive committee of the Soviet of Tumen where, in fact, no Soviet existed. This was not at all an unusual occurrence.

The suppression by force of those Soviets which were not absolutely subservient to the Central Bolshevik Government went on as long as there were any such Soviets. This was especially true in the rural villages among the peasantry. The following statement is by an English trades-unionist, H. V. Keeling, a member of the Lithographic Artists' and Engravers' Society (an English trades-union), who worked in Russia for five years—1914-19:

> In the villages conditions were often quite good, due to the forming of a local Soviet by the inhabitants who were not Bolshevik. The villagers elected the men whom they knew, and as long as they were left alone things proceeded much as usual.
>
> Soon, however, a whisper would reach the district Commissar that the Soviet was not politically straight; he would then come with some Red soldiers and dissolve the committee and order another election, often importing Bolshevik supporters from the towns, and these men the villagers were instructed to elect as their committee. Resistance was often made and an army of Red Guards sent to break it down. Pitched battles often took place, and *in one case of which I can speak from personal knowledge twenty-one of the inhabitants were shot, including the local telegraph-girl operator who had refused to telegraph for reinforcements.*
>
> The practice of sending young soldiers into the villages which were not Bolshevik was very general; care was taken to send men who did not come from the district, so that any scruples might be overcome. Even then it would happen that after the soldiers had got food they would make friends with the people, and so compel the Commissar to send for another set of Red Guards.[2]

[2] *Bolshevism*, by H. V. Keeling, pp. 185-186.

In the chapter dealing with the relation of the Bolsheviki to the peasants and the land question abundant corroboration of Mr. Keeling's testimony is given. The Bolsheviki have, however, found an easier way to insure absolute control of the Soviets: as a general rule they do not depend upon these crude methods of violence. Instead, they have adopted the delightfully simple method of permitting no persons to be placed in nomination whose names are not approved by them. As a first step the anti-Bolshevist parties, such as the

Menshevist Social Democrats, Socialists-Revolutionists of the Right and Center, and the Constitutional Democrats, were excluded by the issuance of a decree that "the right to nominate candidates belongs exclusively to the parties of electors which file the declaration that they acknowledge the Soviet authorities."

The following resolution was adopted by the All-Russian Central Executive Committee on June 14, 1918:

> The representatives of the Social Revolutionary Party (the Right wing and the Center) *are excluded*, and at the same time all Soviets of Workers', Soldiers', Peasants', and Cossacks' Deputies are recommended to expel from their midst all representatives of this faction.

This resolution, which was duly carried into effect, was strictly in accordance with the clause in the Constitution of the Soviet Republic which provides that "guided by the interests of the working-class as a whole, the Russian Socialist Federal Soviet Republic deprives all individuals and groups of rights which could be utilized by them to the detriment of the Socialist Revolution." Thus entire political parties have been excluded from the Soviets by the party in power. It is a noteworthy fact that many of those persons in this country, Socialists and others, who have been most vigorous in denouncing the expulsion from the New York Legislature of the elected representatives of the Socialist Party are, at the same time, vigorous supporters of the Bolsheviki. Comment upon the lack of moral and intellectual integrity thus manifested is unnecessary.

Let us consider the testimony of three other witnesses of unquestionable competence: J. E. Oupovalov, chairman of the Votkinsk Metal Workers' Union, is a Social Democrat, a working-man. He was a member of the local Soviet of Nizhni-

Novgorod. Three times under Czar Nicholas II this militant Socialist and trades-unionist was imprisoned for his activities on behalf of his class. Here, then, is a witness who is at once a Russian, a Socialist, a trades-unionist, and a wage-worker, and he writes of matters of which he has intimate personal knowledge. He does not indulge in generalities, but is precise and specific in his references to events, places, and dates:

> In February, 1919, after the conclusion of the shameful Brest-Litovsk Treaty, the Soviet of Workmen's Delegates met in Nizhni-Novgorod for the purpose of electing delegates to the All-Russian Congress, which would be called upon to decide the question of peace. The Bolsheviks and the Left Social-Revolutionaries obtained a chance majority of two votes in the Soviet. *Taking advantage of this, they deprived the Social Democrats and Right Social-Revolutionaries of the right to take part in the election of delegates.* The expelled members of the Soviet assembled at a separate meeting and decided to elect independently a proportionate number of delegates. *But the Bolsheviks immediately sent a band of armed Letts and we were dispersed.*
>
> In March, 1918, the Sormovo workmen demanded the re-election of the Soviet. After a severe struggle the re-elections took place, the Mensheviks and the Social-Revolutionaries obtaining a majority. But the former Bolshevist Soviet *refused to hand over the management to the newly elected body, and the latter was dispersed by armed Red Guards on April 8th.* Similar events took place in Nizhni-Novgorod, Kovrov, Izhevsk, Koloma, and other places. Who, therefore, would venture to assert that power in Russia belongs to the Soviets?

Equally pertinent and impressive is the testimony of J. Strumillo, also a Social Democrat and trades-unionist. This militant working-man is a member of the Social Democratic Party, to which both Lenin and Trotsky formerly belonged. He is also a wage-worker, an electric fitter. He is an official of the Metal Workers' Union and a member of the Hospital Funds Board for the town of Perm. He says:

... the Labor masses began to draw away from Bolshevism. This became particularly evident after the Brest-Litovsk Peace, which exposed the treacherous way in which the Bolsheviks had handed over the Russian people to the German Junkers. Everywhere re-elections began to take place for the Soviets of Workmen's Delegates and for the trades-unions. On seeing that the workmen were withdrawing from them, the Bolsheviks started by forbidding the re-elections to be held, and finally *declared that the Bolsheviks alone had the right to elect and be elected. Thus an enormous number of workmen were disfranchised....* The year 1918 saw the complete suppression of the Labor movement and of the Social Democratic Party. *All over Russia an order was issued from Moscow to exclude representatives of the Social Democratic Party from the Soviets, and the party itself was declared illegal.*

V. M. Zenzinov, a member of the Central Committee of the Party of Socialists-Revolutionists, came to this country in February, 1919, and spent several weeks, during which time the present writer made his acquaintance. Zenzinov was many times arrested under czarism for his revolutionary activities, and more than once sent into Siberian exile. He was a member of the Constituent Assembly, and later, in September, 1918, at the Ufa Conference, was elected member of the Directory. It will be remembered that the Directory was forcibly overthrown and the Kolchak Government set up in its place. Zenzinov is an anti-Bolshevik, but his testimony is not to be set aside on that account. He says: "The Soviet Government is not even a true Soviet régime, for the Bolsheviki have expelled the representatives of all the other political parties from the Soviets, either by force or by other similar means. The Soviet Government is a government of the Bolshevist Party, pure and simple; it is a party dictatorship—not even a dictatorship of the proletariat."

The apologists for the Bolsheviki in this country have frequently denied the charge that the Soviets were thus packed and that anti-Bolshevist parties were not given equal rights to secure representation in them. Of the facts there can be no question, but it is interesting to find such a well-known pro-Bolshevist writer as Mr. Arthur Ransome stating, in the London *Daily News*, January 11, 1919, that "the Mensheviki now stand definitely on the Soviet platform" and that "a decree has accordingly been passed *readmitting* them to the Soviets." Does not the statement that a decree had been passed "readmitting" this Socialist faction to the Soviets constitute an admission that until the passing of the decree mentioned that faction, at least, had been denied representation in the Soviets? Yet this same Mr. Ransome, in view of this fact, which was well known to most students of Russian conditions, and of which he can hardly have been ignorant, addressed his eloquent plea to the people of America on behalf of the Soviet Government as the true representative of the Russian people!

Even the trades-unions are not wholly assured of the right of representation in the Soviets. Only "if their declared relations to the Soviet Government are approved by the Soviet authorities" can they vote or nominate candidates. Trades-unions may solemnly declare that they "acknowledge the Soviet authorities," but if their immediate relations with the People's Commissaries are not good—if they are engaged in strikes, for example—there is little chance of their getting the approval of the Soviet authorities, without which they cannot vote. Finally, no union, party, faction, or group can nominate whomever it pleases; all candidates must be acceptable to, and approved by, the central authority!

Numerous witnesses have testified that the Soviets under Bolshevism are "packed"; that they are not freely elected bodies, in many cases. Thus H. V. Keeling writes:

The elections for the various posts in our union and local Soviet were an absolute farce. I had a vote and naturally consulted with friends whom to vote for. They laughed at me and said it was all arranged, "we have been told who to vote for." I knew some of these "nominated" men quite well, and will go no farther than saying that they were not the best workmen. It is a simple truth that no one except he be a Bolshevik was allowed to be elected for any post.[3]

[3] Keeling, op. cit., p. 159.

In *A Memorandum on Certain Aspects of the Bolshevist Movement in Russia*, published by the State Department of the United States, January, 1920, the following statement by an unnamed Russian appears in a report dated July 2, 1919:

Discontent and hatred against the Bolsheviks are now so strong that a shock or the knowledge of approaching help would suffice to make the people rise and annihilate the Communists. Considering this discontent and hatred, it would seem that elections to different councils should produce candidates of other parties. Nevertheless all councils consist of Communists. The explanation is very plain. That freedom of election of which the Bolsheviks write and talk so much consists in the free election of certain persons, a list of which had already been prepared. For instance, if in one district six delegates have to be elected, seven to eight names are mentioned, of which six can be chosen. Very characteristic in this respect were the elections February last in the district of ——, Moscow Province, where I have one of my estates. Nearly all voters, about 200, of which twelve Communists, came to the district town. Seven delegates had to be elected and only seven names were on the prepared list, naturally all Communists. The local Soviet invited the twelve communistic voters to a house, treated them with food, tea, and sugar, and gave each ten rubles per day; the others received nothing, not even housing. But they, knowing what they had to expect from former experiences, had provided for such an emergency and decided to remain to the end. The day of election was fixed and put off from day to day. After four postponements the Soviet saw no way out. The result was that the seven delegates elected by all against twelve votes belonged to the Octobrists and Constitutional-Democrats. But these seven and a number of the wealthier voters were immediately arrested as agitators against the Soviet Republic. New elections were announced three days later, but this time the place was surrounded by machine-guns. The next day official papers announced the unanimous election of Communists in the district of Verea. After a short time peasant revolts started. To put down these, Chinese and Letts were sent and about 300 peasants were killed. Then began arrests, but it is not known how many were executed.

Finally, there is the testimony of the workman, Menshekov, member of the Social Democratic Party, who was himself given an important position in one of the largest factories of Russia, the Ijevsky factory, in the Urals, when the Bolsheviki assumed control. This simple workman was not, and is not, a "reactionary monarchist," but a Social Democrat. He belonged to the same party as Lenin and Trotsky until the withdrawal of these men and their followers and the creation of the Communist Party. Menshekov says:

One of the principles which the Bolsheviki proposed is rule by the Workers' Councils. In June, 1918, we were told to elect one of 135 delegates. We did, and only fifty pro-Bolsheviki got in. *The Bolshevist Government was dissatisfied with this result and ordered a second election.* This time only twenty pro-Bolsheviki were elected. Now, I happen to have been elected a member of this Workers' Council, from which I was further elected to sit on the Executive Council. According to the Bolsheviki's own principle, the Executive Council has to do the whole administration. Everything is under it. But the Bolshevist Government withheld this right from us. For two weeks we sat and did nothing; then the Bolsheviki solved the problem for themselves. They arrested some of us—I was arrested myself—and, instead of an elected Council, *the Red Government appointed a Council of selected Communists*, and formed there, as everywhere, a special privileged class.[4]

[4] *Menshekov's account is from a personal communication to the present writer, who has carefully verified the statements made in it.*

All such charges have been scouted by the defenders of the Bolsheviki in this country and in England. On March 22, 1919, the *Dyelo Naroda*, organ of the Socialists-Revolutionists, reproduced the following official document, which fully sustains the accusation that the ordering of the "election" of certain persons to important offices is not "an invention of the capitalist press":

Order of the Department of Information and Instruction of the Executive Committee of the Soviet of Workers' and Peasants' Delegates of the Melenkovski District:

No. 994. Town of Melenki (Prov. of Vladimir)
Feb. 25, 1919

To the Voinovo Agricultural Council:

The Provincial Department instructs you, on the basis of the Constitution of the Soviet (Russian Socialist Federative Soviet Republic). Section 43, Sub-section 6, letter *a*, to proceed without fail with elections for an Agricultural Executive Committee.

The following *must be elected* to the committee: As president, Nikita Riabov; as member, Ivan Soloviev; and as secretary, Alexander Krainov. These people, as may be gathered from the posts to which they are named, *must be elected without fail*. The non-fulfilment of this Order will result in those responsible being severely punished. Acknowledge the carrying out of these instructions to Provincial Headquarters by express.

Head of Provincial Section.

[Signed] J. Nazarov.

Surely there never was a greater travesty of representative government than this—not even under czarism! This is worse than anything that obtained in the old "rotten boroughs" of England before the great Reform Act. Yet our "Liberals" and "Radicals" hail this vicious reactionary despotism with gladness.

If it be thought that the judgment of the present writer is too harsh, he is quite content to rest upon the judgment pronounced by such a sympathizer as Mr. Isaac Don Levine has shown himself to be. In the New York *Globe*, January 5, 1920, Mr. Levine said: "To-day Soviet Russia is a dictatorship, not of the proletariat, but for the proletariat. It certainly is not democracy." And again: "*The dictatorship of the proletariat in Russia is really a dictatorship of the Bolshevist or Communist Party. This is the great change wrought in Soviet Russia since 1918. The Soviets ceased functioning as parliamentary bodies.* Soviet elections, which were frequent in 1918, are very rare now. In Russia, where things are moving so fast and opinions are changing so rapidly, the majority of the present Soviets are obsolete and do not represent the present view of the masses."

If the government is really a dictatorship of the Communist Party—which does not include in its membership 1 per cent. of the people of Russia—if the Soviets have ceased functioning as parliamentary bodies, if the majority of the Soviets are obsolete and do not represent the present view of the masses, the condemnation expressed in this chapter is completely justified.

IV
THE UNDEMOCRATIC SOVIET STATE

M r. Lincoln Steffens is a most amiable idealist who possesses an extraordinary genius for idealizing commonplace and even sordid realities. He can always readily idealize a perfectly rotten egg into a perfectly good omelet. It is surely significant that, in spite of his very apparent efforts to justify and even glorify the Soviet Government and the men who have imposed it upon Russia, even Mr. Steffens has to admit its autocratic character. He says:

> The soviet form of government, which sprang up so spontaneously all over Russia, is established.
>
> This is not a paper thing; not an invention. Never planned, it has not yet been written into the forms of law. It is not even uniform. It is full of faults and difficulties; clumsy, and in its final development it is not democratic. The present Russian Government is the most autocratic government I have ever seen. *Lenin, head of the Soviet Government, is farther removed from the people than the Czar was, or than any actual ruler in Europe is.*
>
> The people in a shop or an industry are a soviet. These little informal soviets elect a local soviet; which elects delegates to the city or country (community) soviet; which elects delegates to the government (State) soviet. The government soviets together elect delegates to the All-Russian Soviet, which elects commissionnaires (who correspond to our Cabinet, or to a European minority). And these commissionnaires finally elect Lenin. He is thus five or six removes from the people. To form an idea of his stability, independence,

and power, think of the process that would have to be gone through with by the people to remove him and elect a successor. A majority of all the soviets in all Russia would have to be changed in personnel or opinion, recalled, or brought somehow to recognize and represent the altered will of the people.[5]

[5] *Report of Lincoln Steffens, laid before the Committee on Foreign Relations of the United States Senate, September, 1919. Published in The Bullitt Mission to Russia, pp. 111-112. Italics mine.*

This is a very moderate estimate of the government which Lenin and Trotsky and their associates have imposed upon Russia by the old agencies—blood and iron. Mr. Steffens is not quite accurate in his statement that the Soviet form of government "has not yet been written into the forms of law." The report from which the above passage is quoted bears the date of April 2, 1919; at that time there was in existence, and widely known even outside of Russia, the Constitution of the Russian Socialist Federal Soviet Republic, which purports to be "the Soviet form of government ... written into the forms of law." Either it is that or it is a mass of meaningless verbiage. There existed, too, at that time, a very plethora of laws which purported to be the written forms of Soviet government, and as such were published by the Bolshevist Government of Russia. The Fundamental Law of Socialization of the Land, which went into effect in September, 1918; the law decreeing the Abolition of Classes and Ranks, dated November 10, 1917; the law creating Regional and Local Boards of National Economy, dated December 23, 1917; the law creating The People's Court, November 24, 1917; the Marriage and Divorce Laws, December 18, 1917; the Eight Hour Law, October 29, 1917, and the Insurance Law, November 29, 1917, are a few of the bewildering array of laws and decrees which seem to indicate that the Soviet form of government has "been written into the forms of law."

It is in no hypercritical spirit that attention is called to this rather remarkable error in the report of Mr. Steffens. It is because the Soviet form of government has "been written into the forms of law" with so much thoroughness and detail that we are enabled to examine Bolshevism at its best, as its protagonists have conceived it, and not merely as it appears in practice, in its experimental stage, with all its mistakes, abuses, and failures. After all, a written constitution is a formulation of certain ideals to be attained and certain principles to be applied as well as very imperfect human beings can do it. Given a worthy ideal, it would be possible to make generous allowance for the deficiencies of practice; to believe that these would be progressively overcome and more or less constant and steady progress made in the direction of the ideal. On the other hand, when the ideal itself is inferior to the practice, when by reason of the good sense and sound morality of the people the actual political life proves superior to the written constitution and laws, it is not difficult to appreciate the fact. In such circumstances we are not compelled to discredit the right practice in order to condemn the wrong theory. It is true that as a general rule mankind sets its ideals beyond its immediate reach; but it is also true that men sometimes surpass their ideals. Most men's creeds are superior to their deeds, but there are many men whose deeds are vastly better than their creeds.

Similarly, while the political life of nations generally falls below the standards set in their formal constitutions and laws, exceptions to this rule are by no means rare. Constitutions are generally framed by political theorists and idealists whose inveterate habit it is to overrate the mental and moral capacity of the great majority of human beings and to underrate the force of selfishness, ignorance, and other defects of imperfect humanity. On the other hand, constitutions have sometimes been framed by selfish and ignorant despots, inferior in character and intelligence to the majority of the human beings to be governed by the constitutions so devised. Under the former conditions political realities fail to attain the high levels of the ideals; under the latter conditions they rise above them. Finally, people outgrow constitutions as they outgrow most other political devices and social arrangements. In old civilizations it is common to find political life upon a higher level than the formal constitutions, which, unrepealed and unamended, have in fact become obsolete, ignored by the people of a wiser and more generous age.

The writer of these pages fully believes that the political reality in Russia is already better than the ignoble ideal set by the Bolshevist constitution. The fundamental virtues of the Russian people, their innate tolerance, their democracy, and their shrewd sense have mitigated, and tend to increasingly mitigate, the rigors of the new autocracy. Once more it is demonstrated that "man is more than constitutions"; that adequate resources of human character can make a tolerable degree of comfort possible under any sort of constitution, just as lack of those resources can make life intolerable under the best constitution ever devised. Men have attained a high degree of civilization and comfort in spite of despotically conceived constitutions, and, on the other hand, the evils of Tammany Hall under a Tweed developed in spite of a constitution conceived in a spirit more generous than any modern nation had hitherto known. Great spiritual and moral forces, whose roots are deeply embedded in the soil of historical development, are shaping Russia's life. Already there is discernible much that is better than anything in the constitution imposed upon her.

A more or less vague perception of this fact has led to much muddled thinking; because the character of the Russian people and the political and economic conditions prevailing have led to a general disregard of much of Bolshevist theory, because men and women in Russia are finding it possible to set aside certain elements of Bolshevism, and thereby attain increasingly tolerable conditions of life, we are asked to believe that Bolshevism is less evil than we feared it to be. To call this "muddled thinking" is to put a strain upon charity of judgment. The facts are not capable of such interpretation by minds disciplined by the processes of straight and clear thinking. What they prove is that, fortunately for mankind, the wholesomeness of the thought and character of the average Russian has proved too strong to be overcome by the false ideas and ideals of the Bolsheviki and their contrivances. The Russian people live, not because they have found good in Bolshevism, but because they have found means to circumvent Bolshevism and set it aside. What progress is being made in Russia to-day is not the result of Bolshevism, but of the growing power of those very qualities of mind and heart which Bolshevism sought to destroy.

Bolshevism is autocratic and despotic in its essence. Whoever believes — as the present writer does — that the only rational and coherent hope for the progress of civilization lies in the growth of democracy must reject Bolshevism and all its works and ways. It is well to remember that whatever there is of freedom and good will in Russia, of democratic growth, exists in fundamental defiance and antagonism to Bolshevism and would be crushed if the triumph of the latter became complete. It is still necessary, therefore, to judge Bolshevism by its ideal and the logical implications of its ideal; not by what results where it is made powerless by moral or economic forces which it cannot overcome, but by what it aims at doing and will do if possible. It is for this reason that we must subject the constitution of Bolshevist Russia to careful analysis and scrutiny. In this document the intellectual leaders of

Bolshevism have set forth in the precise terms of organic law the manner in which they would reconstruct the state.

In considering the political constitution of any nation the believer in democratic government seeks first of all to know the extent and nature of the franchise of its citizens, how it is obtained, what power it has, and how it is exercised. The almost uniform experience of those nations which have developed free and responsible self-government has led to the conclusion that the ultimate sovereignty of the citizens must be absolute; that suffrage must be equal, universal, direct, and free; that it must be exercised under conditions which do not permit intimidation, coercion, or fraud, and that, finally, the mandate of the citizens so expressed must be imperative. The validity of these conclusions may not be absolute; it is at least conceivable that they may be revised. For that matter, a reversion to aristocracy is conceivable, highly improbable though it may be. With these uniform results of the experience of many nations as our criteria, let us examine the fundamental suffrage provisions of the Constitution of the Russian Socialist Federal Soviet Republic and the provisions relating to elections. These are all set forth in Article IV, Chapters XIII to XV, inclusive:

Article IV

Chapter XIII
THE RIGHT TO VOTE

64. The right to vote and to be elected to the Soviets is enjoyed by the following citizens of both sexes, irrespective of religion, nationality, domicile, etc., of the Russian Socialist Federal Soviet Republic, who shall have completed their eighteenth year by the day of election:

(*a*) All who have acquired the means of livelihood through labor that is productive and useful to society, and also persons engaged in housekeeping which enables the former to do productive work, *i.e.*, laborers and employees of all classes who are employed in industry, trade, agriculture, etc., and peasants and Cossack agricultural laborers who employ no help for the purpose of making profits.

(*b*) Soldiers of the army and navy of the Soviets.

(*c*) Citizens of the two preceding categories who have in any degree lost their capacity to work.

Note 1: Local Soviets may, upon approval of the central power, lower the age standard mentioned herein.

Note 2: Non-citizens mentioned in Section 20 (Article II. Chapter V) have the right to vote.

65. The following persons enjoy neither the right to vote nor the right to be voted for, even though they belong to one of the categories enumerated above, namely:

(*a*) Persons who employ hired labor in order to obtain from it an increase in profits.

(*b*) Persons who have an income without doing any work, such as interest from capital, receipts from property, etc.

(*c*) Private merchants, trade and commercial brokers.

(*d*) Monks and clergy of all denominations.

(*e*) Employees and agents of the former police, the gendarme corps, and the *Okhrana* (Czar's secret service), also members of the former reigning dynasty.

(*f*) Persons who have in legal form been declared demented or mentally deficient, and also persons under guardianship.

(*g*) Persons who have been deprived by a Soviet of their rights of citizenship because of selfish or dishonorable offenses, for the period fixed by the sentence.

Chapter XIV
ELECTIONS

66. Elections are conducted according to custom on days fixed by the local Soviets.

67. Election takes place in the presence of an election committee and the representative of the local Soviet.

68. In case the representative of the Soviet cannot for valid causes be present, the chairman of the election meeting replaces him.

69. Minutes of the proceedings and results of elections are to be compiled and signed by the members of the election committee and the representative of the Soviet.

70. Detailed instructions regarding the election proceedings and the participation in them of professional and other workers' organizations are to be issued by the local Soviets, according to the instructions of the All-Russian Central Executive Committee.

Chapter XV
THE CHECKING AND CANCELLATION OF ELECTIONS AND RECALL OF THE DEPUTIES

71. The respective Soviets receive all the records of the proceedings of the election.

72. The Soviet appoints a commission to verify the election.

73. This commission reports the results to the Soviet.

74. The Soviet decides the question when there is doubt as to which candidate is elected.

75. The Soviet announces a new election if the election of one candidate or another cannot be determined.

76. If an election was irregularly carried on in its entirety, it may be declared void by a higher Soviet authority.

77. The highest authority in relation to questions of elections is the All-Russian Central Executive Committee.

78. Voters who have sent a deputy to the Soviet have the right to recall him, and to have a new election, according to general provisions.

It is quite clear that the suffrage here provided for is not universal; that certain classes of people commonly found in modern civilized nations in considerable numbers are not entitled to vote. There may be some doubt as to the precise meaning of some of the paragraphs in Chapter XIII, but it is certain that, if the language used is to be subject to no esoteric interpretation, the following social groups are excluded from the right to vote: (*a*) all persons who employ hired labor for profit, including farmers with a single hired helper; (*b*) all persons who draw incomes from interest, rent, or profit; (*c*) all persons engaged in private trade, even to the smallest shopkeeper; (*d*) all ministers of religion of every kind; (*e*) all persons engaged in work which is not defined by the proper authorities as "productive and useful to society"; (*f*) members of the old royal family and those formerly employed in the old police service.

It is obvious that a very large part of the present voting population of this country would be disfranchised if we should adopt these restrictions or anything like them. It may be fairly argued in reply, however, that the disfranchisement would be—and now is, in Russia—a temporary condition only; that the object of the discriminations, and of other political and economic arrangements complementary to them, is to force people out of such categories as are banned and penalized with disfranchisement—and that this is being done in Russia. In other words, people are to be forced to cease hiring labor for profit, engaging in private trade, being ministers of religion, living on incomes derived from interest, rent, or profits. They are to be forced into service that is "productive and useful to society," and when that is accomplished they will become qualified to vote. Thus practically universal suffrage is possible, in theory at any rate.

So much may be argued with fair show of reason. We may dispute the assumption that there is anything to be gained by disfranchising a man because he engages in trade, and thereby possibly confers a benefit upon those whom he serves. We may doubt or deny that there is likely to accrue any advantage to society from the disfranchisement of all ministers of religion. We may believe that to suppress some of the categories which are discriminated against would be a disaster, subversive of the life of society even. When all this has been admitted it remains the fact that it is possible to conceive of a society in which there are no employers, traders, recipients of capitalist incomes, or ministers of religion; it is possible to conceive of such a society in which, even under this constitution, only a very small fraction of the adult population would be disfranchised. Of course, it is so highly improbable that it borders on the fantastic; but it is, nevertheless, within the bounds of conceivability that practically universal suffrage might be realized within the limits of this instrument.

Let us examine, briefly, the conditions under which the franchise is to be exercised: we do not find any provision for that secrecy of the ballot which experience and ordinary good sense indicate as the only practicable method of eliminating coercion, intimidation, and vote-trafficking. Nor do we find anything like a uniform method of voting. The holding of elections "conducted according to custom on days fixed by the local Soviets"—themselves elective bodies—makes possible an amount of political manipulation and intrigue which almost staggers the imagination. Not until human beings attain a far greater degree of perfection than has ever yet been attained, so far as there is any record, will it be safe or prudent to endow any set of men with so much arbitrary power over the manner in which their fellows may exercise the electoral franchise.

There is one paragraph in the above-quoted portions of the Constitution of Soviet Russia which alone opens the way to a despotism which is practically unlimited. Paragraph 70 of Chapter XIV provides that: "Detailed instructions regarding the election proceedings *and the participation in them of professional and other workers' organizations* are to be issued by the local Soviets, *according to the instructions of the All-Russian Central Executive Committee.*" Within the scope of this general statement every essential principle of representative government can be lawfully abrogated. Elsewhere it has been shown that trades-unions have been denied the right to nominate or vote for candidates unless "their declared relations to the Soviet Government are approved by the Soviet authorities"; that parties are permitted to nominate only such candidates as are acceptable to, and approved by, the central authority; that specific orders to elect certain favored candidates have actually been issued by responsible officials. Within the scope of Paragraph 70 of Chapter XIV, all these things are clearly permissible. No limit to the "instructions" which may be given by the All-Russian Central Executive Committee is provided by the Constitution itself. It cannot be argued that the danger of evil practices occurring is an imaginary one merely; the concrete examples cited in the previous chapter show that the danger is a very real one.

In this connection it is important to note Paragraph 23 of Chapter V, Article VI, which reads as follows:

> Being guided by the interests of the working-class as a whole, the Russian Socialist Federal Soviet Republic deprives all individuals and groups of rights which could be utilized by them to the detriment of the Socialist Revolution.

This means, apparently, that the Council of People's Commissars can at any time disfranchise any individual or group or party which aims to overthrow their rule. This power has been used with tremendous effect on many occasions.

Was it this power which caused the Bolsheviki to withhold the electoral franchise from all members of the teaching profession in Petrograd, we wonder? According to Section 64 of Chapter XIII of the Soviet Constitution, the "right to vote and to be elected to the Soviets" belongs, first, to "all who have acquired the means of livelihood through labor that is productive and useful to society." Teachers employed in the public schools and other educational institutions—especially those controlled by the state—would naturally be included in this category, without any question, one would suppose, especially in view of the manner in which the Bolsheviki have paraded their great passion for education and culture. Nevertheless, it seems to be a fact that, up to July, 1919, the teaching profession of Petrograd was excluded from representation in the Soviet. The following paragraph from the *Izvestia* of the Petrograd Soviet, dated July 3, 1919, can hardly be otherwise interpreted:

> Teachers and other cultural-educational workers this year *for the first time* will be able, in an organized manner through their union, to take an active part in the work of the Petrograd Soviet of Deputies. *This is the first and most difficult examination for the working intelligentsia of the above-named categories.* Comrades and citizens, scholars, teachers, and other cultural workers, stand this test in a worthy manner!

Let us now turn our attention to those provisions of the Constitution of the Russian Socialist Federal Soviet Republic which concern the general political organization of the Soviet state. These are contained in Article III, Chapters VI to XII, inclusive, and are as follows:

Article III

Construction of the Soviet Power

A. Organization of the Central Power

Chapter VI
THE ALL-RUSSIAN CONGRESS OF SOVIETS OF WORKERS', PEASANTS', COSSACKS', AND RED ARMY DEPUTIES

24. The All-Russian Congress of Soviets is the supreme power of the Russian Socialist Federal Soviet Republic.

25. The All-Russian Congress of Soviets is composed of representatives of urban Soviets (one delegate for 25,000 voters), and of representatives of the provincial (*Gubernia*) congresses of Soviets (one delegate for 125,000 inhabitants).

Note 1: In case the Provincial Congress is not called before the All-Russian Congress is convoked, delegates for the latter are sent directly from the County (*Oyezd*) Congress.

Note 2: In case the Regional (*Oblast*) Congress is convoked indirectly, previous to the convocation of the All-Russian Congress, delegates for the latter may be sent by the Regional Congress.

26. The All-Russian Congress is convoked by the All-Russian Central Executive Committee at least twice a year.

27. A special All-Russian Congress is convoked by the All-Russian Central Executive Committee upon its own initiative, or upon the request of local

Soviets having not less than one-third of the entire population of the Republic.

28. The All-Russian Congress elects an All-Russian Central Executive Committee of not more than 200 members.

29. The All-Russian Central Executive Committee is entirely responsible to the All-Russian Congress of Soviets.

30. In the periods between the convocation of the Congresses, the All-Russian Central Executive Committee is the supreme power of the Republic.

Chapter VII
THE ALL-RUSSIAN CENTRAL EXECUTIVE COMMITTEE

31. The All-Russian Central Executive Committee is the supreme legislative, executive, and controlling organ of the Russian Socialist Federal Soviet Republic.

32. The All-Russian Central Executive Committee directs in a general way the activity of the Workers' and Peasants' Government and of all organs of the Soviet authority in the country, and it co-ordinates and regulates the operation of the Soviet Constitution and of the resolutions of the All-Russian Congresses and of the central organs of the Soviet power.

33. The All-Russian Central Executive Committee considers and enacts all measures and proposals introduced by the Soviet of People's Commissars or by the various departments, and it also issues its own decrees and regulations.

34. The All-Russian Central Executive Committee convokes the All-Russian Congress of Soviets, at which time the Executive Committee reports on its activity and on general questions.

35. The All-Russian Central Executive Committee forms a Council of People's Commissars for the purpose of general management of the affairs of the Russian Socialist Federal Soviet Republic, and it also forms departments

(People's Commissariats) for the purpose of conducting the various branches.

36. The members of the All-Russian Central Executive Committee work in the various departments (People's Commissariats) or execute special orders of the All-Russian Central Executive Committee.

Chapter VIII
THE COUNCIL OF PEOPLE'S COMMISSARS

37. The Council of People's Commissars is intrusted with the general management of the affairs of the Russian Socialist Federal Soviet Republic.

38. For the accomplishment of this task the Council of People's Commissars issues decrees, resolutions, orders, and, in general, takes all steps necessary for the proper and rapid conduct of government affairs.

39. The Council of People's Commissars notifies immediately the All-Russian Central Executive Committee of all its orders and resolutions.

40. The All-Russian Central Executive Committee has the right to revoke or suspend all orders and resolutions of the Council of People's Commissars.

41. All orders and resolutions of the Council of People's Commissars of great political significance are referred for consideration and final approval to the All-Russian Central Executive Committee.

Note: Measures requiring immediate execution may be enacted directly by the Council of People's Commissars.

42. The members of the Council of People's Commissars stand at the head of the various People's Commissariats.

43. There are seventeen People's Commissars: (*a*) Foreign Affairs, (*b*) Army, (*c*) Navy, (*d*) Interior, (*e*) Justice, (*f*) Labor, (*g*) Social Welfare, (*h*) Education, (*i*) Post and Telegraph, (*j*) National Affairs, (*k*) Finances, (*l*) Ways of Communication, (*m*) Agriculture, (*n*) Commerce and Industry, (*o*) National Supplies, (*p*) State Control, (*q*) Supreme Soviet of National Economy, (*r*) Public Health.

44. Every Commissar has a Collegium (Committee) of which he is the President, and the members of which are appointed by the Council of People's Commissars.

45. A People's Commissar has the individual right to decide on all questions under the jurisdiction of his Commissariat, and he is to report on his decision to the Collegium. If the Collegium does not agree with the Commissar on some decisions, the former may, without stopping the execution of the decision, complain of it to the executive members of the Council of People's Commissars or to the All-Russian Central Executive Committee.

Individual members of the Collegium have this right also.

46. The Council of People's Commissars is entirely responsible to the All-Russian Congress of Soviets and the All-Russian Central Executive Committee.

47. The People's Commissars and the Collegia of the People's Commissariats are entirely responsible to the Council of People's Commissars and the All-Russian Central Executive Committee.

48. The title of People's Commissar belongs only to the members of the Council of People's Commissars, which is in charge of general affairs of the Russian Socialist Federal Soviet Republic, and it cannot be used by any other representative of the Soviet power, either central or local.

Chapter IX
AFFAIRS IN THE JURISDICTION OF THE ALL-RUSSIAN CONGRESS AND THE ALL-RUSSIAN CENTRAL EXECUTIVE COMMITTEE

49. The All-Russian Congress and the All-Russian Central Executive Committee deal with questions of state, such as:

(*a*) Ratification and amendment of the Constitution of the Russian Socialist Federal Soviet Republic.

(*b*) General direction of the entire interior and foreign policy of the Russian Socialist Federal Soviet Republic.

(*c*) Establishing and changing boundaries, also ceding territory belonging to the Russian Socialist Federal Soviet Republic.

(*d*) Establishing boundaries for regional Soviet unions belonging to the Russian Socialist Federal Soviet Republic, also settling disputes among them.

(*e*) Admission of new members to the Russian Socialist Federal Soviet Republic, and recognition of the secession of any parts of it.

(*f*) The general administrative division of the territory of the Russian Socialist Federal Soviet Republic and the approval of regional unions.

(*g*) Establishing and changing weights, measures, and money denominations in the Russian Socialist Federal Soviet Republic.

(*h*) Foreign relations, declaration of war, and ratification of peace treaties.

(*i*) Making loans, signing commercial treaties and financial agreements.

(*j*) Working out a basis and a general plan for the national economy and for its various branches in the Russian Socialist Federal Soviet Republic.

(*k*) Approval of the budget of the Russian Socialist Federal Soviet Republic.

(*l*) Levying taxes and establishing the duties of citizens to the state.

(*m*) Establishing the bases for the organization of armed forces.

(*n*) State legislation, judicial organization and procedure, civil and criminal legislation, etc.

(*o*) Appointment and dismissal of the individual People's Commissars or the entire Council, also approval of the President of the Council of People's Commissars.

(*p*) Granting and canceling Russian citizenship and fixing rights of foreigners.

(*q*) The right to declare individual and general amnesty.

50. Besides the above-mentioned questions, the All-Russian Congress and the All-Russian Central Executive Committee have charge of all other affairs which, according to their decision, require their attention.

51. The following questions are solely under the jurisdiction of the All-Russian Congress:

(*a*) Ratification and amendment of the fundamental principles of the Soviet Constitution.

(*b*) Ratification of peace treaties.

52. The decision of questions indicated in Paragraphs (*c*) and (*h*) of Section 49 may be made by the All-Russian Central Executive Committee only in case it is impossible to convoke the Congress.

B. Organization of Local Soviets

Chapter X
THE CONGRESSES OF THE SOVIETS

53. Congresses of Soviets are composed as follows:

(*a*) Regional: of representatives of the urban and county Soviets, one representative for 25,000 inhabitants of the county, and one representative for 5,000 voters of the cities—but not more than 500 representatives for the entire region—or of representatives of the provincial Congresses, chosen on the same basis, if such a Congress meets before the regional Congress.

(*b*) Provincial (*Gubernia*): of representatives of urban and rural (*Volost*) Soviets, one representative for 10,000 inhabitants from the rural districts, and one representative for 2,000 voters in the city; altogether not more than 300 representatives for the entire province. In case the county Congress meets before the provincial, election takes place on the same basis, but by the county Congress instead of the rural.

(*c*) County: of representatives of rural Soviets, one delegate for each 1,000 inhabitants, but not more than 300 delegates for the entire county.

(*d*) Rural (*Volost*): of representatives of all village Soviets in the *Volost*, one delegate for ten members of the Soviet.

Note 1: Representatives of urban Soviets which have a population of not more than 10,000 persons participate in the county Congress; village Soviets of districts less than 1,000 inhabitants unite for the purpose of electing delegates to the county Congress.

Note 2: Rural Soviets of less than ten members send one delegate to the rural (*Volost*) Congress.

54. Congresses of the Soviets are convoked by the respective Executive Committees upon their own initiative, or upon request of local Soviets comprising not less than one-third of the entire population of the given district. In any case they are convoked at least twice a year for regions, every three months for provinces and counties, and once a month for rural districts.

55. Every Congress of Soviets (regional, provincial, county, or rural) elects its Executive organ—an Executive Committee the membership of which shall not exceed: (*a*) for regions and provinces, twenty-five; (*b*) for a county, twenty; (*c*) for a rural district, ten. The Executive Committee is responsible to the Congress which elected it.

56. In the boundaries of the respective territories the Congress is the supreme power; during intervals between the convocations of the Congress, the Executive Committee is the supreme power.

Chapter XI
THE SOVIET OF DEPUTIES

57. Soviets of Deputies are formed:

(*a*) In cities, one deputy for each 1,000 inhabitants; the total to be not less than fifty and not more than 1,000 members.

(*b*) All other settlements (towns, villages, hamlets, etc.) of less than 10,000 inhabitants, one deputy for each 100 inhabitants; the total to be not less than three and not more than fifty deputies for each settlement.

Term of the deputy, three months.

Note: In small rural sections, whenever possible, all questions shall be decided at general meetings of voters.

58. The Soviet of Deputies elects an Executive Committee to deal with current affairs; not more than five members for rural districts, one for every fifty members of the Soviets of cities, but not more than fifteen and not less than three in the aggregate (Petrograd and Moscow not more than forty). The Executive Committee is entirely responsible to the Soviet which elected it.

59. The Soviet of Deputies is convoked by the Executive Committee upon its own initiative, or upon the request of not less than one-half of the membership of the Soviet; in any case at least once a week in cities, and twice a week in rural sections.

60. Within its jurisdiction the Soviet, and in cases mentioned in Section 57, Note, the meeting of the voters is the supreme power in the given district.

Chapter XII
JURISDICTION OF THE LOCAL ORGANS OF THE SOVIETS

61. Regional, provincial, county, and rural organs of the Soviet power and also the Soviets of Deputies have to perform the following duties:

(*a*) Carry out all orders of the respective higher organs of the Soviet power.

(*b*) Take all steps for raising the cultural and economic standard of the given territory.

(*c*) Decide all questions of local importance within their respective territories.

(*d*) Co-ordinate all Soviet activity in their respective territories.

62. The Congresses of Soviets and their Executive Committees have the right to control the activity of the local Soviets (*i.e.*, the regional Congress controls all Soviets of the respective region; the provincial, of the respective province, with the exception of the urban Soviets, etc.); and the regional and provincial Congresses and their Executive Committees have in addition the right to

overrule the decisions of the Soviets of their districts, giving notice in important cases to the central Soviet authority.

63. For the purpose of performing their duties, the local Soviets, rural and urban, and the Executive Committees form sections respectively.

It is a significant and notable fact that nowhere in the whole of this remarkable document is there any provision which assures to the individual voter, or to any group, party, or other organization of voters, assurance of the right to make nominations for any office in the whole system of government. Incredible as it may seem, this is literally and exactly true. The urban Soviet consists of "one deputy for each 1,000 inhabitants," but there is nowhere a sentence prescribing how these deputies are to be nominated or by whom. The village Soviet consists of "one deputy for each 100 inhabitants," but there is nowhere a sentence to show how these deputies are to be nominated, or wherein the right to make nominations is vested. The *Volost* Congress is composed of "representatives of all village Soviets" and the County Congress (*Oyezd*) of "representatives of rural Soviets." In both these cases the representatives are termed "delegates," but there is no intimation of how they are nominated, or what their qualifications are. The Provincial Congress (*Gubernia*) is composed of "representatives of urban and rural (*Volost*) Soviets." In this case the word "representatives" is maintained throughout; the word "delegates" does not appear. In this provision, as in the others, there is no intimation of how they are nominated, or whether they are elected or designated.

It can hardly be gainsaid that the Constitution of the Russian Socialist Federal Soviet Republic is characterized by loose construction, vagueness where definiteness is essential, and a marked deficiency of those safeguards and guaranties which ought to be incorporated into a written constitution. There is, for example, no provision for that immunity of parliamentary representatives from arrest for libel, sedition, and the like, which is enjoyed in practically all other countries. Even under Czar Nicholas II this principle of parliamentary immunity was always observed until November, 1916, when the ferment of revolution was already manifesting itself. It requires no expert legal knowledge or training to perceive that the fundamental instrument of the political and legal system of Soviet Russia fails to provide adequate protection for the rights and liberties of its citizens.

Let us consider now another matter of cardinal importance, the complex and tedious processes which intervene between the citizen-voter and the "Council of People's Commissars."

(1) The electorate is divided into two groups or divisions, the urban and the rural. Those entitled to vote in the city form, in the first instance, the Soviet of the shop, factory, trades-union, or professional association, as the case may be. Those entitled to vote in the rural village form, in the first instance, the village Soviet.

(2) The Soviets of the shops, factories, trades-unions, and professional associations choose, in such manner as they will, representatives to the urban Soviet. The urban Soviets are not all based on equal representation, however. According to announcements in the official Bolshevist press, factory workers in Petrograd are entitled to one representative in the Petrograd Soviet for every 500 electors, while the soldiers and sailors are entitled to one representative for every 200 members. Thus two soldiers' votes count for exactly as much as five workmen's votes. Those entitled to vote in the village Soviets choose representatives to a rural Soviet (*Volost*), and this body, in turn, chooses representatives to the county Soviet (*Oyezd*). This latter body is equal in power to the urban Soviet; both are represented in the Provincial Soviet (*Gubernia*). The

village peasant is one step farther removed from the Provincial Soviet than is the city worker.

(3) Both the urban Soviets of the city workers' representatives and the county Soviets of the peasants' representatives are represented in the Provincial Soviet. There appears at this point another great inequality in voting power. The basis of representation is one member for 2,000 city *voters* and one for 10,000 *inhabitants* of rural villages. At first this seems to mean—and has been generally understood to mean—that each city worker's vote is equal to the votes of *five* peasants. Apparently this is an error. The difference is more nearly three to one than five to one. Representation is based on the number of *city voters* and the number of *village inhabitants*.

(4) The Provincial Congress (*Gubernia*) sends representatives to the Regional Congress. Here again the voting power is unequal: the basis of representation is one representative for 5,000 *city voters* and one for "25,000 inhabitants of the county." The discrimination here is markedly greater than in the case of the Provincial Congresses for the following reason: The members of these Regional Congresses are chosen by the *Gubernias*, which include representatives of city workers as well as representatives of peasants, the former being given three times proportionate representation of the latter. Obviously, to again apply the same principle and choose representatives of the *Gubernias* to the Regional Congresses on the same basis of three to one has a cumulative disadvantage to the peasant.

(5) The All-Russian Congress of Soviets is composed of delegates chosen by the Provincial Congresses, which represent city workers and peasants, as already shown, *and of representatives sent direct from the urban Soviets*.

From Voter to National Government—Russia and U. S. A.[6]

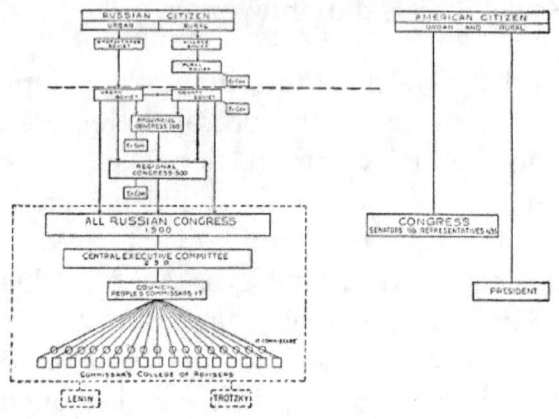

[6] *In all the Soviets, from County Soviets onward, city voters have a larger vote in proportion to numbers than rural voters. (See text.)*

It will be seen that at every step, from the county Soviet to the All-Russian Congress of Soviets, elaborate care has been taken to make certain that the representatives of the city workers are not outnumbered by peasants' representatives. The peasants, who make up 85 per cent. of the population, are systematically discriminated against.

(6) We are not yet at the end of the intricate Soviet system of government. While the All-Russian Congress of Soviets is nominally the supreme power in the state, it is too unwieldy a body to do more than discuss general policies. It meets twice a year for this purpose. From its membership of 1,500 is chosen the All-Russian Central Executive Committee of "not more than 200 members." This likewise is too unwieldy a body to function either quickly or well.

(7) The All-Russian Central Executive Committee selects the Council of People's Commissars of seventeen members, each

Commissar being at the head of a department of the government.

A brief study of the diagram on the preceding page will show how much less directly responsive to the electorate than our own United States Government is this complicated, bureaucratic government of Soviet Russia.

V
THE PEASANTS AND THE LAND

A

t

the time of the Revolution the peasantry comprised 85 per cent. of the population. The industrial wage-earning class—the proletariat—comprised, according to the most generous estimate, not more than 3 to 4 per cent. That part of the proletariat which was actively interested in the revolutionary social change was represented by the Social Democratic Party, which was split into factions as follows: on the right the moderate "defensist" Mensheviki; on the left the radical "defeatist" Bolsheviki; with a large center faction which held a middle course, sometimes giving its support to the right wing and sometimes to the left. Each of these factions contained in it men and women of varying shades of opinion and diverse temperaments. Thus among the Mensheviki were some who were so radical that they were very close to the Bolsheviki, while among the latter were some individuals who were so moderate that they were very close to the Mensheviki.

That part of the peasantry which was actively interested in revolutionary social change was represented by the peasant Socialist parties, the Party of Socialists-Revolutionists, and the Populists, or People's Socialists. The former alone possessed any great numerical strength or political significance. In this party, as in the Social Democratic Party, there was a moderate right wing and a radical left wing with a strong centrist element. In this party also were found in each of the wings men and women whose views seemed barely distinguishable from those generally characteristic of the other. In a general way, the relations of the Socialists-Revolutionists and the Social Democrats were characterized by a tendency on the part of the Socialists-Revolutionists of the Right to make common cause with the Menshevist Social Democrats and a like tendency on the part of the Socialists-Revolutionists of the Left to make common cause with the Bolshevist Social Democrats.

This merging of the two parties applied only to the general program of revolutionary action; in particular to the struggle to overthrow czarism. Upon the supreme basic economic issue confronting Russia they were separated by a deep and wide gulf. The psychology of the peasants was utterly unlike that of the urban proletariat. The latter were concerned with the organization of the state, with factory legislation, with those issues which are universally raised in the conflict of capitalists and wage-earners. The consciousness of the Social Democratic Party was proletarian. On the other hand, the peasants cared very little about the organization of the state or any of the matters which the city workers regarded as being of cardinal importance. They were "land hungry"; they wanted a distribution of the land which would increase their individual holdings. The passion for private possession of land is strong in the peasant of every land, the Russian peasant being no exception to the rule. Yet there is perhaps one respect in which the psychology of the Russian peasant differs from that of the French peasant, for example. The Russian peasant is quite as deeply interested in becoming an individual landholder; he is much less interested in the idea of absolute ownership. Undisturbed possession of an adequate acreage, even though unaccompanied by the title of absolute ownership, satisfies the Russian.

The moderate Social Democrats, the Mensheviki, and the Socialists-Revolutionists stood for substantially the same solution of the land problem prior to the Revolution. They wanted to confiscate the lands of great estates, the Church and the Crown, and to turn them over to democratically elected and governed local bodies. The Bolsheviki, on the other hand, wanted all land to be nationalized and in place of millions of small owners they wanted state ownership and control. Large scale agriculture on government-owned lands by government employees and more or less rapid extinction of private ownership and operation was their ideal. The Socialists-Revolutionists denounced this program of nationalization, saying that it would make the peasants "mere wage-slaves of the state." They wanted "socialization" of all land, including that of the small peasant owners. By socialization they meant taking all lands "out of private ownership of persons into the public ownership, *and their management by democratically organized leagues of communities with the purpose of an equitable utilization."*

The Russian peasant looked upon the Revolution as, above everything else, the certain fulfilment of his desire for redistribution of the land. There were, in fact, two issues which far outweighed all others—the land problem and peace. All classes in Russia, even a majority of the great landowners themselves, realized that the distribution of land among the peasants was now inevitable. Thus, interrogated by peasants,

Rodzianko, President of the Fourth Duma, a large landowner, said:

"Yes, we admit that the fundamental problem of the Constituent Assembly is not merely to construct a political system for Russia, but likewise *to give back to the peasantry the land which is at present in our hands.*"

The Provisional Government, under Lvov, dominated as it then was by landowners and bourgeoisie, never for a moment sought to evade this question. On March 15, 1917, the very day of its formation, the Provisional Government by a decree transferred all the Crown lands—approximately 12,000,000 acres—to the Ministry of Agriculture as state property. Two weeks later the Provisional Government conferred upon the newly created Food Commissions the right to take possession of all vacant and uncultivated land, to cultivate it or to rent it to peasants who were ready to undertake the cultivation. This order compelled many landowners to turn their idle lands over to peasants who were willing and ready to proceed with cultivation. On April 21, 1917, the Provisional Government by a decree created Land Commissions throughout the whole of Russia. These Land Commissions were created in every township (*Volost*), county (*Oyezd*), and province (*Gubernia*). They were to collect all information concerning landownership and local administrative agencies and make their reports to a superior national body, the All-Russian Land Commission, which, in turn, would prepare a comprehensive scheme for submission to the Constituent Assembly. On May 18, 1917, the Provisional Government announced that the question of the transfer of the land to the peasants was to be left wholly to the Constituent Assembly.

These local Land Commissions, as well as the superior national commission, were democratically chosen bodies, thoroughly representative of the peasantry. As might be expected, they were to a very large extent guided by the representatives of the Party of Socialists-Revolutionists. There was never any doubt concerning their attitude toward the peasants' demand for distribution of the land. On the All-Russian Land Commission were the best-known Russian authorities on the land question and the agrarian problem. Professor Posnikov, the chairman; Victor Chernov, leader of the Socialists-Revolutionists; Pieshekhonov; Rakitnikov; the two Moslovs; Oganovsky; Vikhliaev; Cherenekov; Veselovsky, and many other eminent authorities were on this important body. To the ordinary non-Russian these names will mean little, perhaps, but to all who are familiar with modern Russia this brief list will be a sufficient assurance that the commission was governed by liberal idealism united to scientific knowledge and practical experience.

The Land Commissions were not created merely for the purpose of collating data upon the subject of landownership and cultivation. That was, indeed, their avowed and ostensible object; but behind that there was another and much more urgent purpose. In the first place, as soon as the revolutionary disturbances began, peasants in many villages took matters into their own hands and appropriated whatever lands they could seize. Agitators had gone among the peasantry—agitators of the Party of Socialists-Revolutionists not less than of the Bolsheviki—and preached the doctrine of "the expropriation of the expropriators." They told the peasants to seize the land and so execute the will of the people. So long as czarism remained the peasants held back; once it was destroyed, they threw off their restraint and began to seize the land for themselves. The Revolution was here. Was it not always understood that when the Revolution came they were to take the land?

Numerous estates were seized and in some cases the landowners were brutally murdered by the frenzied peasants. On some of the large estates the mansions of the owners, the laborers' cottages, stables, cattle-sheds, and corn-stacks were burned and the valuable agricultural machinery destroyed. Whenever this happened it was a great calamity, for on the large estates were the model farms, the agricultural experiment stations of Russia. And while this wanton and foolish destruction was going on there was a great dearth of food for the army at the front. Millions of men had to be fed and it was necessary to make proper provision for the conservation of existing food crops and for increased production. Nor was it only the big estates which were thus attacked and despoiled; in numerous instances the farms of the "middle peasants" — corresponding to our moderately well-to-do farmers — were seized and their rightful owners driven away. In some cases very small farms were likewise seized. Something had to be done to save Russia from this anarchy, which threatened the very life of the nation. The Land Commissions were made administrative organs to deal with the land problems as they arose, to act until the new Zemstvos could be elected and begin to function, when the administrative work of the commissions would be assumed by the Land Offices of the Zemstvos.

There was another very serious matter which made it important to have the Land Commissions function as administrative bodies. Numerous landowners had begun to divide their estates, selling the land off in parcels, thus introducing greater complexity into the problem, a more numerous class of owners to be dealt with. In many cases, moreover, the "sales" and "transfers" were fictitious and deceptive, the new "owners" being mere dummies. In this manner the landowners sought to trick and cheat the peasants. It was to meet this menace that the Provisional Government, on July 12, 1917, by special decree put a stop to all land speculation and forbade the transfer of title to any land, outside of the cities, except by consent of the local Land Commission approved by the Ministry of Agriculture.

Chernov, who under Kerensky became Minister of Agriculture, was the creator of the Land Commissions and the principal author of the agrarian program of the Provisional Government as this was developed from March to October. How completely his policy was justified may be judged from the fact that while most of the landlords fled to the cities at the outbreak of the Revolution in March, fearing murderous riotings such as took place in 1906, in June they had nearly all returned to their estates. The Land Commissions had checked the peasant uprisings; they had given the peasants something to do toward a constructive solution, and had created in their minds confidence that they were going to be honestly dealt with; that the land would be distributed among them before long. In other words, the peasants were patiently waiting for freedom and land to be assured by legal and peaceful means.

Then the Bolsheviki began to rouse the peasants once more and to play upon their suspicions and fears. Simultaneously their propagandists in the cities and in the villages began their attacks upon the Provisional Government. To the peasants they gave the same old advice: "Seize the land for yourselves! Expropriate the landlords!" Once more the peasants began to seize estates, to sack and burn manor houses, and even to kill landowners. The middle of July saw the beginning of a revival of the "Jacqueries," and in a few weeks they had become alarmingly common. The propagandists of the Party of Socialists-Revolutionists did their best to put an end to the outrages, but the peasants were not so easily placated as they had been in March and April. Hope long deferred had brought about a state of despair and desperation. The poor, bewildered peasants could not understand why such a simple matter as the distribution of the land—for so it seemed to them—should require months of preparation. They were ready to believe the Bolshevist propagandists who told them that the delay was intended to enable the bourgeoisie to betray the toilers, and that if they wanted the land they must take it for themselves. "You know how the Socialists-Revolutionists always talked to you aforetime," said these skilful demagogues; "they told you then to seize the land, but now they only tell you to wait, just as the landlords tell you. They have been corrupted; they are no longer true representatives of your interest. We tell you, what you have long known, that if you want the land you must seize it for yourselves!"

Anarchy among the peasants grew apace. Some of the wisest of the leaders of the Russian revolutionary movement urged the Provisional Government to hurry, to revise its plan, and, instead of waiting for the Constituent Assembly to act upon the land program, to put it into effect at once. The All-Russian Land Commission hastened its work and completed the formulation of a land program. The Provisional Government stuck to its original declaration that the program must be considered and approved or rejected by the Constituent Assembly. In October, at the Democratic Conference in Petrograd, the so-called Pre-Parliament, Prokopovich, the well-known Marxian economist, who had become Minister of Commerce and Labor, uttered a solemn warning that "the disorderly seizing of land was ruining agriculture and threatening the towns and the northern provinces with famine."

It is one of the numerous tragedies of the Russian Revolution that at the very time this warning was issued Kerensky had in his possession two plans, either of which might have averted the catastrophe that followed. One of them was the completed program of the All-Russian Land Commission, largely Chernov's work. It had already been approved by the Provisional Government. It was proposed that Kerensky should make a fight to have the Cabinet proclaim this program to be law, without waiting for the Constituent Assembly. The other plan was very simple and crude. It was that all the large estates be seized at once, as a measure of military necessity, and that in the distribution of the land thus taken peasant soldiers with honorable discharges be given preference. In either case, Kerensky would have split his Cabinet.

When we consider the conditions which prevailed at that time, the extreme military and political weakness, and the vast stakes at issue, it is easy to understand why Kerensky decided to wait for the Constituent Assembly. It is easy enough to say now, after the event, that Kerensky's decision was wrong; that his only chance to hold the confidence of the peasants was to do one of two things, declare immediate peace or introduce sweeping land reforms. Certainly, that seems fairly plain now. At that time, however, Kerensky faced the hard fact that to do either of these things meant a serious break in the Cabinet, another crisis, the outcome of which none could foretell.

Moreover, we must bear in mind that Kerensky himself and those with whom he was working were inspired by a very genuine and sincere passion for democracy. They believed in the Constituent Assembly. They had idealized it. To them it was in the nature of a betrayal of the Revolution that a matter of such fundamental importance should be disposed of by a small handful of men, rather than by the representatives of the people duly elected, upon a democratic basis, for that purpose. The Provisional Government was pledged to leave the Constituent Assembly free and untrammeled to deal with the land problem: how could it violate its pledge and usurp the functions of the Assembly? If Kerensky's course was a mistaken one, it was so only because conscientious loyalty to principle is not invariably expedient in politics; because the guile and dishonesty of his opponents triumphed over his simple honesty and truthfulness.

On October 20, 1917, the Provisional Government enacted a law which marked a further step in the preparation of the way for the new system of land tenure. The new law extended the control of the Land Offices of the Zemstvos—where these existed, and of the Land Commissions, where the Zemstvos with their Land Offices did not yet exist—over all cultivated land. It was thus made possible for the provisions of a comprehensive land law to be applied quickly, with a minimum amount of either disturbance or delay.

From the foregoing it will be readily seen that the Bolshevist *coup d'état* interfered with the consummation of a most painstaking, scientific effort to solve the greatest of all Russian problems. Their apologists are fond of claiming that the Bolsheviki can at least be credited with having solved the land problem by giving the land to the peasants. The answer to that preposterous claim is contained in the foregoing plain and unadorned chronological record, the accuracy of which can easily be attested by any person having access to a reasonably good library. In so far as the Bolsheviki put forward any land program at all, they adopted, for reasons of political expediency, the program which had been worked out by the Land Commissions under the Provisional Government—the so-called Chernov program. With that program they did nothing of any practical value, however. Where the land was distributed under their régime it was done by the peasants themselves. In many cases it was done in the primitive, violent, destructive, and anarchical ways of the "Jacqueries" already described, adding enormously to Russia's suffering and well-nigh encompassing her destruction. By nothing else is the malefic character and influence of Bolshevism more clearly shown than by the state in which it placed the land problem, just when it was about to be scientifically and democratically solved.

When the Constituent Assembly met on January 5, 1918, the proposed land law was at once taken up. The first ten paragraphs had been adopted when the Assembly was dispersed by Trotsky's Red Guards. The entire bill was thus not acted upon. The ten paragraphs which were passed give a very good idea of the general character and scope of the measure:

In the name of the peoples of the Russian State, composing the All-Russian Constituent Assembly, be it ordained that:

1. Right of ownership to land within the limits of the Russian Republic is henceforth and forever abolished.

2. All lands contained within the boundaries of the Russian Republic with all their underground wealth, forests, and waters become the property of the people.

3. The control of all lands, the surface and under the surface, and all forests and waters belongs to the Republic, as expressed in the forms of its central administrative organs and organs of local self-government on the principles enacted by this law.

4. Those territories of the Russian Republic which are autonomous in a juridico-governmental conception, are to realize their agrarian plans on the basis of this law and in accord with the Federal Constitution.

5. The aims of the government forces and the organs of local self-government in the sphere of the control of lands, underground riches, forests, and waters constitute: (*a*) The creation of conditions most favorable to the greater exploitation of the natural wealth of the land and the highest development of

productive forces; (*b*) The equitable distribution of all natural wealth among the population.

6. The right of any person or institution to land, underground resources, forests, and waters is limited only to the utilization thereof.

7. All citizens of the Russian Republic, and also unions of such citizens and states and social institutions, may become users of land, underground resources, forests, and waters, without regard to nationality or religion.

8. The land rights of such users are to be obtained, become effective, and cease under the terms laid down by this law.

9. Land rights belonging at present to private persons, groups, and institutions, in so far as they conflict with this law, are herewith abrogated.

10. The transformation of all lands, underground strata, forests, and waters, belonging at present to private persons, groups, or institutions, into popular property is to be made without recompense to such owners.

After they had dispersed the Constituent Assembly the Bolsheviki published their famous "Declaration of the Rights of the Laboring and Exploited People," containing their program for "socialization of the land," taken bodily from the Socialists-Revolutionists. This declaration had been first presented to the Constituent Assembly when the Bolsheviki demanded its adoption by that body. The paragraphs relating to the socialization of the land read:

1. To effect the socialization of the land, private ownership of land is abolished, and the whole land fund is declared common national property and transferred to the laborers without compensation, on the basis of equalized use of the soil.

All forests, minerals, and waters of state-wide importance, as well as the whole inventory of animate and inanimate objects, all estates and agricultural enterprises, are declared national property.

This meant literally nothing from the standpoint of practical politics. Its principal interest lies in the fact that it shows that the Bolsheviki accepted in theory the essence of the land program of the elements comprised in the Provisional Government and in the Constituent Assembly, both of which they had overthrown. Practically the declaration could have no effect upon the peasants. Millions of them had been goaded by the Bolsheviki into resorting to anarchistic, violent seizing of lands on the principle of "each for himself and the devil take the hindmost." These would now be ready to fight any attempt made by the Soviet authorities to "socialize" the land they held. Millions of other peasants were still under the direction of the local Land Commissions, most of which continued to function, more or less *sub rosa*, for some time. And even when and where the local Land Commissions themselves did not exist, the plans they had prepared were, in quite a large measure, put into practice when local land divisions took place.

The Bolsheviki were powerless to make a single constructive contribution to the solution of the basic economic problem of Russia. Their "socialization decree" was a poor substitute for the program whence it had been derived; they possessed no machinery and no moral agencies to give it reality. It remained a pious wish, at best; perhaps a far harsher description would be that much more nearly true. Later on, when they went into the villages and sought to "socialize" them, the Bolsheviki found that they had not solved the land problem, but had made it worse than it had been before.

We have heard much concerning the nationalization of agriculture in Soviet Russia, and of the marvelous success attending it. The facts, as they are to be found in the official publications of the Soviet Government and the Communist Party, do not sustain the roseate accounts which have been published by our pro-Bolshevist friends. By July, 1918, the month in which the previously decreed nationalization of industry was enforced, some tentative steps toward the nationalization of agriculture had already been taken. Maria Spiridonova, a leader of the extreme left wing of the Socialists-Revolutionists, who had co-operated with the Bolsheviki, bitterly assailed the Council of the People's Commissaries for having resorted to nationalization of the great estates, especially in the western government. In a speech delivered in Petrograd, on July 16th, Spiridonova charged that "the great estates were being taken over by government departments and were being managed by officials, on the ground that state control would yield better results than communal ownership. Under this system the peasants were being reduced to the state of slaves paid wages by the state. Yet the law provided that these estates should be divided among the peasant communes to be tilled by the peasants on a co-operative basis." It appears that this policy was adopted in a number of instances where the hostility to the Bolsheviki manifested by the peasants made the division of the land among them "undesirable." Nationalization upon any large scale was not resorted to until some months later. Nationalization of the agriculture of the country as a whole has never been attempted, of course. There could not be such a nationalization of agriculture without first nationalizing the land, and that, popular opinion to the contrary notwithstanding, has never been done in Russia as yet. The *Economicheskaya Zhizn* (No. 229) declared, in November, 1919, that "in spite of the fact that the decree announcing the nationalization of the land is now two years old, *this nationalization has not yet been carried out."*

It was not until March, 1919, according to a report by N. Bogdanov in *Economicheskaya Zhizn*, November 7, 1919, that nationalized agriculture really began on a large scale. From this report we learn something of the havoc which had been wrought upon the agricultural industry of Russia from March, 1917 to 1919:

A considerable portion of the estates taken over by the People's Commissariat of Agriculture could not be utilized, due to the lack of various accessories, such as harness, horseshoes, rope, small instruments, etc.

The workers were very fluctuating, entirely unorganized, politically inert—all this due to the shortage of provisions and organization. The technical forces could not get used to the village; besides, we did not have sufficient numbers of agronomists (agricultural experts) familiar with the practical organization of large estates. The regulations governing the social management of land charged the representatives of the industrial proletariat with a leading part in the work of the Soviet estates. But, torn between meeting the various requirements of the Republic, of prime importance, the proletariat could not with sufficient speed furnish the number of organizers necessary for agricultural management.

The idea of centralized management on the Soviet estates has not been properly understood by the local authorities, and the work of organization from the very beginning had to progress amid bitter fighting between the provincial Soviet estates and the provincial offices of the Department of Agriculture. This struggle has not as yet ceased.

Thus, the work of nationalizing the country's agriculture began in the spring—*i.e.,* a half-year later than it should have, and without any definite territory (every inch of it had to be taken after a long and strenuous siege on the part of the surrounding population); with insufficient and semi-ruined equipment; without provisions; without an apparatus for organization and without the necessary experience for such work; with the agricultural workers engaged in the Soviet estates lacking any organization whatever.

Naturally, the results of this work are not impressive.

Within the limits of the Soviet estates the labor-union of agricultural proletariat has developed into a large organization.

In a number of provinces the leading part in the work of the Soviet estates has been practically assumed by the industrial proletariat, which has furnished a number of organizers, whose reputation has been sufficiently established.

Estimating the results of the work accomplished, we must admit that we have not yet any fully nationalized rural economy. But during the eight months of work in this direction all the elements for its organization have been accumulated.

A preliminary familiarity with individual estates and with agricultural regions makes it possible to begin the preparation of a national plan for production on the Soviet estates and for a systematic attempt to meet the manifold demands made on the nationalized estates by the agricultural industries: sugar, distilling, chemical, etc., as well as by the country's need for stock-breeding, seeds, planting, and other raw materials.

The greatest difficulties arise in the creation of the machinery of organization. The shortage of agricultural experts is being replenished with great difficulty, for the position of the technical personnel of the Soviet estates, due to their weak political organization, is extremely unstable. The mobilization of the proletarian forces for the work in the Soviet estates gives us ground to believe that in this respect the spring of 1920 will find us sufficiently prepared.

The ranks of proletarian workers in the Soviet estates are drawing together. True, the level of their enlightenment is by no means high, but "in union there is strength," and this force if properly utilized will rapidly yield positive results.

The sole purpose of these quotations is to show that at best the "nationalization of agriculture" in Russia, concerning which we have heard so much, is only an experiment that has just been begun; that it bears no very important relation to the industry as a whole. It would be just as true to say, on the basis of the agricultural experiment stations of our national and state governments, that we have "nationalized agriculture" as to make that claim for Russia. *The records show that the "nationalized" farms did not produce enough food to maintain the workers employed on them.*

Apart from the nationalization of a number of large estates upon the basis of wage labor under a centralized authority, the Committee for the Communization of Agricultural Economy was formed for the purpose of establishing agricultural communes. At the same time—February, 1919—the Central Executive Committee of the Soviets called on the Provincial Soviets to take up this work of creating agricultural communes. Millions of rubles were spent for this purpose, but the results were very small. In March, 1919, *Pravda* declared that "15,000 communes were registered, but we have no proofs as to their existence anywhere except on paper." The *Izvestia* of the Central Executive Committee, May, 1919, complained that "the number of newly organized communes is growing smaller from month to month; the existing communes are becoming disintegrated, twenty of them having been disbanded during March." City-bred workers found themselves helpless on the land and in conflict with the peasants. On the other hand, the peasants would not accept the communes, accompanied as these were with Soviet control. In the same number of the *Izvestia* of the Central Executive Committee, Nikolaiev, a well-known Bolshevik, declared:

> The communes are absolutely contradictory to the mode of living of our toiling peasant masses, as these communes demand not only the abolition of property rights, to implements and means of production, but the division of products according to program.

At the Congress of Trades-unions, which met in Moscow in May, 1919, the possibility of using the communes as means of relieving the wide-spread unemployment and distress among the city workers was discussed by Platonov, Rozanov, and other noted Bolsheviki. The closing down of numerous factories and the resulting unemployment of large masses of workmen had brought about an appalling amount of hunger. It was proposed, therefore, that communes be formed in the villages under the auspices of the trades-unions, and as branches of the unions, parcels of land being given to the unions. In this way, it was argued, employment would be found for the members of the unions and the food-supply of the cities would be materially increased. While approving the formation of communes, the Congress voted down the proposal.

On June 8, 1919, there was established the Administration of Industrial Allotments. The object of this new piece of bureaucratic machinery was the increase of agricultural production through land allotments attached to, or assigned to, industrial establishments, and their cultivation by the workers. This scheme, which had been promulgated as early as February, 1919, was a pathetic anticlimax to the ambitious program with which the Bolshevist Utopia-builders set out. It was neither more nor less than the "allotment gardens" scheme so long familiar in British cities. Such allotment gardens were common enough in the industrial centers of the United States during the war. As an emergency measure for providing vegetables they were useful and even admirable; as a contribution to the solution of the agricultural problem in its largest sense their value was insignificant. Yet we find the *Economicheskaya Zhizn*, in November, 1919, indulging in the old intoxicating visions of Utopia, and seeing in these allotments the means whereby the cities could be relieved of their dependence upon the rural villages for food:

Out of the hitherto frenzied rush of workmen into villages, brought about by hunger, a healthy proletariat movement was born, aiming at the creation of their own agriculture by means of allotments attached to the works. This movement resulted, on February 15, 1919, in a decree which granted to factory and other proletariat groups the right to organize their own rural economy.... The enthusiasm of the workmen is impressive.... *The complete emancipation of the towns from the villages in the matter of food-supply appears to be quite within the realms of possibility in the near future, without the unwieldy, expensive, and inefficient machinery of the People's Commissariat of Food Supply, and without undue irritation of the villages.* This will, besides, relieve enormously the strain on the crippled railways. And, what is even more important, it points out a new and the only right way to the nationalization of the land and to the socialization of agriculture. And, indeed, in spite of the fact that the decree announcing the nationalization of the land is now two years old, *this nationalization has not yet been carried out.* The attitude of the peasant to the land, psychologically as well as economically, is still that of the small landowner. He still considers the land his property, for, as before, it is he, and not the state, that draws both the absolute and the differential rent, and he is fighting for it, with the food detachments, with all his power. If there is any difference at all it is that the rent which formerly used to find its way into the wide pockets of the landowners now goes into the slender purse of the peasant. The difference, however, in the size of the respective pockets is becoming more and more insignificant.... In order to make the approach to socialization of the land possible, it is necessary that the Soviet authorities should, besides promulgating decrees, actually take possession of the land, and the authorities can only do this with the help of the industrial proletariat, whose dictatorship it represents.

How extremely childish all this is! How little the knowledge of the real problem it displays! If the official organ of the Supreme Economic Council and the People's Commissaries of Finance, Commerce and Trade and Food knew no better than this after two such years as Russia had passed through, how can there be any hope for Russia until the reckless, ignorant, bungling experimenters are overthrown? Pills of

Podophyllum for earthquakes would be less grotesque than their prescription for Russia's ailment.

VI

THE BOLSHEVIKI AND THE PEASANTS

In the fierce fratricidal conflict between the Bolsheviki and the democratic anti-Bolshevist elements so much bitterness has been engendered that anything approaching calm, dispassionate discussion and judgment has been impossible for Russians, whether as residents in Russia, engaged in the struggle, or as *émigrés*, impotent to do more than indulge in the expression of their emotions, practically all Russians everywhere have been—and still are—too intensely partizan to be just or fair-minded. And non-Russians have been subject to the same distorting passions, only to a lesser degree. Even here in the United States, while an incredibly large part of the population has remained utterly indifferent, wholly uninterested in the struggle or the issues at stake, it has been practically impossible to find anywhere intelligent interest dissociated from fierce partizanship.

The detachment and impartiality essential to the formation of sound and unbiased judgment have been almost non-existent. The issues at stake have been too vast and too fundamental, too vitally concerned with the primal things of civilization, the sources of some of our profoundest emotions, to permit cool deliberation. Moreover, little groups of men and women with strident cries have hurled the challenge of Bolshevism into the arena of our national life, and that at a time of abnormal excitation, at the very moment when our lives were pulsing with a fiercely emotional patriotism. As a result of these conditions there has been little discriminating discernment in the tremendous riot of discussion of Russian Bolshevism which has raged in all parts of the land. It has been a frenzied battle of epithet and insult, calumny and accusation.

It is not at all strange or remarkable that their opponents, in Russia and outside of it, have been ready to charge against the Bolsheviki every evil condition in Russia, including those which have long existed under czarism and those which developed during and as a result of the war. The transportation system had been reduced to something nearly approaching chaos before the Revolution of March, 1917, as all reasonably well-informed people know. Yet, notwithstanding these things, it is a common practice to charge the Bolsheviki with the destruction of the transportation system and all the evil results following from it. Industrial production declined greatly in the latter part of 1916 and the early weeks of 1917. The March Revolution, by lessening discipline in the factories, had the effect of lessening production still further. The demoralization of industry was one of the gravest problems with which Kerensky had to deal. Yet it is rare to find any allowance made for these important facts in anti-Bolshevist polemics. The Bolsheviki are charged with having wrought all the havoc and harm; there is no discrimination, no intellectual balance.

Similarly, many of their opponents have charged against the Russian Bolsheviki much brutality and crime which in fairness should be attributed rather to inherent defects of the peasant character, themselves the product of centuries of oppression and misrule. There is much that is admirable in the character of the Russian peasant, and many western writers have found the temptation to idealize it irresistible. Yet it is well to remember that it is not yet sixty years since serfdom was abolished; that under a very thin veneer there remain ignorant selfishness, superstition, and the capacity for savage brutality which all primitive peoples have. Nothing is gained, nobody is helped to an understanding of the Russian problem, if emphasis is laid upon the riotous seizures of land by the peasants in the early stages of the Bolshevist régime and no attention paid to the fact that similar riotings and land seizures were numerous and common in 1906, and that as soon as the Revolution broke out in March, 1917, the peasant uprisings began. Undoubtedly the Bolsheviki must be held responsible for the fact that they deliberately destroyed the discipline and restraint which the Land Commissions exercised over the peasants; that they instigated them to riot and anarchy at the very time when a peaceful and orderly solution of the land problem was made certain. It is not necessary to minimize their crime against Russian civilization: only it is neither true nor wise to attribute the brutal character of the peasant to Bolshevism.

The abolition of the courts of justice and the forms of judicial procedure threw upon the so-called "People's Tribunals" the task of administering justice—a task which the peasants of whom the village tribunals were composed, many of them wholly illiterate and wholly unfit to exercise authority, could not be expected to discharge other than as they did, with savage brutality. Here is a list of cases taken from a single issue (April 26, 1918) of the *Dyelo Naroda* (*People's Affair*), organ of the Socialists-Revolutionists:

In Kirensk County the People's Tribunal ordered a woman, found guilty of extracting brandy, to be inclosed in a bag and repeatedly knocked against the ground until dead.

In the Province of Tver the People's Tribunal has sentenced a young fellow "to freeze to death" for theft. In a rigid frost he was led out, clad only in a shirt, and water was poured on him until he turned into a piece of ice. Out of pity somebody cut his tortures short by shooting him.

In Sarapulsk County a peasant woman, helped by her lover, killed her husband. For this crime the People's Tribunal sentenced the woman to be buried alive and her lover to die. A grave was dug, into which first the body of the killed lover was lowered, and then the woman, hands and feet bound, put on top. She had been covered by almost fifteen feet of earth when she still kept on yelling "Help!" and "Have pity, dear people!" The peasants, who witnessed the scene, later said, "But the life of a woman is as lasting as that of a cat."

In the village of Bolshaya Sosnovka a shoemaker killed a soldier who tried to break in during the night. The victim's comrades, also soldiers, created a "Revolutionary Tribunal," which convicted the shoemaker to "be beheaded at the hands of one of his comrades to whose lot it should fall to perform the task." The shoemaker was put to death in the presence of a crowd of thousands of people.

In the village of Bootsenki five men and three women were accused of misconduct. The local peasant committee undertook to try them. After a long trial the committee reached the verdict to punish them by flogging, giving each one publicly thirty-five strokes with the rod. One of the women was pregnant and it was decided to postpone the execution in her case until she had been delivered. The rest were severely flogged. In connection with this affair an interesting episode occurred. One of the convicted received only sixteen strokes instead of thirty-five. At first no attention was paid to it. The next day, however, rumors spread that the president of the committee had been bribed, and had thus mitigated the punishment.

Then the committee decreed to flog the president himself, administering to him fifty strokes with the rod.

In the village of Riepyrky, in Korotoyansk County, the peasants caught a soldier robbing and decided to drown him. The verdict was carried out by the members of the Revolutionary Tribunal in the presence of all the people of the village.

In the village of Vradievka, in Ananyensky County, eleven thieves, sentenced by the people, were shot.

In the district of Kubanetz, in the Province of Petrograd, carrying out the verdict of the people, peasants shot twelve men of the fighting militia who had been caught accepting bribes.

These sentences speak for themselves. They were not expressions of Bolshevist savagery, for in the village tribunals there were very few Bolsheviki. As a matter of fact, the same people who meted out these barbarous sentences treated the agents of the Soviet Government with equally savage brutality. The Bolsheviki had unleashed the furious passion of these primitive folk, destroyed their faith in liberty within the law, and replaced it by license and tyranny. Thus had they recklessly sown dragons' teeth.

As early as December, 1917, the Bolshevist press was discussing the serious conditions which obtained among the peasants in the villages. It was recognized that no good had resulted from the distribution of the land by the anarchical methods which had been adopted. The evils which the leaders of the Mensheviki and the Socialists-Revolutionists had warned against were seen to be very stern realities. As was inevitable, the land went, in many cases, not to the most needy, but to the most powerful and least scrupulous. In these cases there was no order, no wisdom, no justice, no law save might. It was the old, old story of

> Let him take who has the power;
>
> And let him keep who can.

All that there was of justice and order came from the organizations set up by the Provisional Government, the organizations the Bolsheviki sought to destroy. Before they had been in power very long the new rulers were compelled to recognize the seriousness of the situation. On December 26, 1917, *Pravda* said:

> Thus far not everybody realizes to what an extent the war has affected the economic condition of the villages. The increase in the cost of bread has been a gain only for those selling it. The demolition of the estates of the landowners has enriched only those who arrived at the place of plunder in carriages driven by five horses. By the distribution of the landowners' cattle and the rest of their property, those gained most who were in charge of the distribution. In charge of the distribution were committees, which, as everybody was complaining, consisted mainly of wealthy peasants.

One of the most terrible consequences of the lawless anarchy that had been induced by the Bolsheviki was the internecine strife between villages, which speedily assumed the dimensions of civil war. It was common for the peasants in one village to arm themselves and fight the armed peasants of a neighboring village for the possession of the lands of an estate. At the instigation of the Bolsheviki and of German agents, many thousands of peasants had deserted from the army, taking with them their weapons and as much ammunition as they could. "Go back to your homes and take your guns with you. Seize the land for yourselves and defend it!" was the substance of this propaganda. The peasant soldiers deserted in masses, frequently terrorizing the people of the villages and towns through which they passed. Several times the Kerensky Government attempted to disarm these masses of deserters, but their number was so great that this was not possible, every attempt to disarm a body of them resolving itself into a pitched battle. In this way the villages became filled with armed men who were ready to use their weapons in the war for booty, a sort of savage tribal war, the village populations being the tribes. In his paper, *Novaya Zhizn*, Gorky wrote, in June, 1918:

> All those who have studied the Russian villages of our day clearly perceive that *the process of demoralization and decay is going on there with remarkable speed*. The peasants have taken the land away from its owners, divided it among themselves, and destroyed the agricultural implements. *And they are getting ready to engage in a bloody internecine struggle for the division of the booty.* In certain districts the population has consumed the entire grain-supply, including the seed. In other districts the peasants are hiding their grain underground, for fear of being forced to share it with starving neighbors. This situation cannot fail to lead to chaos, destruction, and murder.[7]

[7] *Italics mine.—J. S.*

As a matter of fact the "bloody internecine struggle" had been going on for some time. Even before the overthrow of Kerensky there had been many of these village wars. The Bolshevist Government did not make any very serious attempt to interfere with the peasant movements for the distribution of land for some time after the *coup d'état*. It was too busy trying to consolidate its position in the cities, and especially to organize production in the factories. There was not much to be done with the farms at that season of the year. Early in the spring of 1918 agents of the Soviet Government began to appear in the villages. Their purpose was to supervise and regulate the distribution of the land. Since a great deal of the land had already been seized and distributed by the peasants, this involved some interference on the part of the central Soviet power in matters which the peasants regarded themselves as rightfully entitled to settle in their own way.

This gave rise to a bitter conflict between the peasants and the central Soviet authorities. If the peasants had confiscated and partitioned the land, however inequitably, they regarded their deed as conclusive and final. The attempt of the Soviet agents to "revise" their actions they regarded as robbery. The central Soviet authorities had against them all the village population with the exception of the disgruntled few. If the peasants had not yet partitioned the land they were suspicious of outsiders coming to do it. The land was their own; the city men had nothing to do with it. In hundreds of villages the commissions sent by the Bolsheviki to carry out the provisions of the land program were mobbed and brutally beaten, and in many cases were murdered. The issue of *Vlast Naroda* (*Power of the People*) for May, 1918, contained the following:

In Bielo all members of the Soviets have been murdered.

In Soligalich two of the most prominent members of the Soviets have literally been torn to pieces. Two others have been beaten half dead.

In Atkarsk several members of the Soviets have been killed. In an encounter between the Red Guards and the masses, many were killed and wounded. The Red Guards fled.

In Kleen a crowd entered by force the building occupied by the Soviets, with the intention of bringing the deputies before their own court of justice. The latter fled. The Financial Commissary committed suicide by shooting himself, in order to escape the infuriated crowd.

In Oriekhovo-Zooyevo the deputies work in their offices guarded by a most vigilant military force. Even on the streets they are accompanied by guards armed with rifles and bayonets.

In Penza an attempt has been made on the lives of the Soviet members. One of the presiding officers has been wounded. The Soviet building is now surrounded with cannon and machine-guns.

In Svicherka, where the Bolsheviki had ordered a St. Bartholomew night, the deputies are hunted like wild animals.

In the district of Kaliasinsk the peasantry has decidedly refused to obey orders of the Soviets to organize an army by compulsion. Some of the recruiting officers and agitators have been killed.

Similar acts become more numerous as time goes on. The movement against the Soviets spreads far and wide, affecting wider and wider circles of the people.

The warfare between villages over confiscated land was a very serious matter. Not only did the peasants confiscate and divide among themselves the great estates, but they took the "excess" lands of the moderately well-to-do peasants in many instances—that is, all over and above the average allotment for the village. Those residing in a village immediately adjoining an estate thus confiscated had, all other things being equal, a better chance to get the lands than villagers a little farther distant, though the latter might be in greater need of the land, owing to the fact that their holdings were smaller. Again, the village containing many armed men stood a better chance than the village containing few. Village made war against village, raising armed forces for the purpose. We get a vivid picture of this terrible anarchy from the following account in the *Vlast Naroda*:

The village has taken away the land from the landlords, farmers, wealthy peasants, and monasteries. It cannot, however, divide it peacefully, as was to be expected.

The more land there is the greater the appetite for it; hence more quarrels, misunderstandings, and fights.

In Oboyansk County many villages refused to supply soldiers when the Soviet authorities were mobilizing an army. In their refusal they stated that "in the spring soldiers will be needed at home in the villages," not to cultivate the land, but to protect it with arms against neighboring peasants.

In the Provinces of Kaluga, Kursk, and Voronezh peasant meetings adopted the following resolutions:

"All grown members of the peasant community have to be home in the spring. Whoever will then not return to the village or voluntarily stay away will be forever expelled from the community.

"These provisions are made for the purpose of having as great a force as possible in the spring when it comes to dividing the land."

The peasantry is rapidly preparing to arm and is partly armed already. The villages have a number of rifles, cartridges, hand-grenades, and bombs.

Some villages in the Nieshnov district in the Province of Mohilev have supplied themselves with machine-guns. The village of Little Nieshnov, for instance, has decided to order fifteen machine-guns and has organized a Red Army in order to be able better to defend a piece of land taken away from the landlords, and, as they say, that "the neighboring peasants should not come to cut our hay right in front of our windows, like last year." When the neighboring peasants "heard of the decision" they also procured machine-guns. They have formed an army and intend to go to Little Nieshnov to cut the hay on the meadows "under the windows" of the disputed owners.

In the Counties of Schigrovsk, Oboyansk, and Ruilsk, in the Province of Kursk, almost every small and large village has organized a Red Guard and is making preparations for the coming spring war. In these places the peasants have taken rich booty. They took and devastated 160 estates, 14 breweries, and 26 sugar refineries. Some villages have even marked the spot where the machine-guns will have to be placed in the spring. In Volsk County in the Province of Saratov five large villages—Kluchi, Pletnevka, Ruibni, Shakhan, and Chernavka—expect to have war when the time comes to divide the 148,500 acres of Count Orlov-Denisov's estate. Stubborn fights for meadows and forests are already going on. They often result in skirmishes and murder.

There are similar happenings in other counties of the province; for instance, in Petrov, Balashov, and Arkhar.

In the Province of Simbirsk there is war between the community peasants and shopkeepers. The former have decided to do away with "Stolypin heirs," as they call the shopkeepers. The latter, however, have organized and are ready for a stubborn resistance. Combats have already taken place. The peasants demolish farms, and the farmers set fire to towns, villages, threshing-floors, etc.

We have received from the village of Khanino, in the Province of Kaluga, the following letter:

"The division of the land leads to war. One village fights against the other. The wealthy and strong peasants have decided not to let the poor share the land taken away from the landlords. In their turn, the poor peasants say, 'We will take away from you bourgeois peasants not only the lands of the landlords, but also your own. We, the toilers, are now the government.' This leads to constant quarrels and fights. The population of the neighboring village consists of so-called natives and of peasants brought by landlords from the Province of Orlov. The natives now say to those from Orlov: 'Get away from our land and return to your Province of Orlov. Anyhow, we shall drive you away from here.' The peasants from Orlov, however, threaten 'to kill all the natives.' Thus there are daily encounters."

In another village the peasants have about 5,400 acres of land, which they bought. For some reason or other they failed to cultivate it last year. Therefore the peasants of a neighboring village decided to take it away from them as "superfluous property which is against the labor status." The owners, however, declared:

"First kill us and then you will be able to take away our land."

In some places the first battles for land have already taken place.

In the Province of Tambov, near the village of Ischeina, a serious encounter has taken place between the peasants of the village of Shleyevka and Brianchevka. Fortunately, among the peasants of Brianchevka was a wise man, "the village Solomon," who first persuaded his neighbors to put out for the peasants of Shleyevka five buckets of brandy. The latter actually took the ransom and went away, thus leaving the land to the owners.

In some instances the Bolsheviki instigated the peasants to massacre hundreds of innocent people in adjacent villages and towns. They did not stop, or even protest against, the most savage anti-Jewish pogroms. Charles Dumas, the well-known French Socialist, a Deputy in Parliament, after spending fifteen months in Russia, published his experiences and solemnly warned the Socialists of France against Bolshevism. His book[8] is a terrible chronicle of terrorism, oppression, and anarchy, all the more impressive because of its restraint and careful documentation. He cites the following cases:

[8] La Vérité sur les Bolsheviki, *par Charles Dumas.*

On March 18, 1918, the peasants of an adjoining village organized, in collusion with the Bolsheviki, a veritable St. Bartholomew night in the city of Kuklovo. About five hundred bodies of the victims were found afterward, most of them "Intellectuals." All residences and stores were plundered and destroyed, the Jews being among the worst sufferers. Entire families were wiped out, and for three days the Bolsheviki would not permit the burial of the dead.

In May, 1918, the city of Korocha was the scene of a horrible massacre. Thirty officers, four priests, and three hundred citizens were killed.

In May, 1918, the relations of the Soviet Government to the peasantry were described by Gorky as the war of the city against the country. They were, in fact, very similar to the relations of conquering armies to the subjugated but rebellious and resentful populations of conquered territories. On May 14th a decree was issued regarding the control of grain, the famous compulsory grain registration order. This decree occupies so important a place in the history of the struggle, and contains so many striking features, that a fairly full summary is necessary:[9]

9 *The entire text is given as an appendix at the end of the volume.*

While the people in the consuming districts are starving, there are large reserves of unthreshed grain in the producing districts. This grain is in the hands of the village bourgeoisie—"tight-fisted village dealers and profiteers"—who remain "deaf and indifferent to the wailings of starving workmen and peasant poverty" and hold their grain in the hope of forcing the government to raise the price of grain, selling only to the speculators at fabulous prices. "An end must be put to this obstinacy of the greedy village grain-profiteers." To abolish the grain monopoly and the system of fixed prices, while it would lessen the profits of one group of capitalists, would also "make bread completely inaccessible to our many millions of workmen and would subject them to inevitable death from starvation." Only food grains absolutely necessary for feeding their families, on a rationed basis, and for seed purposes should be permitted to be held by the peasants. *"The answer to the violence of grain-growers toward the starving poor must be violence toward the bourgeoisie."*

Continuing its policy of price-fixing and monopolization of the grain-supply, the government decreed "a merciless struggle with grain speculators," compulsion of "each grain-owner to declare the surplus above what is needed to sow the fields and for personal use, according to established normal quantities, until the new harvest, and to surrender the same within a week after the publication of this decision in each village." The workmen and poor peasants were called upon "to unite at once for a merciless struggle with grain-hoarders." All persons having a surplus of grain and failing to bring it to the collecting-points, and those wasting grain on illicit distillation of alcohol, were to be regarded as "enemies of the people." They were to be turned over to the Revolutionary Tribunal, which would "imprison them for ten years, confiscate their entire property, and drive them out forever from the communes"; while the distillers must, in addition, "be condemned to compulsory communal work."

To carry out this rigorous policy it was provided that any person who revealed an undeclared surplus of grains should receive one-half the value of the surplus when it was seized and confiscated, the other half going to the village commune. "For the more successful struggle with the food crisis" extraordinary powers were conferred upon the People's Food Commissioner, appointed by the Soviet Government. This official was empowered to (1) publish at his discretion obligatory regulations regarding the food situation, "exceeding the usual limits of the People's Food Commissioner's competence"; (2) to abrogate the orders of local food bodies and other organizations contravening his own plans and orders; (3) to demand from all institutions and organizations the immediate carrying out of his regulations; (4) *"to use armed forces in case resistance is shown to the removal of grains or other food products*; (5) to dissolve or reorganize the food agencies where they might resist his orders; (6) to discharge, transfer, commit to the Revolutionary Tribunal, or subject to arrest officers and employees of all departments and public organizations in case of interference with his orders; (7) to transfer the powers of such officials, departments, and institutions," with the approval of the Council of People's Commissaries.

It is not necessary here to discuss the merits of these regulations, even if we possessed the complete data without which the merit of the regulations cannot be determined. For our present purpose it is sufficient to recognize the fact that the peasants regarded the regulations as oppressive and vigorously resisted their enforcement. They claimed that the amount of grain—and also of potatoes—they were permitted to keep was insufficient; that it meant semi-starvation to them. The peasant Soviets, where such still existed, jealous of their rights, refused to recognize the authority of the People's Food Commissaries. No material increase in the supply of "surplus grain" was observed. The receiving-stations were as neglected as before. The poor wretches who, inspired by the rich reward of half the value of the illegal reserves reported, acted as informers were beaten and tortured, and the Food Commissaries, who were frequently arrogant and brutal in their ways, were attacked and in some cases killed.

The Soviet Government had resort to armed force against the peasants. On May 30, 1918, the Council of People's Commissaries met and decided that the workmen of Petrograd and Moscow must form "food-requisitioning detachments" and "advance in a crusade against the village bourgeoisie, calling to their assistance the village poor." From a manifesto issued by the Council of People's Commissaries this passage is quoted:

> The Central Executive Committee has ordered the Soviets of Moscow and Petrograd to mobilize 10,000 workers, to arm them and to equip them for a campaign for the conquest of wheat from the rapacious and the monopolists. This order must be put into operation within a week. Every worker called upon to take up arms must perform his duty without a murmur.

This was, of course, a mobilization for war of the city proletariat against the peasantry. In an article entitled, "The Policy of Despair," published in his paper, the *Novaya Zhizn*, Gorky vigorously denounced this policy:

> The war is declared, the city against the country, a war that allows an infamous propaganda to say that the worker is to snatch his last morsel of bread from the half-starved peasant and to give him in return nothing but Communist bullets and monetary emblems without value. Cruel war is declared, and what is the more terrible, a war without an aim. The granaries of Russia are outside of the Communistic Paradise, but rural Russia suffers as much from famine as urban Russia.

We are profoundly persuaded—and Lenin and many of the intelligent Bolsheviks know this very well—that to collect wheat through these methods that recall in a manner so striking those employed by General Eichhorn (a Prussian general of enduring memory for cruelty) in Ukrainia, will never solve the food crisis. They know that the return to democracy and the work of the local autonomies will give the best results, and meantime they have taken this decisive step on the road to folly.

How completely the Bolshevist methods failed is shown by the official Soviet journal, *Finances and National Economy* (No. 38), November, 1918. The following figures refer to a period of three months in the first half of 1918, and show the number of wagon-loads demanded and the number actually secured:

1918	Wagon-loads Demanded	Wagon-loads Secured	Percentage of Demand Realized
April	20,967	1,462	6.97
May	19,780	1,684	7.02
June	17,370	786	4.52

In explanation of these figures the apologists of Bolshevist rule have said that the failure was due in large part to the control of important grain-growing provinces by anti-Bolshevist forces. This is typical of the half-truths which make up so much of the Bolshevist propaganda. Of course, important grain districts *were* in the control of the anti-Bolshevist forces, *but the fact was known to the Bolsheviki and was taken into account in making their demands.* Otherwise, their demands would certainly have been much greater. Let us, however, look at the matter from a slightly different angle and consider how the scheme worked in those provinces which were wholly controlled by the Bolsheviki, and where there were no "enemy forces." The following figures, taken from the same Soviet journal, refer to the month of June, 1918:

Province	Wagon-loads Demanded	Wagon-loads Secured	Percentage of Demand Realized
Voronezh	1,000	2	0.20
Viatka	1,300	14	1.07
Kazan	400	2	0.50
Kursk	500	7	1.40
Orel	300	8	2.67
Tambo	675	98	14.51

On June 11, 1918, a decree was issued establishing the so-called Pauper Committees, or Committees of the Poor. The decree makes it quite clear that the object was to replace the village Soviets by these committees, which were composed in part of militant Bolsheviki from the cities and in part of the poorest peasants in the villages, including among these the most thriftless, idle, and dissolute. Clause 2 of the decree of June 11th provided that "both local residents and chance visitors" might be elected. Those not admitted were those known to be exploiters and "tight-fists," those owning commercial or industrial concerns, and those hiring labor. An explanatory note was added which stated that those using hired labor for cultivating land up to a certain area might be considered eligible. An official description of these Committees of the Poor was published in *Pravda*, in February, 1919. Of course, the committees had been established and working for something over six months when *Pravda* published this account:

> A Committee of the Poor is a close organization formed in all villages of the very poorest peasants to fight against the usurers, rich peasants, and clergy, who have been exploiting the poorest peasants and squeezing out their life-blood for centuries under the protection of emperors. *Only such of the very poorest peasants as support the Soviet authority are elected members of these committees.* These latter register all grain and available foodstuffs in their villages, as well as all cattle, agricultural implements, carts, etc. It is likewise their duty to introduce the new land laws issued by order of the Soviets of the Workers', Soldiers', Peasants', and Cossacks' Deputies.
>
> The fields are cultivated with the implements thus registered, and the harvest is divided among those who have worked in accordance with the law. The surplus is supplied to the starving cities in return for goods of all kinds that the villagers need. *The motto of the Communist-Bolshevist Party is impressed upon all members of these committees*—namely, "Help the poor; do not injure the peasant of average means, but treat usurers, clergy, and all members of the White Army without mercy."

Even this account of these committees of the poor indicates a terrible condition of strife in the villages. These committees were formed to take the place of the Soviets, which the Food Commissars, in accordance with the wide powers conferred upon them, could order suppressed whenever they chose. Where the solidarity of the local peasantry could not be broken up "chance visitors," poor wretches imported for the purpose, constituted the entire membership of such committees. In other cases, a majority of the members of the committees were chosen from among the local residents. There was no appeal from the decision of these committees. Any member of such a committee having a grudge against a neighbor could satisfy it by declaring him to be a hoarder, could arrest him, seize his property and have him flogged or, as sometimes happened, shot. The military detachments formed to secure grain and other foodstuffs had to work with these committees where they already existed, and to form them where none yet existed.

The *Severnaya Oblast*, July 4, 1918, published detailed instructions of how the food-requisitioning detachments were to proceed in villages where committees of the poor had not yet been formed. They were to first call a meeting, not of all the peasants in a village, but only of the very poorest peasants and such other residents as were well known to be loyal supporters of the Soviet Government. From the number thus assembled five or seven must be selected as a committee. When formed this committee must demand, as a first step, the surrendering of all arms by the rest of the population. This disarming of the people must be very vigorously and thoroughly carried out; refusal to surrender arms to the committee, or concealing arms from the committee, involved severe punishment. Persons guilty of either offense might be ordered shot by the Committee of the Poor, the Food Commissar or the Revolutionary Tribunal. After the disarmament had been proclaimed, three days' notice was to be served upon the peasants to deliver their "surplus" grain — that is, all over and above the amount designated by the committee — at the receiving station. Failure to do this entailed severe penalties; destroying or concealing grain was treason and punishable by death at the hands of a firing-squad.

The war between the peasantry, on the one hand, and the Bolshevist officials, the food-requisitioning detachments and the pauper committees, on the other, went on throughout the summer of 1918. The first armed detachments reached the villages toward the end of June. From that time to the end of December the sanguinary struggle was maintained. According to *Izvestia* of the Food Commissariat, December, 1918, the Food Army consisted of 3,000 men in June and 36,500 in

December. In the course of the struggle this force had lost 7,309 men, killed, wounded, and sick. In other words, the casualties amounted to 30 per cent. of the highest number ever engaged. These figures of themselves bear eloquent witness to the fierce resistance of the peasantry. It was a common occurrence for a food-requisitioning detachment to enter a village and begin to search for concealed weapons and grain and to be at once met with machine-gun and rifle-fire, the peasants treating them as robbers and enemies. Sometimes the villagers were victorious and the Bolshevist forces were driven away. In almost every such case strong reinforcements were sent, principally Lettish or Chinese troops, to subdue the rebel village and wipe out the "counter-revolutionaries" and "bourgeoisie"—that is to say, nine-tenths of the peasants in the village.

Under these conditions things went from bad to worse. Naturally, there was some increase in the amount of grain turned in at the receiving stations, but the increase was not commensurate with the effort and cost of obtaining it. In particular, it did not sustain the host of officials, committees, inspectors, and armed forces employed in intimidating the peasants. One of the most serious results was the alarming decline of cultivation. The incentive to labor had been taken away from the hard-working, thrifty peasants. Their toil was penalized, in fact. A large part of the land ordinarily tilled was not planted that autumn and for spring sowing there was even less cultivation. The peasants saw that the industrious and careful producers had most of the fruits of their labors taken from them and were left with meager rations, which meant semi-starvation, while the idle, thriftless, and shiftless "poorest peasants" fared much better, taking from the industrious and competent. Through the peasantry ran the fatal cry: "Why should we toil and starve? Let us all be idle and live well as 'poor peasants'!"

Thus far, we have followed the development of the agrarian policy of the Bolsheviki through two stages: First of all, peasant Soviets were recognized and regarded as the basis of the whole system of agricultural production. It was found that these did not give satisfactory results; that each Soviet cared only for its own village prosperity; that the peasants held their grain for high prices while famine raged in the cities. Then, secondly, all the village Soviets were shorn of their power and all those which were intractable—a majority of them—suppressed, their functions being taken over by state-appointed officials, the Food Commissars and the Committees of the Poor acting under the direction of these. As we shall see in subsequent chapters, these stages corresponded in a very striking way to the first two stages of industrial organization under Bolshevist rule.

The chairman of the Perm Committee of the Party of Socialists-Revolutionists, M. C. Eroshkin, visited the United States in the winter of 1918-19. It was the good fortune of the present writer to become acquainted with this brilliant Russian Socialist leader and to obtain much information from him. Few men possess a more thorough understanding of the Russian agrarian problem than Mr. Eroshkin, who during the régime of the Provisional Government was the representative for the Perm District of the Ministry of Agriculture and later became a member of the Provisional Government of Ural. In March, 1919, he said:

> The Russian peasant could, in all fairness, scarcely be suspected of being a capitalist, and even according to the Soviet constitution, no matter how twisted, he could not be denied a vote. But fully aware that the peasants constitute a majority and are, as a whole, opposed to the Bolsheviki, the latter have destroyed the Soviets in the villages and instead of these they have created so-called "Committees of the Poor"—*i.e.*, aggregations of inebriates, propertyless, worthless, and work-hating peasants. For, whoever wishes to

work can find work in the Russian village which is always short of agricultural help. These "Committees of the Poor" have been delegated to represent the peasantry of Russia.

Small wonder that the peasants are opposed to this scheme which has robbed them of self-government. Small wonder that their hatred for these "organizations" reaches such a stage that entire settlements are rising against these Soviets and their pretorians, the Red Guardsmen, and in their fury are not only murdering these Soviet officials, but are practising fearful cruelties upon them, as happened in December, 1918, in the Governments of Pskov, Kaluga, and Tver.

By removing and arresting all those delegates who are undesirable to them, the Bolsheviki have converted these Soviets into organizations loyal to themselves, and, of course, fear to think of a true general election, for that will seal their doom at once.

Mr. Eroshkin, like practically every other leader of the Russian peasants' movement, is an anti-Bolshevik and his testimony may be regarded as biased. Let us, therefore, consider what Bolshevist writers have said in their own press.

Izvestia of the Provincial Soviets, January 18, 1919, published the following:

The Commissaries were going through the Tzaritzin County in sumptuous carriages, driven by three, and often by six, horses. A great array of adjutants and a large suite accompanied these Commissaries and an imposing number of trunks followed along. They made exorbitant demands upon the toiling population, coupled with assaults and brutality. Their way of squandering money right and left is particularly characteristic. In some houses the Commissaries gambled away and spent on intoxicants large sums. The hard-working population looked upon these orgies as upon complete demoralization and failure of duty to the world revolution.

In the same official journal, four days later, January 22, 1919, Kerzhentzev, the well-known Bolshevik, wrote:

The facts describing the village Soviet of the Uren borough present a shocking picture which is no doubt typical of all other corners of our provincial Soviet life. The chairman of this village Soviet, Rekhalev, and his nearest co-workers have done all in their power to antagonize the population against the Soviet rule. Rekhalev himself has often been found in an intoxicated condition and he has frequently assaulted the local inhabitants. *The beating-up of visitors to the Soviet office was an ordinary occurrence.* In the village of Bierezovka *the peasants have been thrashed not only with fists, but have often been assaulted with sticks, robbed of their footwear, and cast into damp cellars on bare earthen floors.* The members of the Varnavinsk *Ispolkom* (Executive Committee), Glakhov, Morev, Makhov, and others, have gone even farther. They have organized "requisition parties" which were nothing else but organized pillagings, in the course of which *they have used wire-wrapped sticks on the recalcitrants.* The abundant testimony, verified by the Soviet Commission, portrays a very striking picture of violence. When these members of the Executive Committee arrived at the township of Sadomovo they commenced to assault the population and to rob them of their household belongings, such as quilts, clothing, harness, etc. No receipts for the requisitioned goods were given and no money paid. *They even resold to others on the spot some of the breadstuffs which they had requisitioned.*

In the same paper (No. 98), March 9, 1919, another Bolshevist writer, Sosnovsky, reported on conditions in the villages of Tver Province as follows:

The local Communist Soviet workers behave themselves, with rare exception, in a disgusting manner. Misuse of power is going on constantly.

Izvestia published, January 5, 1919, the signed report of a Bolshevist official, Latzis, complaining that "in the Velizsh county of the Province of Vitebsk *they are flogging the peasants by the authority of the local Soviet Committee.*" On May 14, 1919, the same journal published the following article concerning conditions in this province:

Of late there has been going on in the village a really scandalous orgy. It is necessary to call attention to the destructive work of the scoundrels who worked themselves into responsible positions. Evidently all the good and unselfish beginnings of the workmen's and peasants' authority were either purposely or unintentionally perverted by these adventurers in order to undermine the confidence of the peasants in the existing government in order to provoke dissatisfaction and rebellion. It is no exaggeration to say that no open counter-revolutionary or enemy of the proletariat has done as much harm to the Socialist republic as the charlatans of this sort. Take, as an instance, the third district of the government of Vitebsk, the county of Veliashkov. Here the taxes imposed upon the peasants were as follows: "P. Stoukov, owning 17 dessiatines, was compelled to pay a tax of 5,000 rubles, while U. Voprit, owning 24 dessiatines, paid only 500 rubles. S. Grigoriev paid 2,000 on 29 dessiatines, while Ivan Tselov paid 8,000 on 23 dessiatines." (Quoting some more instances, the writer adds that the soil was alike in all cases. He then brings some examples of the wrongs committed by the requisitioning squads.)

The same issue of this Soviet organ contained the report of an official Bolshevist investigation of the numerous peasant uprisings. This report stated that "The local communists behave, with rare exceptions, abominably, and it was only with the greatest difficulty that we were able to explain to the peasants that we were also communists."

Izvestia also published an appeal from one Vopatin against the intolerable conditions prevailing in his village in the Province of Tambov:

Help! we are perishing! At the time when we are starving do you know what is going on in the villages? Take, for instance, our village, Olkhi. Speculation is rife there, especially with salt, which sells at 40 rubles a pound. What does the militia do? What do the Soviets do? When it is reported to them they wave their hands and say, "This is a normal phenomenon." Not only this, but the militiamen, beginning with the chief and including some communists, are all engaged in brewing their own alcohol, which sells for 70 rubles a bottle.

Nobody who is in close touch with the militia is afraid to engage in this work. Hunger is ahead of us, but neither the citizens nor the "authorities" recognize it. The people's judge also drinks, and if one wishes to win a case one only needs to treat him to a drink. We live in a terrible filth. There is no soap. People and horses all suffer from skin diseases. Epidemics are inevitable in the summer. If Moscow will pay no attention to us, then we shall perish. *We had elections for the village and county Soviets, but the voting occurred in violation of the Constitution of the Soviet Government.*

As a result of this a number of village capitalists, who, under the guise of communists, entered the party in order to avoid the requisitions and contributions, were elected. *The laboring peasantry is thus being turned against the government, and this at a time when the hosts of Kolchak are advancing from the east.*

Lenin, in his report to the Eighth Congress of the Communist Party last April, published in *Pravda*, April 9, 1919, faced the seriousness of the situation indicated by these reports. He said:

All class-conscious workmen, of Petrograd, Ivano-Voznesensk, and Moscow, who have been in the villages, tell us of instances of many misunderstandings, of misunderstandings that could not be solved, it seemed, *and of conflicts of the most serious nature*, all of which were, however, solved by sensible workmen who did not speak according to the book, but in language which the people could understand, and not like an officer allowing himself to issue orders, though unacquainted with village life, but like a comrade explaining the situation and appealing to their feelings as toilers. And by such explanation one attained what could not be attained by thousands who conducted themselves like commanders or superiors.

In the *Severnaya Communa*, May 10, 1919, another Bolshevist official, Krivoshayev, reported:

The Soviet workers are taking from the peasants chicken, geese, bread, and butter without paying for it. In some households of these poverty-stricken folk they are confiscating even the pillows and the samovars and everything they can lay their hands on. The peasants naturally feel very bitterly toward the Soviet rule.

Here, then, is a mass of Bolshevist testimony, published in the official press of the Soviet Government and the Communist Party. It cannot be set aside as "capitalist misrepresentation," or as "lying propaganda of the Socialists-Revolutionists." These and other like phrases which have been so much on the lips of our pro-Bolshevist Liberals and Socialists are outworn; they cannot avail against the evidence supplied by the Bolsheviki themselves. If we wanted to draw upon the mass of similar evidence published by the Socialists-Revolutionists and other Socialist groups opposed to the Bolsheviki, it would be easy to fill hundreds of pages. The apologists of Bolshevism have repeatedly assured us that the one great achievement of the Bolsheviki, concerning which there can be no dispute, is the permanent solution of the land problem, and that as a result the Bolsheviki are supported by the great mass of the peasantry. Against that silly fable let one single fact stand as a sufficient refutation: According to the *Severnaya Communa*, September 4, 1919, the Military Supply Bureau of Petrograd alone had sent, up to April 1, 1919, 225 armed military requisitioning detachments to various villages. Does not that fact alone indicate the true attitude of the peasants?

Armed force did not bring much food, however. The peasants concealed and hoarded their supplies. They resisted the soldiers, in many instances. When they were overcome they became sullen and refused to plant more than they needed for their own use. Extensive curtailment of production was their principal means of self-defense against what they felt to be a great injustice. According to *Economicheskaya Zhizn* (No. 54), 1919, this was the principal reason for the enormous decline of acreage under cultivation—a decline of 13,500,000 acres in twenty-eight provinces—and the main cause of the serious shortage of food grains. Instead of exporting a large surplus of grain, Tambov Province was stricken with famine, and the plight of other provinces was almost as bad.

In the Province of Tambov the peasants rose and drove away the Red Guards. In the Bejetsh district, Tver Province, 17,000 peasants rose in revolt against the Soviet authorities, according to Gregor Alexinsky. A punitive detachment sent there by Trotsky suppressed this rising with great brutality, robbing the peasants, flogging many of them, and killing many others. In Briansk, Province of Orel, the peasants and workmen rose against the Soviet authorities in November, 1919, being led by a former officer of the Fourth Soviet Army named Sapozhnikov. Lettish troops suppressed this uprising in a sanguinary manner. In the villages of Kharkov Province no less than forty-nine armed detachments appeared, seeking to wrest grain from the peasants, who met the soldiers with rifles and machine-guns. This caused Trotsky to send large punitive expeditions, consisting principally of Lettish troops, and many lives were sacrificed. Yet, despite the bloodshed, only a small percentage of the grain expected was ever obtained. There were serious peasant revolts against Soviet rule in many other places.

The District Extraordinary Commissions and the revolutionary tribunals were kept busy dealing with cases of food-hoarding and speculation. A typical report is the following taken from the Bolshevist *Derevenskaia Communa* (No. 222), October 2, 1919. This paper complained that the peasants were concealing and hoarding grain for the purpose of selling it to speculators at fabulous prices:

> Every day the post brings information concerning concealment of grain and other foodstuffs, and the difficulties encountered by the registration commissions in their work in the villages. All this shows the want of consciousness among

> the masses, who do not realize what chaos such tactics introduce into the general life of the country.
>
> No one can eat more than the human organism can absorb; the ration—and that not at all a "famine" one—is fixed. Every one is provided for, and yet—concealment, concealment everywhere, in the hope of selling grain to town speculators at fabulous prices.
>
> How much is being concealed, and what fortunes are made by profiteering, may be seen from the following example: The Goretsky Extraordinary Commission has fined Irina Ivashkevich, a citizeness of Lapinsky village, for burying 25,000 rubles' worth of grain in a hole in her back yard.
>
> Citizeness Irina Ivashkevich has much money, but little understanding of what she is doing.

Neither force nor threats could overcome the resistance of the peasants. In the latter part of November, 1919, sixteen food-requisitioning detachments of twenty-five men each were sent from Petrograd to the Simbirsk Province, according to the *Izvestia* of Petrograd. They were able to secure only 215 tons of grain at a very extraordinary price. Speculation had raised the price of grain to 600 rubles per pood of 36 pounds. The paper *Trud* reported at the same time that the delegates of forty-five labor organizations in Petrograd and Moscow, who left for the food-producing provinces to seek for non-rationed products, returned after two months wholly unsuccessful, having spent an enormous amount of money in their search. Their failure was due in part to a genuine shortage, but it was due in part also to systematic concealment and hoarding for speculation on the part of the peasants. Much of this illicit speculation and trading was carried on with the very Soviet officials who were charged with its suppression![10]

10 *The Bulletin of the Central Executive Committee of the Soviets (No. 25), February 24, 1919, reports such a case. Many other similar references might be quoted. Pravda, July 4, 1919, said that many of those sent to requisition grain from the peasants were themselves "gross speculators."*

How utterly the attempt to wrest the food from the peasants by armed force failed is evidenced by figures published in the Soviet journal, *Finances and National Economy* (No. 310). The figures show the amounts of food-supplies received in Petrograd in the first nine months of 1918 as compared with the corresponding period of the previous year. The totals include flour, rye, wheat, barley, oats, and peas:

	Jan.-Mar. Tons	Apr.-June Tons	July-Sept. Tons	Total for Nine Mos. Tons
In 1913	24,626	24,165	20,438	69,229
In 1918	12,001	5,388	2,241	19,639

If we take barley and oats, which were drawn mainly from the northern and central provinces and from the middle Volga—territories occupied by the Bolsheviki and free from "enemy forces"—we find that the same story is told: in the three months July-September, 1918, 105 tons of barley were received, as against 1,245 tons in the corresponding period of the previous year. Of oats the amount received in the three months of July-September, 1918, was 175 tons as against 3,105 tons in the corresponding period of 1917.

Armed force failed as completely as Gorky had predicted it would. References to the French Revolution are often upon the lips of the leaders of Bolshevism, and they have slavishly copied its form and even its terminology. It might have been expected, therefore, that they would have remembered the French experience with the Law of Maximum and its utter and tragic failure, and that they would have learned something therefrom, at least enough to avoid a repetition of the same mistakes as were made in 1793. There is no evidence of such learning, however. For that matter, is there any evidence that they have learned anything from history?

Not only was armed force used in a vain attempt to wrest the grain from the peasants, but similar methods were relied upon to force the peasants into the Red Army. On May 1, 1919, *Pravda*, official organ of the Communist Party, published the following announcement:

From the Central Committee of the Russian Communist Party.

The Central Committee of the Russian Communist Party announces the following—

To all provincial committees of the Communist Party, to Provincial Military Commissaries.

The All-Russian Central Executive Committee of Soviets, at the session of April 23d, unanimously adopted the decree to bring the middle and poor peasants into the struggle against the counter-revolution. According to this decree, every canton must send 10 to 20 strong, capable soldiers, who can act as nuclei for Red Army units in those places to which they will be sent.

Just as they had resisted all efforts to wrest away their grain and other foodstuffs by force, so the peasants resisted the attempts at forcible mobilization. Conscripted peasants who had been mobilized refused to go to the front and attempted mass desertions in many places, notably, however, in Astrakhan. These struggles went on throughout the early summer of 1919, but in the end force triumphed. On August 12, 1919, Trotsky wrote in *Pravda*:

The mobilization of the 19-year-old and part of the 18-year-old men, the inrush of the peasants who before refused to appear in answer to the mobilization decree, all of this is creating a powerful, almost inexhaustible, source from which to build up our army.... From now on any resistance to local authorities, any attempt to retain and protect any valuable and experienced military worker is deliberate sabotage.... No one should dare to forget that all Soviet Russia is an armed camp.... All Soviet institutions are obliged, immediately, within the next months, not only to furnish officers' schools with the best quarters, but, in general, they must furnish these schools with such material and special aids as will make it possible for the students to work in the most intensive manner....

Bitter as the conflict was during this period and throughout 1919, it was, nevertheless, considerably less violent than during the previous year. This was due to the fact that the Bolsheviki had modified their policy in dealing with the peasants in some very important respects. Precisely as they had manifested particular hatred toward the bourgeoisie in the cities, and made their appeal to the proletariat, so they had, from the very first, manifested a special hatred toward the great body of peasants of the "middle class" — that is to say, the fairly well-to-do and successful peasant — and made their appeal to the very poorest and least successful. The peasants who owned their own farms, possessed decent stock, and perhaps employed some assistance, were regarded as the "rural bourgeoisie" whom it was necessary to expropriate. The whole appeal of the Bolsheviki, so far as the peasant was concerned, was to the element corresponding to the proletariat, owning nothing. The leaders of the Bolsheviki believed that only the poorest section of the peasantry could make common cause with the proletariat; that the greater part of the peasantry belonged with the bourgeoisie. They relied upon the union of the urban proletariat and the poorest part of the peasantry, led by the former, to furnish the sinews of the Revolution. Over and over again Lenin's speeches and writings prior to April, 1919, refer to "the proletariat and the poorest peasants"; over and over again he emphasizes this union, always with the more or less definite statement that "the proletariat" must lead and "the poorest peasants" follow.

In April, 1919, at the Congress of the Russian Communist Party, Lenin read a report on the attitude of the proletariat and the Soviet power to the peasantry which marked a complete change of attitude, despite the fact that Lenin intimated that neither he nor the party had ever believed anything else. "No sensible Socialist ever thought that we might apply violence to the middle peasantry," he said. He even disclaimed any intention to expropriate the rich peasants, if they would refrain from counter-revolutionary tendencies! Of course, in thus affirming his orthodoxy while throwing over an important article of his creed, Lenin was simply conforming to an old and familiar practice. When we remember how he berated the Menshevist Social Democrats and declared them not to be Socialists because their party represented "fairly prosperous peasants,"[11] and the fact that the Soviet Constitution itself sets forth that the dictatorship to be set up is "of the urban and rural proletariat and the poorest peasantry,[12]" Lenin's attempt to make it appear that he had always regarded the middle and rich peasantry with such benign toleration can only move us to laughter.

[11] The New International, *April, 1918.*

[12] *Article II, chap. v, paragraph 9.*

To present Lenin's change of front fairly it is necessary to quote at considerable length from his two speeches at the Congress as reported in *Pravda*, April 5 and 9, 1919:

> During the long period of the bourgeois rule the peasant has always supported the bourgeois authority and was on the side of the bourgeoisie. This is

understandable if one takes into account the economic strength of the bourgeoisie and the political methods of its rule. We cannot expect the middle peasant to come over to our side immediately. But if we direct our policy correctly, then after a certain period hesitation will cease and the peasant may come over to our side. Engels, who, together with Marx, laid the foundations of scientific Marxism—that is, of the doctrine which our party follows constantly and particularly in time of revolution—Engels already established the fact that the peasantry is differentiated with respect to their land holdings into small, middle, and large; and this differentiation for the overwhelming majority of the European countries exists to-day. Engels said, "Perhaps it will not be necessary to suppress by force even the large peasantry in all places." And no sensible Socialist ever thought that we might ever apply violence to the middle peasantry (the smaller peasantry is our friend). This is what Engels said in 1894, a year before his death, when the agrarian question was the burning question of the day. This point of view shows us that truth which is sometimes forgotten, though with which we have always theoretically been in accord. With respect to landlords and capitalists our task is complete expropriation. But we do not permit any violence with respect to the middle peasant. Even with respect to the rich peasant, we do not speak with the same determination as with regard to the bourgeoisie, "Absolute expropriation of the rich peasantry." In our program this difference is emphasized. We say, "The suppression of the resistance of the peasantry, the suppression of its counter-revolutionary tendencies." This is not complete expropriation.

> The fundamental difference in our attitude toward the bourgeoisie and toward the middle peasantry is complete expropriation of the bourgeoisie, but union with the middle peasantry that does not exploit others. This fundamental line *in theory* is recognized by all. *In practice* this line is not always observed strictly, and *local workers have not learned to observe it at all*. When the proletariat overthrew the bourgeois authority and established its own and set about to create a new society, the question of the middle peasantry came into the foreground. Not a single Socialist in the world has denied the fact that the establishment of communism will proceed differently in those countries where there is large land tenure. This is the most elementary of truths and from this truth it follows that as we approach the tasks of

construction our main attention should be concentrated to a certain extent precisely on the middle peasantry. Much will depend on how we have defined our attitude toward the middle peasantry. Theoretically, this question has been decided, but we know from our own experience the difference between the theoretical decision of a question and the practical carrying out of the decision.

... All remember with what difficulty, and after how many months, we passed from workmen's control to workmen's administration of industry, and that was development within our class, within the proletarian class, with which we had always had relations. But now we must define our attitude toward a new class, toward a class which the city workmen do not know. We must define our attitude toward a class which does not have a definite steadfast position. The proletariat as a mass is for Socialism; the bourgeoisie is against Socialism; it is easy to define the relations between two such classes. But when we come to such a group as the middle peasantry, then it appears that this is such a kind of class that it hesitates. The middle peasant is part property-owner and part toiler. He does not exploit other representatives of the toilers. For decades he has had to struggle hard to maintain his position and he has felt the exploitation of the landlord-capitalists. But at the same time he is a property-owner.

Therefore our attitude toward this class presents enormous difficulties. On the basis of our experience of more than a year, and of proletariat work in the village for more than a year, and in view of the fact that there has already taken place a class differentiation in the village, we must be most careful not to be hasty, not to theorize without understanding, not to consider ready what has not been worked out. In the resolution which the committee proposes to you, prepared by the agrarian section, which one of the next speakers will read to you, you will find many warnings on this point. From the economic point of view it is clear that we must go to the assistance of the middle peasant. On this point theoretically there is no doubt. But with our level of culture, with our lack of cultural and technical forces which we could offer to the village, and with that helplessness with which we often go to the villages, comrades often apply compulsion, which spoils the whole cause. Only yesterday one comrade gave me a small pamphlet entitled, *Instructions for Party Activity in the Province of Nizhninovgorod*, a publication of the Nizhninovgorod Committee of the Russian Communist Party (Bolsheviki), and in this pamphlet I read, for example, on page 41, "The decree on the extraordinary revolutionary tax should fall with its whole weight on the shoulders of the village rich peasant speculators, and in general on the middle elements of the peasantry." Now here one may see that people have indeed "understood," or is this a misprint? But it is not admissible for such misprints to appear. Or is this the result of hurried, hasty work, which shows how dangerous haste is in a matter like this? Or have we here simply a failure to understand, though this is the very worst supposition which I really do not wish to make with reference to our comrades at Nizhninovgorod? It is quite possible that this is simply an oversight. Such instances occur in practice, as one of the comrades in the commission has related. The peasants surrounded him and each peasant asked: "Please define, am I a middle peasant or not? I have two horses and one cow. I have two cows and one horse," etc. And so this agitator who was traveling over entire districts had to use a kind of thermometer in order to take each peasant and tell him whether he was a middle peasant or not. But to do this he had to know the whole history and economic life of this particular peasant and his relations to lower and higher groups, and of course we cannot know this with exactness.

Here one must have practical experience and knowledge of local conditions, and we have not these things as yet. We are not at all ashamed to admit this; we must admit this openly. We have never been Utopists and have never imagined that we could build up the communistic society with the pure hands of pure communists who would be born and educated in a pure communistic society. Such would be children's fables. We must build communism on the ruins of capitalism, and only that class which has been tempered in the struggle against capitalism can do this. You know very well that the proletariat is not without the faults and weaknesses of the capitalistic society. It struggles for Socialism, and at the same time against its own defects. The best and most progressive portion of the proletariat which has been carrying on a desperate struggle in the cities for decades was able to imitate in the course of this struggle all the culture of city life, and to a certain extent did acquire it. You know that the village even in the most progressive countries was condemned to ignorance. Of course, the cultural level of the village will be raised by us, but that is a matter of years and years. This is what our comrades everywhere forget, and this is what every word that comes to us from the village portrays with particular clearness, when the word comes not from local intellectuals and local officials, but from people who are watching the work in the village from a practical point of view.

When we speak of the tasks in connection with work in the villages, in spite of all difficulties, in spite of the fact that our knowledge has been directed to the immediate suppression of exploiters, we must nevertheless remember and not forget that in the villages with relation to the middle peasantry the task is of a different nature. All conscious workmen, of Petrograd, Ivanovo-Vosnesensk, and Moscow, who have been in the villages, tell us of instances of many misunderstandings, of misunderstandings that could not be solved, it seemed, and of conflicts of the most serious nature, all of which were, however, solved by sensible workmen who did not speak according to the book, but in language which the people could understand, and not like an officer allowing himself to issue orders though unacquainted with village life, but like a comrade explaining the situation and appealing to their feelings as toilers. And by such explanation one attained what could not be attained by thousands who conducted themselves like commanders or superiors.

The resolution which we now present for your attention is drawn up in this spirit. I have tried in this report to emphasize the main principles behind this resolution, and its general political significance. I have tried to show, and I trust I have succeeded, that from the point of view of the interests of the revolution as a whole we have not made any changes. We have not altered our line of action. The White-Guardists and their assistants shout and will continue to shout that we have changed. Let them shout. That does not disturb us. We are developing our aims in an absolutely logical manner. From the task of suppressing the bourgeoisie we must now transfer our attention to the task of building up the life of the middle peasantry. We must live with the middle peasantry in peace. The middle peasantry in a communistic society will be on our side only if we lighten and improve its economic conditions. If we to-morrow could furnish a hundred thousand first-class tractors supplied with gasolene and machinists (you know, of course, that for the moment this is dreaming), then the middle peasant would say, "I am for the Commune." But in order to do this we must first defeat the international bourgeoisie; we must force them to give us these tractors, or we must increase our own production so that we can ourselves produce them. Only thus is the question stated correctly.

The peasant needs the industries of the cities and cannot live without them and the industries are in our hands. If we approach the situation correctly, then the peasant will thank us because we will bring him the products from the cities—implements and culture. It will not be exploiters who will bring him these things, not landlords, but his own comrades, workers whom he values very deeply. The middle peasant is very practical and values only actual assistance, quite carelessly thrusting aside all commands and instructions from above.

First help him and then you will secure his confidence. If this matter is handled correctly, if each step taken by our group in the village, in the canton, in the food-supply detachment, or in any organization, is carefully made, is carefully verified from this point of view, then we shall win the confidence of the peasant, and only then shall we be able to move forward. Now we must give him assistance. We must give him advice, and this must not be the order of a commanding officer, but the advice of a comrade. The peasant then will be absolutely for us.

... We learned how to overthrow the bourgeoisie and suppress it and we are very proud of what we have done. We have not yet learned how to regulate our relations with the millions of middle peasants and how to win their confidence. We must say this frankly; but we have understood the task and we have undertaken it and we say to ourselves with full hope, complete knowledge, and entire decision: We shall solve this task, and then Socialism will be absolute, invincible.

At the same time, at a meeting of the Moscow Soviet, Kalinin, a peasant and a Bolshevik, was elected president of the Central Executive Committee. His speech, reported in *Severnaya Communa*, April 10, 1919, sounded the same note as the speeches of Lenin—conciliation of the middle peasantry:

> My election is the symbol of the union of the proletariat and the peasantry. At the present moment when all counter-revolutionary forces are pressing in on us, such a union is particularly valuable. The peasantry was always our natural ally, but in recent times one has heard notes of doubt among the peasants; parties hostile to us are trying to drive a wedge between us and the peasantry. *We must convince the middle peasants that the working-class, having in its hands the factories, has not attacked, and will not attack, the small, individual farms of the peasant.* This can be done all the more easily because neither the old nor the new program of communists says that we will forcibly centralize the peasant lands and drive them into communes, etc. Quite to the contrary, we say definitely that we will make every effort to readjust and raise the level of the peasant economic enterprises, helping both technically and in other ways, and I shall adhere to this policy in my new post. Here is the policy we shall follow:

> We shall point out to province, district, and other executive committees that they should make every effort in the course of the collecting of the revolutionary tax, *to the end that it should not be a heavy burden on the middle peasant*; that they should make self-administration less costly and reduce bureaucratic routine. We shall make every effort so that the local executive committees shall not put obstacles in the way of exchange of articles of agriculture and of home consumption between cantons and peasants—that is, the purchase of farm and household utensils that are sold at fairs. We shall try to eliminate all friction and misunderstandings between provinces and cantons. We shall appeal to the local executive committees not only not to interfere with, but, on the contrary, to support, separate peasant economic enterprises which, because of their special character, have a special value. The mole of history is working well for us; the hour of world revolution is near, though we must not close our eyes to the fact that at the present moment it is all the more difficult for us to struggle with counter-revolution because of the disorganization of

our economic life. Frequently they prophesied our failure, but we still hold on and we shall find new sources of strength and support. Further, each of us must answer the question as to how to adjust production, carry out our enormous tasks, and use our great natural resources. In this field the unions of Petersburg and Moscow are doing very much, because they are the organizing centers from whose examples the provinces will learn. Much has been done in preparing products, but much still has to be done. We in Petersburg fed ourselves for three months, from the end of June to the beginning of September, on products from our Petersburg gardens.

The new attitude toward the peasantry revealed in the speeches of Lenin and Kalinin was already manifesting itself in the practical policy of the Soviet power. Greatly alarmed by the spread of famine in the cities, and by the stout resistance of the peasants to the armed requisitioning detachments, which amounted to civil war upon a large scale, they had established in many county towns in the grain-producing provinces central exchanges to which the peasants were urged to bring their grain to be exchanged for the manufactured goods so sorely needed by them. The attitude toward the peasants was more tolerant and friendly; the brutal strife practically disappeared. This did not bring grain to the cities, however, in any considerable quantity. The peasants found that the price offered for their grain was too low, and the prices demanded for the manufactured goods too high. According to *Izvestia* of the Central Executive Committee, No. 443, the fixed price of grain was only 70 per cent. higher than in the month preceding the Bolshevist *coup d'état*, whereas the prices on manufactured goods needed by the peasants, including shoes, clothing, household utensils, and small tools, average more than 2,800 per cent. higher. The peasant saw himself once more as a victim of the frightful parasitism of the cities and refused to part with his grain. The same issue of *Izvestia* explained that the exchange stations "have functioned but feebly and have brought very little relief to the villages";

that the stations soon became storehouses for "bread taken away from the peasants by force at the fixed prices." When cajoling failed to move the peasants the old agencies of force were resorted to. The grain was forcibly taken and the peasants were paid in paper currency so depreciated as to be almost worthless. Thus the villages were robbed of grain and, at the same time, left destitute of manufactured goods.

At the Congress of the Communist Party, following the speeches of Lenin, from which we have quoted, it was decided that the work of securing grain and other foodstuffs should be turned over to the co-operatives. A few days earlier, according to *Pravda*, March 15, 1919, a decree was issued permitting, in a number of provinces, "free sales of products, including foodstuffs." This meant that the peasants were free to bring their supplies of grain out in the open and to sell them at the best prices they could get. The situation was thus somewhat improved, but not everywhere nor for long. Many of the local Soviets refused to adopt the new policy and, as pointed out by the *Izvestia* of the Petrograd Soviet, March 24, 1919, continued to make forced requisitions. There was, however, some limitation upon the arrogant and brutal rule of the local Soviets; some restrictions were imposed upon the dictatorship of the Committees of the Poor.

From an article in *Izvestia*, November 3, 1919, we get some further information concerning the attitude of the peasants toward the Soviet power, and its bearing upon the food question. Only a summary of the article is possible here: "The food conditions are hard, not because Russia, by being cut off from the principal bread-producing districts, does not have sufficient quantities of grain, but principally owing to the class war, *which has become permanent and continuous*. This class war hinders the work of factories and shops" and, by lessening the production of manufactured goods, "naturally renders the exchange of goods between towns and country difficult, *because the peasants consider money of no value, not being able to buy anything with it."* The peasants are not yet "sufficiently farsighted to be quite convinced of the stability of the Soviet power and the inevitability of Socialism." The peasants of the producing provinces "do not willingly enough give the grain to the towns, and this greatly drags on the class war, *which of course ruins them."* The food conditions in the towns promote "counter-revolution," creating the hope that the famine-stricken people in the towns will cease to support the Soviet power. "Thus the peasants by concealing their bread ... render conditions harder, not only for the workmen, but also for themselves." A statistical table shows that from August, 1918, to September, 1919, in the twelve principal provinces, "99,980,000 poods of bread and fodder grains were delivered to the state, which constitutes 38.1 per cent. of the quantity which was to be received according to the state allocation by provinces. The delivery of bread grain equaled 42.5 per cent. Thus these provinces gave less than one-half of what they could and should have given to the state."

Such is the self-confessed record of Bolshevism in rural Russia. It is a record of stupid, blundering, oppressive bureaucracy at its best, and at its worst of unspeakable brutality. In dealing with the peasantry, who make up more than 85 per cent. of the population of Russia, Lenin and Trotsky and their followers have shown no greater wisdom of statesmanship, no stronger love of justice, no greater humanity, than the old bureaucracy of czarism. They have not elevated the life of the peasants, but, on the contrary, have checked the healthy development that was already in progress and that promised so well. They have further brutalized the life of the peasants, deepened their old distrust of government, fostered anarchy, and restored the most primitive methods of living and working. All this they have done in the name of Socialism and Progress!

VII
THE RED TERROR

I

It is frequently asserted in defense of the Bolsheviki that they resorted to the methods of terrorism only after the bourgeoisie had done so; that, in particular, the attempts to assassinate Lenin and other prominent Bolshevist leaders induced terroristic reprisals. Thus the Red Terror is made to appear as the response of the proletariat to the White Terror of the bourgeoisie. This is not true, unless, indeed, we are to take seriously the alleged "attack" on Lenin on January 16, 1918. A shot was fired, it was said, at Lenin while he was riding in his motor-car. No one was arrested and no attempt was made to discover the person who fired the shot. The general impression in Petrograd was that it was a trick, designed to afford an excuse for the introduction of the Terror. The assassination of Uritzky and the attempted assassination of Lenin, in the summer of 1918, were undoubtedly followed by an increase in the extent and savagery of the Red Terror, but it is equally true that long before that time men and women who had given their lives to the revolutionary struggle against czarism, and who had approved of the terroristic acts against individual officials, were staggered by the new mass terrorism which began soon after the Bolsheviki seized the reins of power.

On January 16th, following the alleged "attack" upon Lenin above referred to, Zinoviev, Bouch-Bruyevich, and other leaders of the Bolsheviki raised a loud demand for the Terror. On the 18th, the date set for the opening of the Constituent Assembly, the brutal suppression of the demonstration was to be held, but on the 16th the self-constituted Commissaries of the People adopted a resolution to the effect that any attempt "to hold a demonstration in honor of the Constituent Assembly" would be "put down most ruthlessly." This resolution was adopted, it is said, at the instigation of Bouch-Bruyevich, who under czarism had been a noted defender of religious liberty.

The upholders of the Constituent Assembly proceeded to hold their demonstration. What happened is best told in the report of the event made to the Executive Committee of the International Socialist Bureau by Inna Rakitnikov:

> From eleven o'clock in the morning cortèges, composed principally of working-men bearing red flags and placards with inscriptions such as "Proletarians of All Countries, Unite!" "Land and Liberty!" "Long Live the Constituent Assembly!" etc., set out from different parts of the city. The members of the Executive Committee of the Soviet of Peasants' Delegates had agreed to meet at the Field of Mars, where a procession coming from the Petrogradsky quarter was due to arrive. It was soon learned that a part of the participants, coming from the Viborg quarter, had been assailed at the Liteiny bridge by gun-fire from the Red Guards and were obliged to turn back. But that did not check the other parades. The peasant participants, united with the workers from Petrogradsky quarter, came to the Field of Mars; after having lowered their flags before the tombs of the Revolution of February and sung a funeral hymn to their memory, they installed themselves on Liteinaia Street. New manifestants came to join them and the street was crowded with people. At

the corner of Fourstatskaia Street (one of the streets leading to the Taurida Palace) they found themselves all at once assailed by shots from the Red Guards.

The Red Guard fired *without warning*, something that never before happened, even in the time of czarism. The police always began by inviting the participators to disperse. Among the first victims was a member of the Executive Committee of the Soviet of Peasants' Delegates, the Siberian peasant, Logvinov. An explosive bullet shot away half of his head (a photograph of his body was taken; it was added to the documents which were transferred to the Commission of Inquiry). Several workmen and students and one militant of the Revolutionary Socialist Party, Gorbatchevskaia, were killed at the same time. Other processions of participants on their way to the Taurida Palace were fired into at the same time. On all the streets leading to the palace, groups of Red Guards had been established; they received the order, "Not to spare the cartridges." On that day at Petrograd there were one hundred killed and wounded.[13]

[13] *How the Russian Peasants Fought for a Constituent Assembly. A report to the International Socialist Bureau by Inna Rakitnikov, vice-president of the executive committee of the Soviet of Delegates, placing themselves upon the grounds of the defense of the Constituent Assembly. With a letter-preface by the citizen, E. Roubanovitch, member of the International Socialist Bureau. May 30, 1918. Note: This report is printed in full as Appendix II to Bolshevism, by John Spargo, pp. 331-384.*

What of the brutal murder of the two members of the Provisional Government, F. F. Kokoshkin and A. I. Shingarev? Seized in the middle of December, they were cast into dark, damp, and cold cells in the Peter and Paul Fortress, in the notorious "Trubetskoy Bastion." On the evening of January 18th they were taken to the Marie Hospital. That night Red Guards and sailors forced their way into the hospital and brutally murdered them both. It is true that *Izvestia* condemned the crime, saying: "Apart from everything else it is bad from a political point of view. This is a fearful blow aimed at the Revolution, at the Soviet authorities." It is true, also, that Dybenko, Naval Commissary, published a remarkable order, saying: "The honor of the Revolutionary Fleet must not bear the stain of an accusation of revolutionary sailors having murdered their helpless enemies, rendered harmless by imprisonment. *I call upon all who took part in the murder ... to appear of their own accord before the Revolutionary Tribunal.*"

In the absence of definite proof to the contrary it is perhaps best to regard this outrage as due to the brutal savagery of individuals, rather than as part of a deliberate officially sanctioned policy of terrorism. Yet there is the fact that the sailors and Red Guards, who were armed, had gone straight to the hospital from the office of the Commission for Combating Counter-Revolution, Sabotage, and Profiteering. That this body, which from the first enlisted the services of many of the spies and secret agents of the old régime, had some connection with the murders was generally believed.

At the end of December, 1917, and in January, 1918, there were wholesale massacres in Sebastopol, Simferopol, Eupatoria, and other places. The well-known radical Russian journalist, Dioneo-Shklovsky, quotes Gorky's paper, the *Novaya Zhizn* (*New Life*), as follows:

> The garrison of the Revolutionary Army at Sebastopol has already begun its final struggle against the bourgeoisie. Without much ado they decided simply to massacre all the bourgeoisie. At first they massacred the inhabitants of the two most bourgeois streets in Sebastopol, then the same operation was extended to Simferopol, and then it was the turn of Eupatoria.

In Sebastopol not less than five hundred citizens disappeared during this St. Bartholomew massacre, according to this report, while at Simferopol between two and three hundred officers were shot in the prisons and in the streets. At Yalta many persons—between eighty and one hundred—were thrown into the bay. At Eupatoria the sailors placed the local "bourgeoisie in a barge and sank it."

Of course Gorky's paper was at that time very bitter in its criticisms of the brutal methods of the Bolsheviki, and that fact must be taken into account in considering its testimony. Gorky had been very friendly to the Bolsheviki up to the *coup d'état*, but revolted against their brutality in the early part of their régime. Subsequently, as is well known, he became reconciled to the régime sufficiently to take office under it. The foregoing accounts, as well as those in the following paragraph, agree in all essential particulars with reports published in the Constitutional-Democratic paper, *Nast Viek*. This paper, for some inexplicable reason, notwithstanding its vigorous opposition to the Bolsheviki, was permitted to appear, even when all other non-Bolshevist papers were suppressed.

According to the *Novaya Zhizn*, No. 5, the Soviets in many Russian towns made haste to follow the example of the revolutionary forces at Sebastopol and Simferopol. In the town of Etaritsa the local Red Guard wired to the authorities at the Smolny Institute, Petrograd, for permission to have "a St. Bartholomew's night" (*Yeremeievskaia Notch*). In Tropetz, according to the same issue of Gorky's paper, the commandant presented this report to the Executive Committee of the local Soviet: "The Red Army is quite ready for action. Am waiting for orders to begin a St. Bartholomew's massacre." During the latter part of February and the first week of March, 1918, there were wholesale massacres of officers and other bourgeoisie in Kiev, Rostov-on-Don and Novotcherkassk, among other places. The local Socialists-

Revolutionists paper, *Izvestia*, of Novotcherkassk, in its issue of March 6, 1918, gave an account of the killing of a number of officers.

In the beginning of March, 1918, mass executions were held in Rostov-on-Don. Many children were executed by way of reprisal. The *Russkiya Viedomosti (Russian News)*, in its issue of March 23, 1918, reported that the president of the Municipal Council of Rostov, B. C. Vasiliev, a prominent member of the Social Democratic Party; the mayor of the city; the former chairman of the Rostov-Nakhichevan Council of Workingmen's and Soldiers' Delegates, P. Melnikov; and M. Smirnov, who was chairman of this Soviet at the time—had handed in a petition to the Bolshevist War-Revolutionary Council, asking that they themselves be shot "instead of the innocent children who are executed without law and justice."

A group of mothers submitted to the same Bolshevist tribunal the following heartrending petition:

> If, according to you, there is need of sacrifices in blood and life in order to establish a socialistic state and to create new ways of life, take our lives, kill us, grown mothers and fathers, but let our children live. They have not yet had a chance to live; they are only growing and developing. Do not destroy young lives. Take our lives and our blood as ransom.
>
> Our voices are calling to you, laborers. You have not stained the banner of the Revolution even with the blood of traitors, such as Shceglovitov and Protopopov. Why do you now witness indifferently the bloodshed of our children? Raise your voices in protest. Children do not understand about party strife. Their adherence to one or another party is directed by their eagerness for new impressions, novelty, and the suggestions of elders.
>
> We, mothers, have served the country by giving our sons, husbands, and brothers. Pray, take our last possessions, our lives, but spare our children. Call us one after the other for execution, when our children are to be shot! Every one of

us would gladly die in order to save the life of her children or that of other children.

Citizens, members of the War-Revolutionary Council, listen to the cries of the mothers. We cannot keep silent!

A. Lockerman is a Socialist whose work against czarism brought prison and exile. He was engaged in Socialist work in Rostov-on-Don when the Bolsheviki seized the city in 1918, and during the seventy days they remained its masters. He says:

> The callousness with which the Red soldiers carried out executions was amazing. Without wasting words, without questions, even without any irritation, the Red Army men took those who were brought to them from the street, stripped them naked, put them to the wall and shot them. Then the bodies were thrown out on the embankment and stable manure thrown over the pools of blood.[14]

[14] *A. Lockerman; Les Bolsheviks à l'œuvre, preface par V. Zenzinov, Paris, 1920.*

Such barbarity and terrorism went on wherever the Bolsheviki held control, long before the introduction of a system of organized terror directed by the central Soviet Government. Not only did the Bolshevist leaders make no attempt to check the brutal savagery, the murders, lynchings, floggings, and other outrages, but they loudly complained that the local revolutionary authorities were not severe enough. Zinoviev bewailed the too great leniency displayed toward the "counter-revolutionaries and bourgeoisie." Even Lenin, popularly believed to be less inclined to severity than any of his colleagues, complained, in April, 1918, that "our rule is too mild, quite frequently resembling jam rather than iron." Trotsky with greater savagery said:

> You are perturbed by the mild terror we are applying against our class enemies, but know that a month hence this terror will take a more terrible form on the model of the terror of the great revolutionaries of France. Not a fortress, but the guillotine, will be for our enemies!

Numerous reports similar to the foregoing could be cited to disprove the claim of the apologists of the Bolsheviki that the Red Terror was introduced in consequence of the assassination of Uritzky and the attempt to assassinate Lenin. The truth is that the tyrannicide, the so-called White Terror, was the result of the Red Terror, not its cause. It is true, of course, that the terrorism was not all on the one side. There were many uprisings of the people, both city workers and peasants, against the Bolshevist usurpers. Defenders of the Bolsheviki cite these uprisings and the brutal savagery with which the Soviet officials were attacked to justify the terroristic policy of the Bolsheviki. The introduction of such a defense surely knocks the bottom out of the claim that the Bolsheviki really represented the great mass of the working-people, and that only the aristocracy, the bourgeoisie, and the rich peasants were opposed to them. The uprisings were too numerous, too wide-spread, and too formidable to admit of such an interpretation.

M. C. Eroshkin, who was chairman of the Perm Committee of the Party of Socialists-Revolutionists, and represented the Minister of Agriculture in the Perm district under the Provisional Government, during his visit to the United States in 1919 told the present writer some harrowing stories of uprisings against the Soviets which took on a character of bestial brutality. One of these stories was of an uprising in the Polevsky Works, in Ekaterinburg County, where a mob of peasants, armed with axes, scythes, and sticks, fell upon the members of the Soviet like so many wild animals, tearing fifty of them literally into pieces!

That the government of Russia under the Bolsheviki was to be tyrannical and despotic in the extreme was made evident from the very beginning. By the decree of November 24, 1917, all existing courts of justice were abolished and in their places set up a system of local courts based upon the elective principle. The first judges were to be elected by the Soviets, but henceforth "on the basis of direct democratic vote." It was provided that the judges were to be "guided in their rulings and verdicts by the laws of the governments which had been overthrown only in so far as those laws are not annulled by the Revolution, and do not contradict the revolutionary conscience and the revolutionary conception of right." An interpretative note was appended to this clause explaining that all laws which were in contradiction to the decrees of the Central Executive Committee of the Soviet Government, or the minimum programs of the Social Democratic or Socialists-Revolutionists parties, must be regarded as canceled.

This new "democratic judicial system" was widely hailed as an earnest of the democracy of the new régime and as a constructive experiment of the highest importance. That the decree seemed to manifest a democratic intention is not to be gainsaid: the question of its sincerity cannot be so easily determined. Of course, there is much in the decree and in the scheme outlined that is extremely crude, while the explanatory note referred to practically had the effect of enacting the platforms of political parties, which had never been formulated in the precise terms of laws, being rather general propositions concerning the exact meaning, of which there was much uncertainty. Crude and clumsy though the scheme might be, however, it had the merit of appearing to be democratic. A careful reading of the decree reveals the fact that several most important classes of offenses were exempted from the jurisdiction of these courts, among them all "political offenses." Special revolutionary tribunals were to be charged with "the defense of the Revolution":

> For the struggle against the counter-revolutionary forces by means of measures for the defense of the Revolution and its accomplishments, and also for the trial of proceedings against profiteering, speculation, sabotage, and other misdeeds of merchants, manufacturers, officials, and other persons, Workmen's and Peasants' Revolutionary Tribunals are established, consisting of a chairman and six members, serving in turn, elected by the provincial or city Soviets of Workmen's, Soldiers', and Peasants' Deputies.

Perhaps only those who are familiar with the methods of czarism can appreciate fully the significance of thus associating political offenses, such as counter-revolutionary agitation, with such offenses as illegal speculation and profiteering. Proceedings against profiteers and speculators could be relied upon to bring sufficient popularity to these tribunals to enable them to punish political offenders severely, and with a greater degree of impunity than would otherwise be possible. On December 19, 1917, I. Z. Steinberg, People's Commissar of Justice, issued a decree called "Instructions to the Revolutionary Tribunal," which caused Shcheglovitov, the most reactionary Minister of Justice the Czar ever had, to cry out: "The Cadets repeatedly charged me in the Duma with turning the tribunal into a weapon of political struggle. How far the Bolsheviki have left me behind!" The following paragraphs from this remarkable document show how admirably the institution of the Revolutionary Tribunal was designed for political oppression:

> 1. The Revolutionary Tribunal has jurisdiction in cases of persons (a) who organize uprisings against the authority of the Workmen's and Peasants' Government, actively oppose the latter or do not obey it, or call upon other persons to oppose or disobey it; (b) who utilize their positions in the state or public service to disturb or hamper the regular progress of work in the

institution or enterprise in which they are or have been serving (sabotage, concealing or destroying documents or property, etc.); (*c*) who stop or reduce production of articles of general use without actual necessity for so doing; (*d*) who violate the decrees, orders, binding ordinances, and other published acts of the organs of the Workmen's and Peasants' Government, if such acts stipulate a trial by the Revolutionary Tribunal for their violation; (*e*) who, taking advantage of their social or administrative position, misuse the authority given them by the revolutionary people. Crimes against the people committed by means of the press are under the jurisdiction of a specially instituted Revolutionary Tribunal.

2. The Revolutionary Tribunal for offenses indicated in Article I imposes upon the guilty the following penalties: (1) fine; (2) deprivation of freedom; (3) exile from the capitals, from particular localities, or from the territory of the Russian Republic; (4) public censure; (5) declaring the offender a public enemy; (6) deprivation of all or some political rights; (7) sequestration or confiscation, partial or general, of property; (8) sentence to compulsory public work.

The Revolutionary Tribunal fixes the penalty, being guided by the circumstances of the case and the dictates of the revolutionary conscience.

II. The verdicts of the Revolutionary Tribunal are final. In case of violation of the form of procedure established by these instructions, or the discovery of indications of obvious injustice in the verdict, the People's Commissar of Justice has the right to address to the Central Executive Committee of the Soviets of Workers', Soldiers', and Peasants' Deputies a request to order a second and last trial of the case.

Refusal to obey the Soviet Government, active opposition to it, and calling upon other persons "to oppose or disobey it" are thus made punishable offenses. In view of the uproar of protest raised in this country against the deportation of alien agitators and conspirators, especially by the defenders and upholders of the Bolsheviki who have assured us of the beneficent liberality of the Soviet Utopia, it may be well to direct particular attention to the fact that these "instructions" make special and precise provisions for the deportation of political undesirables. It is set forth that the Revolutionary Tribunal may inflict, among other penalties, "exile from the capitals, from particular localities, *or from the territory of the Russian Republic*," that is, deportation. These penalties, moreover, apply to Russian citizens, not, as in the case of our deportations, to aliens. The various forms of exile thus provided for were common penalties under the old régime.[15]

15 To avoid misunderstanding (though I cannot hope to avert misrepresentation) let me say that this paragraph is not intended to be a defense or a justification of the policy of deporting alien agitators. While admitting the right of our government to deport undesirable aliens, as a corollary to the undoubted right to deny their admission in the first place, I do not believe in deportation as a method of dealing with revolutionary propaganda. On the other hand, I deny the right of the Bolsheviki or their supporters to oppose as reactionary and illiberal a method of dealing with political undesirables which is in full force in Bolshevist Russia, which they acclaim so loudly.

It is interesting to observe, further, that there is no right of appeal from the verdicts of the Revolutionary Tribunal, except that "the People's Commissar of Justice has the right to address to the Central Executive Committee of the Soviets of Workers', Soldiers', and Peasants' Deputies a *request* to order a second and last trial" of any case in which he is sufficiently interested to do so. Unless this official can be convinced that there has been some "violation of the form of procedure" or that there is "obvious injustice in the verdict," and unless he can be induced to make such a "request" to the central Soviet authority, the verdict of the Revolutionary Tribunal is final and absolute. What a travesty upon justice and upon democracy! What an admirable instrument for tyrants to rely upon!

Even this terrible weapon of despotism and oppression did not satisfy the Bolsheviki, however. For one thing, the decree constituting the Revolutionary Tribunal provided that its session must be held in the open; for another, its members must be elected. Consequently, a new type of tribunal was added to the system, the Extraordinary Commission for Combating Counter-Revolution—the infamous *Chresvychaika*. Not since the Inquisitions of the Middle Ages has any civilized nation maintained tribunals clothed with anything like the arbitrary and unlimited authority possessed by the central and local Extraordinary Commissions for Combating Counter-Revolution. They have written upon the pages of Russia's history a record of tyranny and oppression which makes the worst record of czarism seem gentle and beneficent.

It is not without sinister significance that in all the collections of documents which the Bolsheviki and their sympathizers have published to illustrate the workings of the Soviet system, in this country and in Europe, there is not one explaining the organization, functions, methods, and personnel of it's most characteristic institution—more characteristic even than the Soviet. Neither in the several collections published by *The Nation*, the American Association for International Conciliation, the Russian Soviet Government Bureau, nor in the books of writers like John Reed, Louise Bryant, William C. Bullitt, Raymond Robins, William T. Goode, Arthur Ransome, Isaac Don Levine, Colonel Malone, M.P., Lincoln Eyre, Etienne Antonelli, nor any other volume of the kind, can such information be found. This silence is profoundly eloquent.

This much we know about the Chresvychaikas: *The Soviet Government created the All-Russian Extraordinary Commission for Combating Counter-Revolution, Sabotage, and Profiteering, and established it at the headquarters of the former Prefecture of Petrograd, 2, Gorokhovaia Street. Its full personnel has never been made known, but it is well known that many of the spies and confidential agents of the former secret police service entered its employ.* Until February, 1919, it possessed absolutely unlimited powers of arrest, except for the immunity enjoyed by members of the government; its hearings were held in secret; it was not obliged to report even the names of persons sentenced by it; mass arrests and mass sentences were common under its direction; it was not confined to dealing with definite crimes, violations of definite laws, but could punish at will, in any manner it deemed fit, any conduct which it pleased to declare to be "counter-revolutionary."

Those apologists who say that the Bolsheviki resorted to terrorism only after the assassination of Uritzky, and those others who say that terrorism was the answer to the intervention of the Allies, are best answered by the citation of official documentary evidence furnished by the Bolsheviki themselves. In the face of such evidence argument is puerile and vain. In February, 1918, months before either the assassination of Uritzky or the intervention of the Allies took place, the All-Russian Extraordinary Commission issued the following proclamation, which was published in the *Krasnaya Gazeta*, official organ of the Petrograd Soviet, on February 23, 1918:

> The All-Russian Extraordinary Commission to Combat Counter-Revolution, Sabotage, and Speculation, of the Council of People's Commissaries, brings to the notice of all citizens that up to the present time it has been lenient in the struggle against the enemies of the people.
>
> But at the present moment, when the counter-revolution is becoming more impudent every day, inspired by the treacherous attacks of German counter-revolutionists; when the bourgeoisie of the whole world is trying to suppress the advance-guard of the revolutionary International, the Russian proletariat, the All-Russian Extraordinary Commission, acting in conformity with the ordinances of the Council of People's Commissaries, sees *no other way to combat counter-revolutionists*, speculators, marauders, hooligans, obstructionists, and other parasites, *except by pitiless destruction at the place of crime.*
>
> *Therefore the Commission announces that all enemy agents,* and counter-revolutionary agitators, speculators, organizers of uprisings or participants in preparations for uprisings to overthrow the Soviet authority, all fugitives to the Don to join the counter-revolutionary armies of Kaledin and Kornilov and the Polish counter-revolutionary Legions, *sellers or purchasers of arms to be sent to the Finnish White Guard, the*

troops of Kaledin, Kornilov, and Dovbor Musnitsky, or to arm the counter-revolutionary bourgeoisie of Petrograd, will be mercilessly shot by detachments of the Commission at the place of the crime.

PETROGRAD, February 22, 1918.

ALL-RUSSIAN EXTRAORDINARY COMMISSION.

In connection with this ferocious document and its announcement that "counter-revolutionists" would be subject to "pitiless destruction," that "counter-revolutionary agitators" would be "mercilessly shot," it is important to remember that during the summer of 1917, when Kerensky was struggling against "German counter-revolutionists" and plots to overthrow the Revolution, the Bolsheviki had demanded the abolition of the death penalty. Lenin, Trotsky, Kamenev, Zinoviev, and others denounced Kerensky as a "hangman" and "murderer." Where is the moral integrity of these men? Like scorpion stings are the bitter words of the protest of L. Martov, leader of the radical left wing of the Menshevist Social Democrats:

> In 1910 the International Socialist Congress at Copenhagen passed a resolution in favor of starting a campaign in all countries for the abolition of the death penalty.
>
> All the present leaders of the Bolshevist Party—Lenin, Zinoviev, Trotsky, Kamenev, Radek, Rakovsky, Lunarcharsky—voted for this resolution. I saw them all there raising their hands in favor of the resolution declaring war on capital punishment.
>
> Then I saw them in Petrograd in July, 1917, protesting against punishing by death even those who had turned traitors to their country during the war.

> I see them now condemning to death and executing people, bourgeoisie and workmen, peasants and officers alike. I see them now demanding from their subordinates that they should not count the victims, that they should put to death as many opponents of the Bolshevist régime as possible.
>
> And I say to these Bolshevist "judges": "You are malignant liars and perjurers! You have deceived the workmen's International by signing its demand for the universal abolition of the death penalty and by its restoration when you came to power.

No idle threat was the proclamation of February: the performance was fully as brutal as the text. Hundreds of people were shot. The death penalty had been "abolished," and on the strength of that fact the Bolsheviki had been lauded to the skies for their humanity by myopic and perverse admirers in this country and elsewhere outside of Russia. But the shooting of people by the armed detachments of the Extraordinary Commission went on. No court ever examined the cases; no competent jurists heard or reviewed the evidence, or even examined the charges. A simple entry, such as "Ivan Kouzmitch—Robbery—Shot," might cover the murder of a devoted Socialist whose only crime was a simple speech to his fellow-workmen in favor of the immediate convocation of the Constituent Assembly, or calling upon them to unite against the Bolsheviki. And where counter-revolutionary agitation was given as the crime for which men were shot there was nothing to show, in many cases, whether the victim had taken up arms against the Soviet power or merely expressed opinions unfavorable to the régime.

Originally under the direction of Uritzky, who met a well-deserved fate at the hands of an assassin[16] in July, 1918, the All-Russian Extraordinary Commission in turn set up Provincial and District Extraordinary Commissions, all of which enjoyed the same practically unlimited powers. Before February, 1919, these bodies were not even limited in the exercise of the right to inflict the death penalty, except for the immunity enjoyed by members of the government. Any Extraordinary Commission could arrest, arraign, condemn, and execute any person in secret, the only requirement being that *afterward*, if called upon to do so, it must report the case to the local Soviet! A well-known Bolshevist writer, Alminsky, wrote in *Pravda*, October 8, 1918:

<u>16</u> *Uritzky is thus described by Maurice Verstraete:*

"He is a refined sadist, who does his grim work for the love of it.... Uritzky is a hunchback and seems to be revenging himself on all mankind for his deformity. His heart is full of hatred, his nerves are shattered, and his mind depraved. He is the personification of a civilized brute—that is to say, the most cruel of all. Yesterday he was laughing at his own joke. He had ordered twenty men to be executed. Among the condemned was a lover of the girl who was waiting to be examined. Uritzky himself told her of the death of her lover.... The only emotion of which Uritzky is capable is fear. The only person Uritzky obeys is the Swiss ambassador, as he hopes, in return, that the latter will enable him to procure a passport to Switzerland, in case he is forced to escape when the Bolsheviks are overthrown.... Trotsky and Zinoviev are in many ways like Uritzky. They are also cruel, hysterical, and ready to overwhelm the world with blood."—VERSTRAETE, *Mes Cahiers Russes*, p. 350.

The absence of the necessary restraint makes one feel appalled at the "instruction" issued by the All-Russian Extraordinary Commission to "All Provincial Extraordinary Commissions," which says: "The All-Russian Extraordinary Commission is perfectly independent in its work, carrying out house-searches, arrests, executions, of which it *afterward* reports to the Council of the People's Commissaries and to the Central Executive Council." Further, the Provincial and District Extraordinary Commissions "are independent in their activities, and when called upon by the local Executive Council present a report of their work." In so far as house-searches and arrests are concerned, a report made *afterward* may result in putting right irregularities committed owing to lack of restraint. The same cannot be said of executions.... It can also be seen from the "instruction" that personal safety is to a certain extent guaranteed only to members of the government, of the Central Council, and of the local Executive Committees. With the exception of

> these few persons all members of the local committees of the (Bolshevik) Party, of the Control Committees, and of the Executive Committee of the party may be shot at any time by the decision of any Extraordinary Commission of a small district town if they happen to be on its territory, and a report of that made *afterward*.

After the assassination of Uritzky, and the attempted assassination of Lenin, there was instituted a mad orgy of murderous terror without parallel. It was a veritable saturnalia of brutal repression. Against the vain protestation of the defenders of the Bolsheviki that the Red Terror has been grossly exaggerated, it is quite sufficient to set down the exultations and admissions of the Bolsheviki themselves, the records made and published in their own official reports and newspapers. The evidence which is given in the next few pages is only a small part of the immense volume of such evidence that is available, every word of it taken from Bolshevist sources.

Under czarism revolutionary terrorism directed against government officials was almost invariably followed by increased repression; terror made answer to terror. We shall search the records of czarism in vain, however, for evidence of such brutal and blood-lusting rage as the Bolsheviki manifested when their terror was answered by terror. When a young Jew named Kannegiesser assassinated Uritzky the *Krasnaya Gazeta* declared:

> The whole bourgeoisie must answer for this act of terror.... Thousands of our enemies must pay for Uritzky's death.... We must teach the bourgeoisie a bloody lesson.... Death to the bourgeoisie!

This same Bolshevist organ, after the attempt to assassinate Lenin, said:

We will turn our hearts into steel, which we will temper in the fire of suffering and the blood of fighters for freedom. We will make our hearts cruel, hard, and immovable, so that no mercy will enter them, and so that they will not quiver at the sight of a sea of enemy blood. We will let loose the flood-gates of that sea. Without mercy, without sparing, we will kill our enemies in scores of hundreds. Let them be thousands; let them drown themselves in their own blood. For the blood of Lenin and Uritzky, Zinoviev, and Volodarsky, let there be floods of the blood of the bourgeoisie—more blood, as much as possible.

In the same spirit the *Izvestia* declared, "The proletariat will reply to the attempt on Lenin in a manner that will make the whole bourgeoisie shudder with horror." Peters, successor to Uritzky as head of the Extraordinary Commission, said, in an official proclamation, "This crime will be answered by a mass terror." On September 2d, Petrovsky, Commissar for the Interior, issued this call to mass terror:

Murder of Volodarsky and Uritzky, attempt on Lenin, and shooting of masses of our comrades in Finland, Ukrainia, the Don and Czechoslovakia, continual discovery of conspiracies in our rear, open acknowledgment of Right Social Revolutionary Party and other counter-revolutionary rascals of their part in these conspiracies, together with the insignificant extent of serious repressions and mass shooting of White Guards and bourgeoisie on the part of the Soviets, all these things show that notwithstanding frequent pronouncements urging mass terror against the Socialists-Revolutionaries, White Guards, and bourgeoisie no real terror exists.

Such a situation should decidedly be stopped. End should be put to weakness and softness. All Right Socialists-Revolutionaries known to local Soviets should be arrested immediately. Numerous hostages should be taken from the bourgeoisie and officer classes. At the slightest attempt to resist or the slightest movement among the White Guards, mass shooting should be applied at once. Initiative in this matter rests especially with the local executive committees.

Through the militia and extraordinary commissions, all branches of government must take measures to seek out and arrest persons hiding under false names and shoot without fail anybody connected with the work of the White Guards.

All above measures should be put immediately into execution.

Indecisive action on the part of local Soviets must be immediately reported to People's Commissary for Home Affairs.

The rear of our armies must be finally guaranteed and completely cleared of all kinds of White-Guardists, and all despicable conspirators against the authority of the working-class and of the poorest peasantry. Not the slightest hesitation or the slightest indecisiveness in applying mass terror.

Acknowledge the receipt of this telegram.

Transmit to district Soviets.

[Signed] PETROVSKY.[17]

[17] *The text is taken from the Weekly of the All-Russian Extraordinary Commission (No. 1), Moscow, September 21, 1918. The translation used is that published by the U. S. Department of State. It has been verified.*

On September 3, 1918, the *Izvestia* published this news item:

In connection with the murder of Uritzky five hundred persons have been shot by order of the Petrograd Extraordinary Commission to Combat Counter-Revolution. The names of the persons shot, and those of candidates for future shooting, in case of a new attempt on the lives of the Soviet leaders, will be published later.[18]

[18] *Desiring to confine the evidence here strictly to Bolshevist sources, I have passed over much testimony by well-known Socialists-Revolutionists, Social Democrats, and others. Because it has not been possible to have the item referring to the retaliatory massacre in Petrograd satisfactorily verified, I introduce here, by way of corroboration, a statement by the Socialists-Revolutionists leader, Eugene Trupp, published in the organ of the Socialists-Revolutionists, Zemlia i Volia, October 3, 1918:*

"After the murder of Uritzky in Petrograd 1,500 people were arrested; 512, including 10 Socialists-Revolutionists, were shot. At the same time 800 people were arrested in Moscow. It is unknown, however, how many of these were shot. In Nizhni-Novgorod, 41 were shot; in Jaroslavl, 13; in Astrakhan, 12 Socialists-Revolutionists; in Sarapool, a member of the Central Committee of the party of Socialists-Revolutionists, I. I. Teterin; in Penza, about 40 officers."

See also the corroboration of this incident quoted from the Weekly Journal of the Extraordinary Commission, on p. 171.

Two days later, September 5, 1918, a single column of *Izvestia* contained the following paragraphs, headed "Latest News":

Arrest of Right Socialists-Revolutionaries

At the present moment the ward extraordinary commissioners are making mass arrests of Right Socialists-Revolutionaries, since it has become clear that this party is responsible for the recent acts of terrorism (attempt on life of Comrade Lenin and the murder of Uritzky), which were carried out according to a definitely elaborated program.

Arrest of a Priest

For an anti-Soviet sermon preached from the church pulpit, the Priest Molot has been arrested and turned over to the counter-revolutionary section of the All-Russian Extraordinary Commission.

Struggle Against Counter-Revolutionaries

We have received the following telegram from the president of the Front Extraordinary Commission, Comrade Latsis: "The Extraordinary Commission of the Front had shot in the district of Ardatov, for anti-Soviet agitation, 4 peasants, and sent to a concentration camp 32 officers.

"At Arzamas were shot three champions of the Tsarist régime, and one peasant-exploiter, and 14 officers were sent to the concentration camp for anti-Soviet agitation."

House Committee Fined

For failure to execute the orders of the dwelling section of the All-Russian Extraordinary Commission, the house committee at 42, Pokrovka, has been fined 20,000 rubles.

This fine is a punishment for failure to remove from the house register the name of the well-known Cadet Astrov, who disappeared three months ago.

All the movable property of Astrov has been confiscated.

The Arrest of Speculators

On September 3d members of the Section to Combat Speculation of the All-Russian Extraordinary Commission arrested Citizen Pitkevich, who was trying to buy 125 food-cards at 20 rubles each. A search was made in the apartment of Pitkevich, which revealed a store of such cards bearing official stamps.

This section also arrested a certain Bosh, who was speculating in cocaine brought from Pskov.

On September 5, 1918, the Council of the People's Commissaries ordered that the names of persons shot by order of the Extraordinary Commission should be published, with full particulars of their cases, a decision which was flouted by the Extraordinary Commission, as we shall see. The resolution of the Council of People's Commissaries was published in the *Severnaya Communa*, evening edition, November 9, 1918, and reads as follows:

The Council of the People's Commissaries, having considered the report of the chairman of the Extraordinary Commission, finds that under the existing conditions it is most necessary to secure the safety of the rear by means of terror. All persons belonging to the White Guard organizations or involved in conspiracies and rebellion are to be shot. Their names and the particulars of their cases are to be published.

On September 10, 1918, the *Severnaya Communa* published in its news columns the two following despatches:

JAROSLAVL, *September 9th.*—In the whole of the Jaroslavl Government a strict registration of the bourgeoisie and its partizans has been organized. Manifestly anti-Soviet elements are being shot; suspected persons are being interned in concentration camps; non-working sections of the population are being subjected to compulsory labor.

TYER, *September 9th.*—The Extraordinary Commission has arrested and sent to concentration camps over 130 hostages from among the bourgeoisie. The prisoners include members of the Cadet Party, Socialists-Revolutionists of the Right, former officers, well-known members of the propertied class, and policemen.

Two days later, September 12th, the same journal contained the following:

ATKARSK, *September, 11th.*—Yesterday martial law was proclaimed in the town. Eight counter-revolutionaries were shot.

On September 18, 1918, the *Severnaya Communa* published the following evidences of the wide-spread character of the terrorism which the Bolsheviki were practising:

In Sebesh a priest named Kikevitch was shot for counter-revolutionary propaganda and for *saying masses for the late Nicholas Romanov.*

In Astrakhan the Extraordinary Commission has shot ten Socialists-Revolutionists of the Right involved in a plot against the Soviet power. *In Karamyshev a priest named Lubinoff and a deacon named Kvintil have been shot for* revolutionary agitation against the decree separating the Church from the State *and for an appeal to overthrow the Soviet Government.* In Perm, in retaliation for the assassination of Uritzky and for the attempt on Lenin, fifty hostages from among the bourgeois classes and the White Guards were shot.

The shooting of innocent hostages is a peculiarly brutal form of terrorism. When it was practised by the Germans during the war the world reverberated with denunciation. That the Bolsheviki ever were guilty of this crime, so much more odious than anything which can be charged against czarism, has been many times denied, but the foregoing statement from one of their most influential official journals is a complete refutation of all such denials. Perm is more than a thousand miles from Petrograd, where the assassination of Uritzky occurred, and no attempt was ever made to show that the fifty hostages who were shot, or any of them, were guilty of any complicity in the assassination. It was a brutal, malignant retaliation upon innocent people for a crime of which they knew nothing. The famous "Decree No. 903," signed by Trotsky, which called for the taking of hostages as a means of checking desertions from the Red Army, was published in *Izvestia*, September 18, 1918:

> Decree No. 903: Seeing the increasing number of deserters, especially among the commanders, orders are issued to arrest as hostages all the members of the family one can lay hands on: father, mother, brother, sister, wife, and children.

The evening edition of *Severnaya Communa*, September 18, 1918, reported a meeting of the Soviet of the first district of Petrograd, stating that the following resolution had been passed:

> The meeting welcomes the fact that mass terror is being used against the White Guards and higher bourgeois classes, and declares that every attempt on the

life of any of our leaders will be answered by the proletariat by the shooting down not only of hundreds, as the case is now, but of thousands of White Guards, bankers, manufacturers, Cadets, and Socialists-Revolutionists of the Right.

On the following day, September 19th, the same journal quoted Zinoviev as saying:

To overcome our enemies we must have our own Socialist Militarism. We must win over to our side 90 millions out of the 100 millions of population of Russia under the Soviets. *As for the rest, we have nothing to say to them; they must be annihilated.*

Reference has already been made to the fact that the Council of the People's Commissaries ordered that the Extraordinary Commission publish the names of all persons sentenced to be shot, with particulars of their cases, and the further fact that the instruction was ignored. It is well known that great friction developed between the Extraordinary Commissions and the Soviet power. In many places the Extraordinary Commissions not only defied the local Soviets, *but actually suppressed them.* Naturally, there was friction between the Soviet power and its creature. There were loud protests on the part of influential Bolsheviki, who demanded that the *Chresvychaikas* be curbed and restrained and that the power to inflict the death penalty be taken from them. That is why the resolution of September 5th, already quoted, was passed. Nevertheless, in practice secrecy was very generally observed. Trials took place in secret and there was no publication, in many instances, of results. Reporting a meeting of the Executive Committee of the Moscow Soviet, which took place on October 16, 1918, *Izvestia*, the official Bolshevist organ, contained the following in its issue of the next day:

The report of the work of the All-Russian Extraordinary Commission was read at a secret session of the Executive Committee. *But the report and the discussion of it were held behind closed doors and will not be published.* After a debate the doors of the Session Hall were thrown open.

From an article in the *Severnaya Communa*, October 17, 1918, we learn that the Extraordinary Commission "has registered 2,559 counter-revolutionary affairs and 5,000 arrests have been made"; that "at Kronstadt there have been 1,130 hostages. Only 183 people are left; 500 have been shot."

Under the heading, "The Conference of the Extraordinary Commission," *Izvestia* of October 19, 1918, printed the following paragraph:

> PETROGRAD, *October 17th.*—At to-day's meeting of the Conference of the Extraordinary Investigating Commission, Comrades Moros and Baky read reports giving an account of the activities of the Extraordinary Commission in Petrograd and Moscow. Comrade Baky threw light on the work of the district commission of Petrograd after the departure of the All-Russian Extraordinary Commission for Moscow. The total number of people arrested by the Extraordinary Commission amounted to 6,220. *Eight hundred people were shot.*

On November 5, 1918, *Izvestia* said:

> A riot occurred in the Kirsanoff district. The rioters shouted, "Down with the Soviets." They dissolved the Soviet and Committee of the Village Poor. The riot was suppressed by a detachment of Soviet troops. Six ringleaders were shot. The case is under examination.

The *Weekly Journal of the Extraordinary Commissions to Combat Counter-Revolution* is, as the name implies, the official organ in which the proclamations and reports of these Extraordinary Commissions are published. It is popularly nicknamed "The Hangmen's Journal." The issue of October 6, 1918 (No. 3), contains the following:

> We decided to make it a real, not a paper terror. In many cities there took place, accordingly, *mass shootings of hostages*, and it is well that they did. In such business half-measures are worse than none.

Another issue (No. 5), dated October 20, 1918, says:

> Upon the decision of the Petrograd Extraordinary Commission, 500 hostages were shot.

These are typical extracts: it would be possible to quote from this journal whole pages quite similar to them.

How closely the Extraordinary Commissions copied the methods of the Czar's secret police system can be judged from a paragraph that appeared in the *Severnaya Communa*, October 17, 1918:

> The Extraordinary Commission has organized the placing of police agents in every part of Petrograd. The Commission has issued a proclamation to the workmen exhorting them to inform the police of all they know. The bandits, both in word and action, must be forced to recognize that the revolutionary proletariat is watching them strictly.

Here, then, is a formidable array of evidence from Bolshevist sources of the very highest authority. It is only a part of the whole volume of such evidence that is available; nevertheless, it is sufficient, overwhelming, and conclusive. If we were to draw upon the official documentary testimony of the Socialist parties and groups opposed to the Bolsheviki, hundreds of pages of records of *Schrecklichkeit*, even more brutal than anything here quoted, could be easily compiled. Much of this testimony is as reliable and entitled to as much weight as any of the foregoing. Take, for example, the statement of the Foreign Representatives of the Russian Social Democratic

Party upon the shooting of six young students arrested in Petrograd: In the New York *World*, March 22, 1920, Mr. Lincoln Eyre quotes "Red Executioner Peters" as saying: "We have never yet passed the sentence of death on a foreigner, although some of them richly deserved it. The few foreigners who have lost their lives in the Revolution have been killed in the course of a fight or in some such manner." Shall we not set against that statement the signed testimony of responsible and honored spokesmen of the Russian Social Democratic Party?

Three brothers, named Genzelli, French citizens, were arrested and shot without the formality of a trial. They had been officers in the Czar's army, and, with three young fellow-officers, Russians, were discovered at a private gathering, wearing the shoulder-straps indicative of their former military rank. This was their offense. According to a statement issued by the Foreign Representatives of the Russian Social Democratic Party, Lenin was asked at Smolny, "What is to be done with the students?" and replied, "Do with them what you like." The whole six were shot, but it has never been possible to ascertain who issued the order for the execution.

Another example: The famous Schastny case throws a strong light upon one very important phase of the Bolshevist terror. Shall we decline to give credence to Socialists of honorable distinction, simply because they are opposed to Bolshevism? Here are two well-known Socialist writers, one French and the other Russian, long and honorably identified with the international Socialist movement. Charles Dumas, the French Socialist, from whose book[19] quotation has already been made, gives an account of the Schastny case which vividly illustrates the brutality of the Bolsheviki:

---

[19] *La Vérité sur les Bolsheviki*, par Charles Dumas, Paris, 1919.

The Schastny case is the most detestable episode in Bolshevist history. Its most repulsive feature is the parody of legality which the Bolsheviki attempt to attach to a case of wanton murder. Admiral Schastny was the commander of the Baltic Fleet and was put in command by the Bolsheviki themselves. Thanks to his efforts, the Russian war-ships were brought out of Helsingfors harbor in time to escape capture by the Germans on the eve of their invasion of Finland. In general, it was he who contributed largely to the saving of whatever there was left of the Russian fleet. His political views were so radical that even the Bolsheviki tolerated him in their service. Notwithstanding all this, he was accused of complicity in a counter-revolutionary plot and haled before a tribunal. In vain did the judge search for a shred of proof of his guilt. Only one witness appeared against him—Trotsky—who delivered an impassioned harangue full of venom and malice. Admiral Schastny implored the court to allow witnesses for the defense to testify, but the judges decreed that his request was sheer treason. Thereupon the witnesses who were prevented from appearing in court forwarded their testimony in writing, but the court decided not to read their communication. After a simulated consultation, Schastny was condemned to die—a verdict which later stirred even Krylenko, one of his accusers, to say: "That was not a death sentence—that was a summary shooting!"

The verdict was to be carried out in twenty-four hours. This aroused the ire of the Socialists-Revolutionists of the Left, who at that time were represented in the People's Commissariat, and they immediately forwarded, in the name of their party, a sharp protest against the official confirmation of the death sentence. The Commissaries, in reply, ordered the immediate shooting of Schastny.

Apparently Schastny was subjected to torture before his death. He was killed without witnesses, without a priest, and even his lawyer was not notified of the hour of his execution. When his family demanded the surrender of his body to them, it was denied. What, if otherwise, did the Bolsheviki fear, and why did they so assiduously conceal the body of the dead admiral? The same occurred after the execution of Fanny Royd, who shot at Lenin. There is also indisputable evidence that the Bolsheviki are resorting to torture at inquests. The assassin of Commissary Uritzky (whose family, by the way, was entirely wiped out by the Bolsheviki as a matter of principle, without even the claim that they knew anything about the planned attempt) was tortured by his executioners in the Fortress of St. Peter and Paul.

In the modern revolutionary movement of Russia few men have served with greater distinction than L. Martov, and none with greater disinterestedness. His account of the Schastny trial is vibrant with the passionate hatred of tyranny and oppression characteristic of his whole career:

He was accused of conspiring against the Soviet power. Captain Schastny denied it. He asked the tribunal to hear witnesses, including Bolshevist commissaries, who had been appointed to watch him. Who was better qualified to state whether he had really conspired against the Soviet power?

The tribunal refused to hear witnesses. Refused what every court in the world, except Stolypin's field court martials, recognized the worst criminal entitled to.

A man's life was at stake, the life of a man who had won the love and confidence of his subordinates, the sailors of the Baltic Fleet, who protested against the captain's arrest. The life of a man who had performed a marvelous feat! He had somehow managed to take out of Helsingfors harbor all the ships of the Baltic Fleet, and had thus saved them from capture by the Finnish Whites.

It was not the enraged Finnish Whites, nor the German Imperialists, who shot this man. He was put to death by men who call themselves Russian Communists—by Messrs. Medvedeff, Bruno, Karelin, Veselovski, Peterson, members of the Supreme Revolutionary Tribunal.

Captain Schastny was refused the exercise of the right to which every thief or murderer is entitled—*i.e.*, to call in witnesses for the defense. But the witness for the prosecution was heard. This witness was Trotsky, Trotsky, who, as Commissary for War and Naval Affairs, had arrested Captain Schastny.

At the hearing of the case by the tribunal, Trotsky acted, not as a witness, but as a prosecutor. As a prosecutor he declared, "This man is guilty; you must condemn him!" And Trotsky did it after having gagged the prisoner by refusing to call in witnesses who might refute the accusations brought against him.

Not much valor is required to fight a man who has been gagged and whose hands are tied, nor much honesty or loftiness of character.

It was not a trial; it was a farce. There was no jury. The judges were officials dependent upon the authorities, receiving their salaries from the hands of Trotsky and other People's Commissaries. And this mockery of a court passed the death sentence, which was hurriedly carried out before the people, who were profoundly shaken by this order to kill an innocent man, could do anything to save him.

Under Nicholas Romanov one could sometimes stop the carrying out of a monstrously cruel sentence and thus pull the victim out of the executioner's hands.

Under Vladimir Ulianov this is impossible. The Bolshevist leaders slept peacefully when, under the cover of night, the first victim of their tribunal was stealthily being killed.

No one knew who murdered Schastny or how he was murdered. As under the Czars, the executioners' names are concealed from the people. No one knows whether Trotsky himself came to the place of the execution to watch and direct it.

Perhaps he, too, slept peacefully and saw in his dreams the proletariat of the whole world hailing him as the liberator of mankind, as the leader of the universal revolution.

In the name of Socialism, in thy name, O proletariat, blind madmen and vainglorious fools staged this appalling farce of cold-blooded murder.

The evidence we have cited from Bolshevist sources proves conclusively that the Red Terror was far from being the unimportant episode it is frequently represented to have been by pro-Bolshevist writers. It effectually disposes of the assiduously circulated myth that the Extraordinary Commissions were for the most part concerned with the suppression of robbery, crimes of violence, and illegal speculation, and that only in a few exceptional instances did they use their powers to suppress anti-Bolshevist propaganda.

The evidence makes it quite clear that from the early days of the Bolshevist régime until November, 1918, at least, an extraordinary degree of terrorism prevailed throughout Soviet Russia. According to a report published by the All-Russian Extraordinary Commission in February of the present year, not less than 6,185 persons were executed in 1918 and 3,456 in 1919, a total of 9,641 in Moscow and Petrograd alone. Of the total number for the two years, *7,068 persons were shot for counter-revolutionary activities*, 631 for crimes in office — embezzlement, corruption, and so on — 217 for speculation and profiteering, and 1,204 for all other classes of crime.

That these figures understate the extent of the Red Terror is certain. In the first place, the report covers only the work of the Extraordinary Commissions of Moscow and Petrograd. The numerous District Extraordinary Commissions are not reported on. In the next place, there is reason to believe that many of the reports of the Extraordinary Commissions were falsified in order not to create too bad an impression. Quite frequently, as a matter of fact, the number of victims reported by the *Chresvychaikas* was less than the number actually known to have been killed. Moreover, the figures given refer only to the victims of the Extraordinary Commissions, and do not include those sentenced to death by the other revolutionary tribunals. The 9,641 executions — even if we accept the figures as full and complete — refer only to the victims of the Moscow and Petrograd *Chresvychaikas*, men and women put to death without anything like a trial.[20] When to these figures there shall be added the victims of all the District Extraordinary Commissions and of all the other revolutionary tribunals, the real meaning of the Red Terror will begin to appear. But even that will not give us the real measure of the Red Terror, for the simple reason that the many thousands of peasants and workmen who have been slain in the numerous uprisings, frequently taking on the character of pitched battles between armed masses and detachments of Soviet troops, are not included.

[20] *The figures are taken from Russkoe Delo (Prague), March 4, 1920.*

The naïve and impressionable Mr. Goode says of the judicial system of Soviet Russia: "Its chief quality would seem to be a certain simplicity. By a stroke of irony the people's courts aim not only at punishment of evil, but also at reformation of the wrongdoer! A first offender is set free on condition that he must not fall again. Should he do so, he pays the penalty of his second offense together with that to which his first crime rendered him liable."[21] That Mr. Goode should be ignorant of the fact that such humane measures were not unknown or uncommon in the administration of justice by the ordinary criminal courts under czarism is perhaps not surprising. It is somewhat surprising, however, that he should write as though the Soviet courts have made a distinct advance in penology. Has he never heard of the First Offenders Act in his own country, or of our extensive system of suspended sentences, parole, probation, and so on? It is not necessary to deny Mr. Goode's statement, or even to question it. As a commentary upon it, the following article from *Severnaya Communa*, December 4, 1918, is sufficient:

[21] *Bolshevism at Work*, by William T. Goode, pp. 96-97.

> It is impossible to continue silent. It has constantly been brought to the knowledge of the Viborg Soviet (Petrograd) of the terrible state of affairs existing in the city prisons. That people all the time are dying there of hunger; *that people are detained six and eight months without examination, and that in many cases it is impossible to learn why they have been arrested, owing to officials being changed, departments closed, and documents lost.* In order to confirm, or otherwise, these rumors, the Soviet decided to send on the 3d November a commission consisting of the president of the Soviet, the district medical officer, and district military commissar, to visit and report on the "Kresti" prison. Comrades! What they saw and what they heard from the imprisoned is impossible to describe. Not only were all rumors confirmed, but conditions were actually found much worse than had been stated. I was pained and ashamed. I myself was imprisoned under czardom in that same prison. Then all was clean, and prisoners had clean linen twice a month. Now, not only are prisoners left without clean linen, but many are even without blankets, and, as in the past, for a trifling offense they are placed in solitary confinement in cold, dark cells. But the most terrible sights we saw were in the sick-bays. Comrades, there we saw living dead who hardly had strength enough to whisper their complaints that they were dying of hunger. In one ward, among the sick a corpse had lain for several hours, whose neighbors managed to murmur, "Of hunger he died, and soon of hunger we shall all die." Comrades, among them are many who are quite young, who wish to live and see the sunshine. If we really possess a workmen's government such things should not be.

Following the example of Mr. Arthur Ransome, many pro-Bolshevist writers have assured us that after 1918 the Red Terror practically ceased to exist. Mr. Ransome makes a great deal of the fact that in February, 1919, the Central Executive Committee of the People's Commissaries "definitely limited the powers of the Extraordinary Commission."[22] Although he seems to have attended the meeting at which this was done, and talks of "the bitter struggle within the party for and against the almost dictatorial powers of the Extraordinary

Committee," he appears not to have understood what was done. Perhaps it ought not to be expected that this writer of fairy-stories who so naïvely confesses his ignorance of "economics" should comprehend the revolutionary struggle in Russia. Be that how it may, he does not state accurately what happened. He says: "Therefore the right of sentencing was removed from the Extraordinary Commission; but if, through unforeseen circumstances, the old conditions should return, they intended that the dictatorial powers of the Commission should be returned to it until those conditions had ceased." Actually the decision was that the power to inflict the death penalty should be taken from the Extraordinary Commissions, *except where and when martial law existed*. When Krylenko, Diakonov, and others protested against the outrage of permitting the Extraordinary Commissions to execute people without proof of their guilt, *Izvestia* answered in words which clearly reveal the desperate and brutal spirit of Bolshevism: "*If among one hundred executed one was guilty, this would be satisfactory and would sanction the action of the Commission.*"

22 *Russia in 1919, by Arthur Ransome, pp. 108-114.*

As a matter of fact, the resolution which, according to Mr. Ransome, "definitely limited the powers of the Extraordinary Commission," was an evasion of the issue. Not only was martial law in existence in the principal cities, and not only was it easy to declare martial law anywhere in Soviet Russia, but it was a very easy matter for accused persons to be brought to Moscow or Petrograd and there sentenced by the Extraordinary Commission. *This was actually done in many cases after the February decision.* Mr. Ransome quotes Dzerzhinsky to the effect that criminality had been greatly decreased by the Extraordinary Commissions—in Moscow by 80 per cent.!— and that there was now, February, 1919, no longer danger of "large scale revolts." What a pity that the All-Russian Extraordinary Commission did not consult Mr. Ransome before publishing its report in February of this year! That report shows, first, that in 1919 the activities of the Extraordinary Commission were much greater than in 1918; second, that the number of arrests made in 1919 was 80,662 as against 46,348 in 1918; third, that in 1919 the arrests of "ordinary criminals" nearly equaled the total number of arrests made in 1918 for *all causes*, including counter-revolutionary activity, speculation, crimes in office, and general crime. The figures given in the report are: arrests for ordinary crimes only in 1919, 39,957; arrests for all causes in 1918, 47,348. When it is remembered that all the other revolutionary tribunals were active throughout this period, how shall we reconcile this record of the Extraordinary Commission with Mr. Ransome's account? The fact is that crime steadily increased throughout 1919, *and that at the very time Mr. Ransome was in Moscow conditions there were exceedingly bad, as the report of arrests and convictions shows.*

Terrorism continued in Russia throughout 1919, the rose-colored reports of specially coached correspondents to the contrary notwithstanding. There was, indeed, a period in the early summer when the rigors of the Red Terror were somewhat relaxed. This seems to have been connected with the return of the bourgeois specialists to the factories and the officers of the Czar's army to positions of importance in the Red Army. This could not fail to lessen the persecution of the bourgeoisie, at least for a time. In July the number of arrests made by the Extraordinary Commission was small, only 4,301; in November it reached the high level of 14,673. To those who claim that terrorism did not exist in Russia during 1919, the best answer is—this very illuminating official Bolshevist report.

On January 10, 1919, *Izvestia* published an article by Trotsky in which the leader of the military forces of the Soviet Republic dealt with the subject of terrorism. This was, of course, in advance of the meeting which Mr. Ransome so completely misunderstood. Trotsky said:

> By its terror against saboteurs the proletariat does not at all say, "I shall wipe out all of you and get along without specialists." Such a program would be a program of hopelessness and ruin. *While dispersing, arresting, and shooting saboteurs and conspirators*, the proletariat says, "*I shall break your will, because my will is stronger than yours, and I shall force you to serve me.*" Terror as the demonstration of the will and strength of the working-class is historically justified, precisely because the proletariat was able thereby to break the will of the Intelligentsia, pacify the professional men of various categories and work, and gradually subordinate them to its own aims within the fields of their specialties.

On April 2, 1919, *Izvestia* published a proclamation by Dzerzhinsky, president of the All-Russian Extraordinary Commission, warning that "demonstrations and appeals of any kind will be suppressed without pity":

> In view of the discovery of a conspiracy which aimed to organize an armed demonstration against the Soviet authority by means of explosions, destruction of railways, and fires, the All-Russian Extraordinary Commission warns that demonstrations and appeals of any kind will be suppressed without pity. In order to save Petrograd and Moscow from famine, in order to save hundreds and thousands of innocent victims, the All-Russian Extraordinary Commission will be obliged to take the most severe measures of punishment against all who will appeal for White Guard demonstration or for attempts at armed uprising.
>
> [SIGNED] F. Dzerzhinsky,
>
> *President of the All-Russian Extraordinary Commission*

The *Severnaya Communa* of April 2, 1919, contains an official report of the shooting by the Petrograd Extraordinary Commission of a printer named Michael Ivanovsky *"for the printing of proclamations issued by the Socialists-Revolutionists of the Left."* Later several Socialists-Revolutionists, among them Soronov, were shot "for having proclamations and appeals in their possession."

On May 1, 1919, the *Izvestia* of Odessa, official organ of the Soviet in that city, published the following account of the infliction of the death penalty for belonging to an organization. It said:

> The Special Branch of the Staff of the Third Army has uncovered the existence of an organization, the Union of the Russian People, now calling itself "the Russian Union for the People and the State." The entire committee was arrested.

After giving the names of those arrested the account continued:

> The case of those arrested was transferred to the Military Tribunal of the Soviet of the Third Army. Owing to the obvious activity of the members of the Union directed against the peaceful population and the conquests of the Revolution, the Revolutionary Tribunal decided to sentence the above-mentioned persons to death. The verdict was carried out on the same night.

On May 6, 1919, *Severnaya Communa* published the following order from the Defense Committee:

> Order No. 8 of the Defense Committee. The Extraordinary Commission for Combating Counter-Revolution is to take measures to suppress all forms of official crime, and not to hesitate at shooting the guilty. The Extraordinary Committee is bound to indict not only those who are guilty of active crime,

but also those who are guilty of inaction of authority or condonement of crime, bearing in mind that the punishment must be increased in proportion to the responsibility attached to the post filled by the guilty official.

On May 14, 1919, *Izvestia* published an article by a Bolshevist official describing what happened in the Volga district as the Bolsheviki advanced. This article is important because it calls attention to a form of terrorism not heretofore mentioned: it will be remembered that in the latter part of 1918 the Bolsheviki introduced the system of rationing out food upon class lines, giving to the Red Army three times as much food per capita as to the average of the civil population, and dividing the latter into categories. The article under consideration shows very clearly how this system was made an instrument of terrorism:

> Instructions were received from Moscow to forbid free trade, and to introduce the class system of feeding. After much confusion, *this made the population starve in a short time*, and rebel against the food dictatorship.... "Was it necessary to introduce the class system of feeding into the Volga district so haphazardly?" asks the writer. "Oh no. *There was enough bread ready for shipment in that region, and in many places it was rotting, because of the lack of railroad facilities.* The class-feeding system did not increase the amount of bread.... It did create, together with the inefficient policy, and the lack of a distribution system, a state of starvation, which provoked dissatisfaction."

Throughout 1919 the official Bolshevist press continued to publish accounts of the arrest of hostages. Thus *Izvestia* of the Petrograd Soviet of Workmen's and Red Army Deputies (No. 185), August 16, 1919, published an official order by the acting Commandant of the fortified district of Petrograd, a Bolshevist official named Kozlovsky. The two closing paragraphs of this order follow:

> I declare that all guilty of arson, also all those who have knowledge of the same and fail to report the culprits to the authorities, *will be shot forthwith.*

> I warn all that in the event of repeated cases of arson I will not hesitate to adopt extreme measures, *including the shooting of the bourgeoisie's hostages*, in view of the fact that all the White Guards' plots directed against the proletarian state *must be regarded not as the crime of individuals, but as the offense of the entire enemy class.*

That hostages were actually shot, and not merely held under arrest, is clearly stated in the *Severnaya Communa*, March 11, 1919:

> By order of the Military Revolutionary Committee of Petrograd several officers were shot for *spreading untrue rumors that the Soviet authority had lost the confidence of the people.*
>
> All relatives of the officers of the 86th Infantry Regiment (which deserted to the Whites) were shot.

The same journal published, September 2, 1919, the following decree of the War Council of the Petrograd Fortified District:

> It has been ascertained that on the 17th of August there was maliciously cut down in the territory of the Ovtzenskaya Colony about 200 sazhensks of telegraph and telephone wire. In consequence of the above-mentioned criminal offense, the War Council of the Petrograd Fortified District has ordered—
>
> (1) To impose on the Ovtzenskaya Colony a fine of 500,000 rubles; (2) the guarding of the intactness of the lines to be made incumbent upon the population under reciprocal responsibility; and (3) *hostages to be taken.*
>
> Note: The decree of the War Council was carried out on the 30th of August. The following hostages have been taken: Languinen, P. M.; Languinen, Ya. P.; Finck, F. Kh.; Ikert, E. S.; Luneff, F. L.; Dalinguer, P. M.; Dalinguer, P. Ya.; Raw, Ya. I.; Shtraw, V. M.; Afanassieff, L. K.

This drastic order was issued and carried out nearly a month before the district was declared to be in a state of siege.

The *Krasnaya Gazeta*, November 4, 1919, published a significant list of Red Army officers who had deserted to the Whites and of the retaliatory arrests of innocent members of their families. Mothers, brothers, sisters, and wives were arrested and punished for the acts of their relatives in deserting the Red Army. The list follows:

1. Khomutov, D. C. — brother and mother arrested.

2. Piatnitzky, D. A. — mother, sister, and brother arrested.

3. Postnov — mother and sister arrested.

4. Agalakov, A. M. — wife, father, and mother arrested.

5. Haratkviech, B. — wife and sister arrested.

6. Kostylev, V. I. — wife and brother arrested.

7. Smyrnov, A. A. — mother, sister, and father arrested.

8. Chebykin — wife arrested.

In September, 1919, practically all the Bolshevist papers published the following order, signed by Trotsky:

> I have ordered several times that officers with indefinite political convictions should not be appointed to military posts, especially when the families of such officers live on the territory controlled by enemies of the Soviet Power. My orders are not being carried out. In one of our armies an officer whose family lives on the territory controlled by Kolchak was appointed as a commander of a division. Consequently, this commander betrayed his division and went over, together with his staff, to the enemy. Once more I order the Military Commissaries to make a thorough cleansing of all

Commanding Staffs. In case an officer goes over to the enemy, *his family should be made to feel the consequences of his betrayal.*

Early in November, 1919, the Petrograd Extraordinary Commission announced that by its orders forty-two persons had been shot. A number of these were ordinary criminals; several others had been guilty of selling cocaine. Among the other victims we find one Maximovich, "for organizing a mass desertion of Red Army soldiers to the Whites"; one Shramchenko, *"for participating in a counter-revolutionary conspiracy"*; E. K. Kaulbars, "for spying"; Ploozhnikoff and Demeshchenke, *"for exciting the politically unconscious masses and hounding them on against the Soviet Power."*

In considering this terribly impressive accumulation of evidence from the Bolshevist press we must bear in mind that it represents not the criticism of a free press, but only that measure of truth which managed to find its way through the most drastic censorship ever known in any country at any time. Not only were the organs of the anti-Bolshevist Socialists suppressed, but even the Soviet press was not free to publish the truth. Trotsky himself made vigorous protest in the *Izvestia* of the Central Executive Committee (No. 13) against the censorship which "prevented the publication of the news that Perm was taken by the White Guards." A congress of Soviet journalists was held at Moscow, in May, 1919, and made protest against the manner in which they were restrained from criticizing Soviet misrule. The *Izvestia* of the Provincial Executive Committee, May 8, 1919, quotes from this protest as follows:

> The picture of the provincial Soviet press is melancholy enough. We journalists are particularly "up against it" when we endeavor to expose the shortcomings of the local Soviet rule and the local Soviet officials. Immediately we are met with threats of arrest and banishment, *threats*

which are often carried out. In Kaluga a Soviet editor was nearly shot for a remark about a drunken communist.

Under such conditions as are indicated in this protest the evidence we have cited was published. What the record would have been if only there was freedom for the opposition press can only be imagined. In the light of such a mass of authoritative evidence furnished by the Bolsheviki themselves, of what use is it for casual visitors to Russia, like Mr. Goode and Mr. Lansbury, for example, to attempt to throw dust into our eyes and make it appear that acts of terrorism and tyranny are no more common in Russia than in countries like England, France, and America? And how, in the light of such testimony, shall we explain the ecstatic praise of Bolshevism and the Bolsheviki by men and women who call themselves Socialists and Liberals, and who profess to love freedom? It is true that the abolition of the death penalty has now been decreed, the decree going into effect on January 22, 1920. Lenin has declared that this date marks the passing of the policy of blood, and that only a renewal of armed intervention by the Allies can force a return to it. We shall see. This is not the first time the death penalty has been "abolished" by decree during the Bolshevist régime. Some of us remember that on November 7, 1918, the Central Executive Committee in Moscow decreed the abolition of the death penalty and a general amnesty. After that murder, by order of the Extraordinary Commissions, went on worse than before.[23]

[23] *As proofs of these pages are being revised, word comes that the death penalty has been revived—Vide London Times, May 26, 1920.*

In Odessa an investigation was made into the workings of the *Chresvychaika* and a list of fifteen classes of crimes for which the death penalty had been imposed and carried out was published. The list enumerated various offenses, ranging from espionage and counter-revolutionary agitation to "dissoluteness." The fifteenth and last class on the list read, "Reasons unknown." Perhaps these words sum up the only answer to our last question.

VIII

INDUSTRY UNDER SOVIET CONTROL

For the student of the evolution of Bolshevism in Russia there is, perhaps, no task more difficult than to unravel the tangled skein of the history of the first few weeks after the *coup d'état*. Whoever attempts to set forth the development of events during those weeks in an ordered and consecutive narrative, and to present an accurate, yet intelligible, account of the conditions that prevailed, must toil patiently through a bewildering snarled mass of conflicting testimony, charges and counter-charges, claims and counter-claims. Statements concerning apparently simple matters of fact, made by witnesses whose competence and probity are not to be lightly questioned, upon events of which they were witnesses, are simply irreconcilable. Moreover, there is a perfect welter of sweeping generalizations and an almost complete lack of such direct and definite information, statistical and other, as can readily be found relating to both the earlier and the later stages of the Revolution.

Let us first set down the facts concerning which there is substantial agreement on the part of the partizans of the Bolsheviki and the various factions opposed to them, ranging from the Constitutional-Democrats to such factions as the Socialists-Revolutionists of the Left and the "Internationalist" section of the Menshevist Social Democrats, both of which were quite closely allied to the Bolsheviki in sympathy and in theory. At the time when the Bolsheviki raised the cry, "All power to the Soviets!" in October, 1917, arrangements were well under way for the election, upon the most democratic basis imaginable, of a great representative constitutional convention, the Constituent Assembly. Not only had the Bolsheviki nominated their candidates and entered upon an electoral campaign in advocacy of their program; not only were they, in common with all other parties, pledged to the holding of the Constituent Assembly; much more important is the fact that they professed to be, and were by many regarded as, the special champions and defenders of the Constituent Assembly, solicitous above all else for its convocation and its integrity. From June onward Trotsky, Kamenev, and other Bolshevist leaders had professed to fear only that the Provisional Government would either refuse to convoke the Constituent Assembly or in some manner prevent its free action. No small part of the influence possessed by the Bolsheviki immediately prior to the overthrow of Kerensky was due to the fact that, far from being suspected of hostility to the Constituent Assembly, they were widely regarded as its most vigorous and determined upholders. To confirm that belief the Council of the People's Commissaries issued this, its first decree:

In the name of the Government of the Russian Republic, chosen by the All-Russian Congress of Soviets of Workers' and Soldiers' Deputies with participation of peasant deputies, the Council of People's Commissars decrees:

1. The elections for the Constituent Assembly shall take place at the date determined upon—November 12th.

2. All electoral commissions, organs of local self-government, Soviets of Workers', Soldiers', and Peasants' Deputies, and soldiers' organizations on the front should make every effort to assure free and regular elections at the date determined upon.

In the name of the Government of the Russian Republic,

The President of the Council of People's Commissars

Vladimir Ulianov—Lenin.

That was in November, 1917—and the Constituent Assembly has not yet been convoked. In *Pravda*, December 26, 1917, Lenin published a series of propositions to show that the elections, which had taken place since the Bolsheviki assumed power, did not give a clear indication of the real voice of the masses! The elections had gone heavily against the Bolsheviki, and that fact doubtless explains Lenin's disingenuous argument. Later on Lenin was able to announce that no assembly elected by the masses by universal suffrage could be accepted! "The Soviet Republic repudiates the hypocrisy of formal equality of all human beings," he wrote in his *Letter to American Workmen*.

It is quite certain that the political power and influence of the Soviets was never so small at any time since the birth of the Revolution in March as it was when the Bolsheviki raised the cry, "All power to the Soviets!" The reasons for this, if not obvious, are easily intelligible: the mere facts that the election of a thoroughly democratic constitutional convention at an early date was assured, and that the electoral campaign had already begun, were by themselves sufficient to cause many of those actively engaged in the revolutionary struggle to turn their interest from the politics of the Soviets to the greater political issues connected with the campaign for the Constituent Assembly elections. There were other factors at work lessening the popular interest in and, consequently, the political influence of, the Soviets. In the first place, the hectic excitement of the early stages of the Revolution had passed off, together with its novelty, and life had assumed a *tempo* nearer normal; in the second place, city Dumas and the local Zemstvos, which had been elected during the summer, upon a thoroughly democratic basis, were functioning, and, naturally, absorbing much energy which had hitherto been devoted to the Soviets.

Concerning these things there is little room for dispute. The *Izvestia* of the Soviets again and again called attention to the waning power and influence of the Soviets, always cheerfully and with wise appreciation. On September 28, 1917, it said:

> At last a truly democratic government, born of the will of all classes of the Russian people, the first rough form of the future liberal parliamentary régime, has been formed. Ahead of us is the Constituent Assembly, which will solve all questions of fundamental law, and whose composition will be essentially democratic. The function of the Soviets is at an end, and the time is approaching when they must retire, with the rest of the revolutionary machinery, from the stage of a free and victorious people, whose weapons shall hereafter be the peaceful ones of political action.

On October 23, 1917, *Izvestia* published an important article dealing with this subject, saying:

> We ourselves are being called the "undertakers" of our own organization. In reality, we are the hardest workers in constructing the new Russia.... When autocracy and the entire bureaucratic régime fell, we set up the Soviets as barracks in which all the democracy could find temporary shelter. Now, in place of barracks we are building the permanent edifice of a new system, and

naturally the people will gradually leave the barracks for the more comfortable quarters.

Dealing with the lessening activity of the local Soviets, scores of which had ceased to exist, the Soviet organ said:

This is natural, for the people are coming to be interested in the more permanent organs of legislation—the municipal Dumas and the Zemstvos.

Continuing, the article said:

In the important centers of Petrograd and Moscow, where the Soviets were best organized, they did not take in all the democratic elements.... The majority of the intellectuals did not participate, and many workers also; some of the workers because they were politically backward, others because the center of gravity for them was in their unions.... We cannot deny that these organizations are firmly united with the masses, whose every-day needs are better served by them....

That the local democratic administrations are being energetically organized is highly important. The city Dumas are elected by universal suffrage, and in purely local matters have more authority than the Soviets. Not a single democrat will see anything wrong in this....

... Elections to the municipalities are being conducted in a better and more democratic way than the elections to the Soviets.... All classes are represented in the municipalities.... And as soon as the local self-governments begin to organize life in the municipalities, the rôle of the local Soviets naturally ends....

... There are two factors in the falling off of interest in the Soviets. The first we may attribute to the lowering of political interest in the masses; the second to the growing effort of provincial and local governing bodies to organize the building of new Russia.... The more the tendency lies in this latter direction the sooner disappears the significance of the Soviets....

It seems to be hardly less certain, though less capable of complete demonstration, perhaps, that the influence of the

Soviets in the factories was also on the wane. Perhaps it would be fairer to say that there was an increasing sense of responsibility and a lessening of the dangerous recklessness of the earlier stages of the Revolution. The factory Soviets in the time of the Provisional Government varied so greatly in their character and methods that it is rather difficult to accurately represent them in a brief description. Many of them were similar, in practice, to the shop meetings of the trades-unions; others more nearly resembled the Whitley Councils of England. There were still others, however, which asserted practically complete ownership of the factories and forced the real owners out.

On March 20, 1917, *Izvestia* said:

> If any owner of an undertaking who is dissatisfied with the demands made by the workmen refuses to carry on the business, then the workmen must resolutely insist on the management of the work being given over into their hands, under the supervision of the Commissary of the Soviets.

That is precisely what happened in many cases. We must not forget that the Bolsheviki did not introduce Soviet control of industry. That they did so is a very general belief, but, like so many other beliefs concerning Russia, it is erroneous. The longest trial of the Soviet control of industry took place under the régime of the Provisional Government, in the pre-Bolshevist period. Many of the worst evils of the system were developed during that period, though as a result of Bolshevist propaganda and intrigue to a large degree.

Industrial control by the workers, during the pre-Bolshevist period of the Revolution, and especially during the spring and early summer, was principally carried on by means of four distinct types of organization, to all of which the general term "Soviet" was commonly applied. Perhaps a brief description of each of these types will help to interpret the history of this period:

(1) Factory Councils. These may be called the true factory Soviets. They existed in most factories, large and small alike, their size varying in proportion to the number of workers employed. In a small factory the Council might consist of seven or nine members; in a large factory the number might be sixty. The latter figure seems rarely to have been exceeded. Most of the Councils were elected by the workers directly, upon a basis of equal suffrage, every wage-worker, whether skilled or unskilled, male or female, being entitled to vote. Boys and girls were on the same footing as their elders in this respect. Generally the voting was done at mass-meetings, held during working-hours, the ordinary method being a show of hands. While there were exceptions to this rule, it was rare that foremen, technical supervisors, or other persons connected with the management were permitted to vote. In some cases the Council was elected indirectly, that is to say, it was selected by a committee, called the Workshop Committee. The Factory Council was not elected for any specified period of time, as a rule, and where a definite period for holding office was fixed, the right of recall was so easily invoked, and was so freely exercised, that the result was the same as if there had been no such provision. As a result of the nervous tension of the time, the inevitable reaction against long-continued repression, there was much friction at first and recalls and re-elections were common. The present writer has received several reports, from sources of indubitable authority, of factories in which two, and even three, Council elections were held in less than one month! Of course, this is an incidental fact, ascribable to the environment rather than to the institution. The Councils held their meetings during working-hours, the members receiving full pay for the time thus spent. Usually the Council would hold a daily meeting, and it was

not uncommon for the meetings to last all day, and even into the evening—overtime being paid for the extra hours. Emile Vandervelde, the Belgian Socialist Minister of State—a most sympathetic observer—is authority for the statement that in one establishment in Petrograd, employing 8,000 skilled workers, the Factory Council, composed of forty-three men who each earned sixteen rubles per day of eight hours, sat regularly eight hours per day.[24]

[24] Three Aspects of the Russian Revolution, *by Emile Vandervelde, p. 71.*

To describe fully the functions of the Factory Councils would require many pages, so complex were they. Only a brief synopsis of their most important rights and duties is possible here. Broadly speaking, they possessed the right of control over everything, but no responsibility for successful management and administration. In their original form, and where the owners still remained at the head, the Councils did not interfere in such matters as the securing of raw materials, for example. They did not interest themselves in the financial side of the undertaking, at least not to see that its operations were profitable. Their concern was to control the working conditions and to "guard the interests of the workers." They sometimes assumed the right to refuse to do work upon contracts of which they disapproved. Jealous in their exercise of the right to *control*, they would assume no responsibility for *direction*. At the same time, however, they asserted—and generally enforced—their right to determine everything relating to the engaging or dismissal of workers, the fixing of wages, hours of labor, rules of employment, and so on, as well as *the selection of foremen, superintendents, technical experts, and even the principal managers of the establishments*. Professor Ross quotes the statement made by the spokesman of the employers at Baku, adding that the men did strike and win:

They ask that we grant leave on pay for a certain period to a sick employee. Most of us are doing that already. They stipulate that on dismissal an employee shall receive a month's pay for every year he has been in our service. Agreed. They demand that no workman be dismissed without the consent of a committee representing the men. That's all right. They require that we take on new men from a list submitted by them. That's reasonable enough. They know far better than we can whether or not a fellow is safe to work alongside of in a dangerous business like ours. But when they demand control over the hiring and firing of *all* our employees—foremen, superintendents, and managers as well as workmen—we balk. We don't see how we can yield that point without losing the control essential to discipline and efficiency. Yet if we don't sign to-night, they threaten to strike.[25]

[25] *Russia in Upheaval*, by E. A. Ross, p. 277.

(2) Workshop Committees. This term was sometimes used instead of "Factory Councils," particularly in the case of smaller factories, and much confusion in the published reports of the time may be attributed to this fact. Nothing is gained by an arbitrary division of Factory Councils on the basis of size, since there was no material difference in functions or methods. The term "Workshop Committee" was, however, applied to a different organization entirely, which was to be found in practically every large industrial establishment, along with, and generally subordinated to, the Factory Council. These committees usually carried out the policies formulated by the superior Factory Councils. They did the greater part of the work usually performed by a foreman, and their functions were sometimes summed up in the term "collective foremanship." They decided who should be taken on and who employed; they decided when fines or other forms of punishment should be imposed for poor work, sabotage, and other offenses. The foreman was immediately responsible to them. Appeals from the decisions of these committees might be made to the Councils, either by the owners or the workers. Like the Councils, the committees

were elected by universal, equal voting at open meetings; indeed, in some cases, only the Workshop Committee was so elected, being charged with the task of selecting the Factory Council.

(3) Wages Committees. These committees existed in the large establishments, as a rule, especially those in which the labor employed was of many kinds and varying degrees of skill. Like all other factory organizations, they were elected by vote of the employees. Responsible to the Factory Councils, though independently elected, the Wages Committees classified all workers into their respective wage-groups, fixed prices for piece-work, and so on. They could, and frequently did, decide these matters independently, without consulting the management at all.

(4) Committees of Arbitration and Adjustment. These seem to have been less common than the other committees already described. Elected solely by the workers, in the same manner as the other bodies described, they were charged with hearing and settling disputes arising, no matter from what cause. They dealt with the charges brought by individual employees, whether against the employers or against fellow-employees; they dealt, also, with complaints by the workers as a whole against conditions, with disputes over wages, and so on. *In all cases of disputes between workers and employers the decision was left entirely to the elected representatives of the workers.*

The foregoing gives a very fair idea of the proletarian machinery set up in the factories under the Provisional Government. In one factory might be found operating these four popularly elected representative bodies, all of them holding meetings in working-hours and being paid for the time consumed; all of them involving more or less frequent elections. No matter how moderate and restrained the description may be, the impression can hardly fail to be one of appalling wastefulness and confusion. As a matter of fact, there is very general agreement that in practice, after the first few weeks, what seems a grotesque system worked reasonably well, or, at least, far better than its critics had believed possible. Of course, there *was* much overlapping of functions; there *was* much waste. On the other hand, wasteful strikes were avoided and the productive processes were maintained. Of course, the experiment was made under abnormal conditions. Not very much in the way of certain conclusion can be adduced from it. Opponents of the Soviet theory and system will always point to the striking decline of productive efficiency and say that it was the inevitable result of the Soviet control; believers in the theory and the system will say that the inefficiency would have been greater but for the Soviets.

That there was an enormous decline in productive efficiency during the early part of the period of Soviet control cannot be disputed. The evidence of this is too overwhelmingly conclusive. As early as April, 1917, serious reports of this decline began to be made. It was said that in some factories the per capita daily production was less than a third of what it was a few weeks before. The air was filled with charges that the workers were loafing and malingering. On April 11th Tseretelli denounced these "foul slanders" at a meeting of the Petrograd Soviet and was wildly cheered. Nevertheless, one fact stood out—namely, the sharp decline in productivity in almost every line. There were not a few cases in which the owners and highly trained managers were forced out entirely and their places filled by wholly incompetent men possessing no technical training at all. An extreme illustration is quoted by Ross:[26] In a factory in southern Russia the workers forced the owner out and then undertook to run the plant themselves. When they had used up the small supply of raw material they had they began to sell the machines out of the works in order to get money to buy more raw material; then, when they obtained the raw material, they lacked the machinery for working it up. Of course, the incident is simply an illustration of extreme folly, merely. Men misuse safety razors to commit suicide with in extreme cases, and the misuse of Soviet power in isolated cases proves little of value. On the other hand, the case cited by Ross is only an extreme instance of a very general practice. Many factories were taken over in the same way, after the competent directors had been driven out, and were brought to ruin by the Soviets. It was a general practice or, at any rate, a common one, which drew from Skobelev, Minister of Labor, this protest, which *Izvestia* published at the beginning of May:

26 *Ross, op. cit., p. 283.*

> The seizure of factories makes workmen without any experience in management, and without working capital, temporarily masters of such undertakings, but soon leads to their being closed down, or to the subjugation of the workmen to a still harder taskmaster.

On July 10th Skobelev issued another stirring appeal to the workers, pointing out that "the success of the struggle against economic devastation depends upon the productivity of labor, and pointing out the danger of the growing anarchy. The appeal is too long to quote in its entirety, but the following paragraphs give a good idea of it, and, at the same time, indicate how serious the demoralization of the workers had become:

> Workmen, comrades, I appeal to you at a critical period of the Revolution. Industrial output is rapidly declining, the quantity of necessary manufactured articles is diminishing, the peasants are deprived of industrial supplies, we are threatened with fresh food complications and increasing national destitution.

The Revolution has swept away the oppression of the police régime, which stifled the labor movement, and the liberated working-class is enabled to defend its economic interests by the mere force of its class solidarity and unity. They possess the freedom of strikes, they have professional unions, which can adapt the tactics of a mass economic movement, according to the conditions of the present economic crisis.

However, at present purely elemental tendencies are gaining the upper hand over organized movement, and without regard to the limited resources of the state, and without any reckoning as to the state of the industry in which you are employed, and to the detriment of the proletarian class movement, you sometimes obtain an increase of wages which disorganizes the enterprise and drains the exchequer.

Frequently the workmen refuse all negotiations and by menace of violence force the gratification of their demands. They use violence against officials and managers, dismiss them of their own accord, interfere arbitrarily with the technical management, and even attempt to take the whole enterprise into their own hands.

Workmen, comrades, our socialistic ideals shall be attained not by the seizure of separate factories, but by a high standard of economic organization, by the intelligence of the masses, and the wide development of the country's productive forces.... Workmen, comrades, remember not only your rights, but also your duties; think not only of your wishes, but of the possibilities of granting them, not only of your own good, but of the sacrifices necessary for the consolidation of the Revolution and the triumph of our ideals.

In July the per capita output in the munition-works of Petrograd was reported as being only 25 per cent. of what it was at the beginning of the year. In August Kornilov told the Moscow Democratic Conference that the productivity of the workers in the great gun and shell plants had declined 60 per cent., as compared with the three months immediately prior to the Revolution; that the decline at the aeroplane-factories was still greater, not less than 70 per cent. No denial of this came from the representatives of the Soviets. In Petrograd, Nijni-Novgorod, Saratov, and other large centers there was an estimated general decline of production of between 60 and 70 per cent.

The representatives of the workers, the Soviet leaders, said that the decline, which they admitted, was due to causes over which the Soviets had no control to a far greater degree than to any conscious or unconscious sabotage by the workers. They admitted that many of the workers had not yet got used to freedom; that they interpreted it as meaning freedom from work. There was a very natural reaction, they said, against the tremendous pace which had been maintained under the old régime. They insisted, however, that this temporary failing of the workers was a minor cause only, and that far greater causes were (1) deterioration of machinery; (2) withdrawal for military reasons and purposes of many of the most capable and efficient workers; (3) shortage and poor quality of materials.

There is room here for an endless controversy, and the present writer does not intend to enter into it. He is convinced that the three causes named by the Soviet defenders were responsible for a not inconsiderable proportion of the decline in productivity, but that the Soviets and the impaired morale of the workers were the main causes. In the mining of coal and iron, the manufacture of munitions, locomotives, textiles, metal goods, paper, and practically everything else, the available reports show an enormous increase in production cost per unit, accompanied by a very great decline in average per capita production. It is true that there were exceptions to this rule, that there were factories in which, after the first few days of the revolutionary excitation in March, production per capita rose and was maintained at a high level for a long time—until the Bolsheviki secured ascendancy in those factories, in fact. The writer has seen and examined numerous reports indicating this, but prefers to confine himself to the citation of such reports as come with the authority of responsible and trusted witnesses.

Such a report is that of the Social Democrat, the workman Menshekov, concerning the Ijevski factory with its 40,000 workmen, and of the sales department of which he was made manager when full Soviet control was established. In that position he had access to the books showing production for the years 1916, 1917, and 1918, and the figures show that under the Provisional Government production rose, but that it declined with the rise of Bolshevism among the workers and declined more rapidly when the Bolsheviki gained control. Such another witness is the trades-unionist and Social Democrat, Oupovalov, concerning production in the great Sormovo Works, in the Province of Nijni-Novgorod, which during the war employed 20,000 persons. Not only was production maintained, but there was even a marked improvement. The writer has been permitted to examine the documentary evidence in the possession of these men and believes that it fully confirms and justifies the claim that, where there was an earnest desire on the part of the workers to maintain and even to improve production, this proved possible under Soviet control.

The fact seems quite clear to the writer (though perhaps impossible to prove by an adequate volume of concrete evidence) that the impaired morale of the workers which resulted in lessened production was due to two principal causes, namely, Bolshevist propaganda and the lack of an intelligent understanding on the part of masses of workers who were not mentally or morally ready for the freedom which was suddenly thrust upon them. The condition of these latter is readily understood and appreciated. The disciplines and self-compulsions of freedom are not learned in a day. When we reflect upon the conditions that obtained under czarism, we can hardly wonder that so many of the victims of those conditions should have mistaken license for liberty, or that they should have failed to see the vital connection between their own honest effort in the shop and the success of the Revolution they were celebrating.

All through the summer the Bolsheviki were carrying on their propaganda among the workers in the shops as well as among the troops at the front. Just as they preached desertion to the soldiers, so they preached sabotage and advocated obstructive strikes among the workers in the factories. This was a logical thing for them to do; they wanted to break up the military machine in order to compel peace, and a blow at that machine was as effective when struck in the factory as anywhere else. For men who were preaching mass desertion and mutiny at the front, sabotage in the munition-works at the rear, or in the transportation service on which the army depended, was a logical policy. It is as certain as anything can be that the Bolshevist agitation was one of the primary causes of the alarming decrease in the production during the régime of the Provisional Government. On the other hand, the Socialist leaders who supported the Provisional Government waged a vigorous propaganda among the workers, urging them to increase production. Where they made headway, in general there production was maintained, or the decline was relatively small. The counterpart of that patriotism which Kerensky preached among the troops at the front with such magnificent energy was preached among the factory-workers. Here is what Jandarmov says:

It is a mistake to suppose that output was interfered with, for, to do our working-class justice, nowhere was work delayed for more than two days, and in many factories this epoch-making development was taken without a pause in the ordinary routine.

I cannot too strongly insist upon the altogether unanimous idealism of those early days. There was not an ugly streak in that beautiful dawn where now the skies are glowering and red and frightful. I say that output was speeded up. I, as chairman of the first Soviet,[27] assure you that we received fifty-seven papers from workmen containing proposals for increasing the efficiency of the factory; and that spirit lasted three months, figures of output went well up and old closed-down factories were reopened. *New Russia was bursting with energy—the sluice-gates of our character were unlocked.*

27 *That is, "first Soviet" at the Lisvinsk factory, about seventy miles from Perm.*

There must have been a great deal of that exalted feeling among the intelligent working-men of Russia in those stirring times. No one who has known anything of the spiritual passion, of sacrificial quality, which has characterized the Russian revolutionary movement can doubt this. Of course, Jandarmov is referring to the early months before Bolshevism began to spread in that district. Then there was a change. It was the old, old story of rapidly declining production:

> But after the first few months the workers as a whole began to fall under the spell of catchwords and stock phrases. Agitation began among the lower workers. Bolshevism started in the ranks of unskilled labor. They clamored for the reduction of hours and down went the output. The defenders of the idea of the shortest possible working-day were the same men who afterward turned out very fiends of Bolshevism and every disorder. I watched the growing of their madness and the development of their claims, each more impossible than the last.
>
> In the Kiselovski mines the output of 2,000,000 poods monthly dropped to 300,000, and the foundries of Upper Serginski produced 1,200 poods of iron instead of 2,000. Why such a fall? The engineers wondered how workers could reduce output to such an extent if they tried, but one soon ceased to wonder at the disasters that followed in quick succession.
>
> There was anarchy in the factories and a premium on idleness became the order of the day. It was a positive danger to work more than the laziest unskilled laborer, because this was the type of man who always seemed to get to the top of the Soviet. "Traitor to the interests of Labor" you were called if you exceeded the time limit, which soon became two hours a day.[28]

28 *These extracts are from a personal report by Jandarmov, sent to the present writer.*

By September, 1917, a healthy reaction against the abuses of Soviet industrial control was making itself felt in the factories.

The workers were making less extravagant demands and accepting the fact that they could gain nothing by paralyzing production; that reducing the quantity and the quality of production can only result in disaster to the nation, and, most of all, to the workers themselves. In numerous instances the factory Soviets had called back the owners they had forced out, and the managers and technical directors they had dismissed, and restored the authority of foremen. In other words, they ceased to be controlling authorities and became simply consultative bodies. While, therefore, they were becoming valuable democratic agencies, the economic power and influence of the Soviets was waning.

On the day of the *coup d'état*, November 7, 1917, the Bolshevist Military Revolutionary Committee issued a special proclamation which said, "The goal for which the people fought, the immediate proposal of a democratic peace, the abolition of private landed property, *labor control of industry*, the establishment of a Soviet Government—all this is guaranteed." Seven days later, November 14th, a decree was issued, giving an outline of the manner in which the control of industry by the Soviets was to be organized and carried out. The principal features of this outline plan are set forth in the following paragraphs:

(1) In order to put the economic life of the country on an orderly basis, control by the workers is instituted over all industrial, commercial, and agricultural undertakings and societies; and those connected with banking and transport, as well as over productive co-operative societies which employ labor or put out work to be done at home or in connection with the production, purchase, and sale of commodities and of raw materials, and with conservation of such commodities as well as regards the financial aspect of such undertakings.

(2) Control is exercised by all the workers of a given enterprise through the medium of their elected organs, such as factories and works committees,

councils of workmen's delegates, etc., such organs equally comprising representatives of the employees and of the technical staff.

(3) In each important industrial town, province, or district is set up a local workmen's organ of control, which, being the organ of the soldiers', workmen's, and peasants' council, will comprise the representatives of the labor unions, workmen's committees, and of any other factories, as well as of workmen's co-operative societies.

(5) Side by side with the Workmen's Supreme Council of the Labor Unions, committees of inspection comprising technical specialists, accountants, etc. These committees, both on their own initiative or at the request of local workmen's organs of control, proceed to a given locality to study the financial and technical side of any enterprise.

(6) The Workmen's Organs of Control have the right to supervise production, to fix a minimum wage in any undertaking, and to take steps to fix the prices at which manufactured articles are to be sold.

(7) The Workmen's Organs of Control have the right to control all correspondence passing in connection with the business of an undertaking, being held responsible before a court of justice for diverting their correspondence. Commercial secrets are abolished. The owners are called upon to produce to the Workmen's Organs of Control all books and moneys in hand, both relating to the current year and to any previous transactions.

(8) The decisions of the Workmen's Organs of Control are binding upon the owners of undertakings, and cannot be nullified save by the decision of a Workmen's Superior Organ of Control.

(9) Three days are given to the owners, or the administrators of a business, to appeal to a Workmen's Superior Court of Control against the decisions filed by any of the lower organs of Workmen's Control.

(10) In all undertakings, the owners and the representatives of workmen and of employees delegated to exercise control on behalf of the workmen, are responsible to the government for the maintenance of strict order and discipline, and for the conservation of property (goods). Those guilty of

misappropriating materials and products, of not keeping books properly, and of similar offenses, are liable to prosecution.

It was not until December 27, 1917—seven weeks after their arbitrary seizure of the reins of government—that the Bolsheviki published the details of their scheme. Both the original preliminary outline and the later carefully elaborated scheme made it quite evident that, no matter how loudly and grandiloquently Lenin, Trotsky, Miliutin, Smedevich, and others might talk about the "introduction" of workers' control, in point of fact they were only thinking of giving a certain legal status to the Soviet system of control already in operation. That system, as we have already seen, had been in their hands for some time. They had used it to destroy efficiency, to cripple the factories and assist in paralyzing the government and the military forces of the nation. Now that they were no longer an opposition party trying to upset the government, but were themselves the *de facto* government, the Bolsheviki could no longer afford to pursue the policy of encouraging the factory Soviets to sabotage. Maximum production was the first necessity of the Bolshevist Government, quite as truly as it had been for the Provisional Government, and as it must have been for any other government. Sabotage in the factories had been an important means of combating the Provisional Government, but now it must be quickly eliminated. So long as they were in the position of being a party of revolt the Bolshevist leaders were ready to approve the seizure of factories by the workers, regardless of the consequences to industrial production or to the military enterprises dependent upon that production. As the governing power of the nation, in full possession of the machinery of government, such ruinous action by the workers could not be tolerated. For the same reasons, the demoralization of the army, which they had laboriously fostered, must now be arrested.

In the instructions to the All-Russian Council of Workers' Control, published December 27, 1917, we find no important *extension* of the existing Soviet control; we do, however, find its *legalization with important limitations*. These limitations, moreover, are merely legalistic formulations of the modifications already developed in practice and obtaining in many factories. A comparison of the full text of the instructions with the account of the system of factory control under the Provisional Government will demonstrate this beyond doubt.[29] The control in each enterprise is to be organized "either by the Shop or Factory Committee or by the General Assembly of workers and employees of the enterprise, who elect a Special Commission of Control" (Article I). In "large-scale enterprises" the election of such a Control Commission is compulsory. To the Commission of Control is given sole authority to "enter into relations with the management upon the subject of control," though it may give authorization to other workers to enter into such relations if it sees fit (Article III). The Control Commission must make report to the general body of workers and employees in the enterprise "at least twice a month" (Article IV). The article (No. 5) which deals with and defines the "Duties and Privileges of the Control Commission" is so elaborate that it is almost impossible to summarize it without injustice. It is, therefore, well to quote it in full.

[29] *This important document is printed in full at the end of the book as an Appendix.*

V. The Control Commission of each enterprise is required:

1. To determine the stock of goods and fuel possessed by the plant, and the amount of these needed respectively for the machinery of production, the technical personnel, and the laborers by specialties.
2. To determine to what extent the plant is provided with everything that is necessary to insure its normal operation.
3. To forecast whether there is danger of the plant closing down or lowering production, and what the causes are.
4. To determine the number of workers by specialties likely to be unemployed, basing the estimate upon the reserve supply and the expected receipts of fuel and materials.
5. To determine the measures to be taken to maintain discipline in work among the workers and employees.
6. To superintend the execution of the decisions of governmental agencies regulating the buying and selling of goods.
7. *(a)* To prevent the arbitrary removal of machines, materials, fuel, etc., from the plant without authorization from the agencies which regulate economic affairs, and to see that inventories are not tampered with.

(b) To assist in explaining the causes of the lowering of production and to take measures for raising it.
8. To assist in elucidating the possibility of a complete or partial utilization of the plant for some kind of production (especially how to pass from a war to a peace footing, and what kind of production should be undertaken), to determine what changes should be made in the equipment of the plant and in the number of its personnel, to accomplish this purpose; to determine in what period of time these changes can be effected; to determine what is necessary in order to make them, and the probable amount of production after the change is made to another kind of manufacture.
9. To aid in the study of the possibility of developing the kinds of labor required by the necessities of peace-times, such as the methods of using three shifts of workmen, or any other method, by furnishing information on the possibilities of housing the additional number of laborers and their families.

10. To see that the production of the plant is maintained at the figures to be fixed by the governmental regulating agencies, and until such time as these figures shall have been fixed to see that the production reaches the normal average for the plant, judged by a standard of conscientious labor.

11. To co-operate in estimating costs of production of the plant upon the demand of the higher agency of workers' control or upon the demand of the governmental regulating institutions.

It is expressly stipulated that only the owner has "the right to give orders to the directors of the plant"; that the Control Commission "does not participate in the management of the plant and has no responsibility for its development and operation" (Article VII). It is also definitely stated that the Control Commission has no concern with financial management of the plant (Article VIII). Finally, while it has the right to "recommend for the consideration of the governmental regulating institutions the question of the sequestration of the plant or other measures of constraint upon the plant," the Control Commission "has not the right to seize and direct the enterprise" (Article IX). These are the principal clauses of this remarkable document relating to the functions and methods of the Soviet system of control in the factory itself; other clauses deal with the relations of the factory organizations to the central governmental authority and to the trades-unions. They prescribe and define a most elaborate system of bureaucracy.

So much for the *imperium in imperio* of the Soviet system of industrial control conceived by the Bolsheviki. In many important respects it is much more conservative than the system itself had been under Kerensky. It gives legal form and force to those very modifications which had been brought about, and it specifically prohibits the very abuses the Bolshevist agitators had fostered and the elimination of which they had everywhere bitterly resisted. Practically every provision in the elaborate decree of instructions limiting the authority of the workers, defining the rights of the managers, insisting upon the maintenance of production, and the like, the Kerensky government had endeavored to introduce, being opposed and denounced therefor by the Bolsheviki. It is easy to imagine how bitterly that decree of instructions on Workers' Control would have been denounced by Lenin and Trotsky had it been issued by Kerensky's Cabinet in July or August.

Let us not make the mistake, however, of assuming that because the Bolsheviki in power thus sought to improve the system of industrial control, to purge it of its weaknesses—its reckless lawlessness, sabotage, tyranny, dishonesty, and incompetence—that there was actually a corresponding improvement in the system itself. The pro-Bolshevist writers in this country and in western Europe have pointed to these instructions, and to many other decrees conceived in a similar spirit and couched in a similar tone, as conclusive evidence of moderation, constructive statesmanship, and wise intention. Alas! in statesmanship good intention is of little value. In politics and social polity, as in life generally, the road to destruction is paved with "good intentions." The Lenins and Trotskys, who in opposition and revolt were filled with the fury of destruction, might be capable of becoming builders under the influence of a solemn recognition of the obligations of authority and power. But for the masses of the people no such change was possible. Such miracles do not happen, except in the disordered imaginations of those whose minds are afflicted with moral Daltonism and that incapacity for sequential thinking which characterizes such a wide variety of subnormal mentalities.

By their propaganda the Bolsheviki had fostered an extremely anti-social consciousness, embracing sabotage, lawlessness, and narrow selfishness; the manner in which they had seized the governmental power, and brutally frustrated the achievement of that great democratic purpose which had behind it the greatest collective spiritual impulse in the history of the nation, greatly intensified that anti-social consciousness. Now that they were in power these madmen hoped that in the twinkling of an eye, by the mere issuance of decrees and manifestoes, they could eradicate the evil thing. Canute's command to the tide was not one whit more vain than their verbose decrees hurled against the relentless and irresistible sequence of cause and effect. Loafing, waste, disorder, and sabotage continued in the factories, as great a burden to the Bolshevist oligarchs as they had been to the democrats. Workers continued to "seize" factories as before, and production steadily declined to the music of an insatiable demand on the part of the workers for more pay. There was no change in the situation, except in so far as it grew worse. The governmental machine grew until it became like an immense swarm of devastating locusts, devouring everything and producing nothing. History does not furnish another such record of industrial chaos and ruinous inefficiency.

Five days after the seizure of power by the Bolsheviki, the Commissar of Labor, Shliapnikov, issued a protest against sabotage and violence. Naturally, he ascribed the excesses of the workers to provocation by the propertied classes. That "proletarian consciousness" upon which the Bolsheviki based their faith must have been sadly lacking in the workers if, at such a time, they were susceptible to the influence of the "propertied classes." The fact is that the destructive anarchical spirit they had fostered was now a deadly menace to the Bolsheviki themselves. Shliapnikov wrote:

> The propertied classes are endeavoring to create anarchy and the ruin of industry by provoking the workmen to excesses and violence over the question of

foremen, technicians, and engineers. They hope thereby to achieve the complete and final ruin of all the mills and factories. The revolutionary Commission of Labor asks you, our worker-comrades, to abstain from all acts of violence and excess. By a joint and creative work of the laboring masses and proletarian organizations, the Commission of Labor will know how to surmount all obstacles in its way. The new revolutionary government will apply the most drastic measures against all industrials and those who continue to sabotage industry, and thereby prevent the carrying out of the tasks and aims of the great proletarian and peasant Revolution. Executions without trial and other arbitrary acts will only damage the cause of the Revolution. The Commission of Labor calls on you for self-control and revolutionary discipline.

In January, 1918, Lenin read to a gathering of party workers a characteristic series of numbered "theses," which *Izvestia* published on March 8th of that year. In that document he said:

1. The situation of the Russian Revolution at the present moment is such that almost all workmen and the overwhelming majority of the peasants undoubtedly are on the side of the Soviet authority, and of the social revolution started by it. To that extent the success of the socialistic revolution in Russia is guaranteed.

2. At the same time the civil war, caused by the frantic resistance of the propertied classes which understand very well that they are facing the last and decisive struggle to preserve private property in land, and in the means of production, has not as yet reached its highest point. The victory of the Soviet authority in this war is guaranteed, but inevitably some time yet must pass, inevitably a considerable exertion of strength will be required, a certain period of acute disorganization and chaos, which always attend any war and in particular a civil war, is inevitable, before the resistance of the bourgeoisie will be crushed.

3. Further, this resistance takes less and less active and non-military forms: sabotage, bribing beggars, bribing agents of the bourgeoisie who have pushed themselves into the ranks of the Socialists in order to ruin the latter's cause, etc. This resistance has proved stubborn, and capable of assuming so

many different forms, that the struggle against it will inevitably drag along for a certain period, and will probably not be finished in its main aspects before several months. And without a decisive victory over this passive and concealed resistance of the bourgeoisie and its champions, the success of the socialistic revolution is impossible.

4. Finally, the organizing tasks of the socialistic reorganization of Russia are so enormous and difficult that a rather prolonged period of time is also required to solve them, in view of the large number of petty bourgeois fellow-travelers of the socialistic proletariat, and of the latter's low cultural level.

5. All these circumstances taken together are such that from them result *the necessity, for the success of Socialism in Russia, of a certain interval of time, not less than a few months*, in the course of which the socialistic government must have its hands absolutely free, in order to triumph over the bourgeoisie, first of all in its own country, and in order to adopt broad and deep organizing activity.

The greatest significance of Lenin's words lies in their recognition of the seriousness of the non-military forms of resistance, sabotage, and the like, and of the "low cultural level" of the "socialistic proletariat." Reading the foregoing statements carefully and remembering Lenin's other utterances, both before and after, we are compelled to wonder whether he is intellectually dishonest, an unscrupulous trickster playing upon the credulity of his followers, or merely a loose thinker adrift and helpless on the swift tides of events. "For the success of Socialism ... not less than *a few months*" we read from the pen of the man who, in June of the previous year, while on his way from Switzerland, had written "Socialism cannot now prevail in Russia"; the same man who in May, 1918, was to tell his comrades "it is hardly to be expected that the even more developed coming generation will accomplish a complete transition to Socialism"; who later told Raymond Robins: "The Russian Revolution will probably fail. We have not developed far enough in the capitalist stage, we are too primitive to realize the Socialist state."[30]

[30] Vide testimony of Robins before U. S. Senate Committee.

And yet—"the success of Socialism ... not less than a few months!"

By the latter part of February, 1918, it was quite clear that the Soviet control of industry was "killing the goose that laid the golden eggs"; that it was ruining the industrial life of the nation. The official press began to discuss in the most serious manner the alarming decline in production and the staggering financial losses incurred in the operation of what formerly had been profitable enterprises. At the Extraordinary Congress of Soviets, in March, 1918, the seriousness of the situation caused great alarm and a desperate appeal was made to the workers to increase production, refrain from sabotage, and practise self-discipline. The congress urged "a merciless struggle against chaos and disorganization." Lenin himself pointed out that confiscation of factories by the workers was ruining Russia. The very policy they had urged upon the workers, the seizure of the factories, was now seen as a menace.

On April 28, 1918, Lenin said: "If we are to expropriate at this pace, we shall be certain to suffer a defeat. The organization of production under proletarian control is notoriously very much behind the expropriation of big masses of capital."[31] He had already come to realize that the task of transforming capitalist society to a Socialist society was not the easy matter he had believed shortly before. In September he had looked upon the task of realizing Socialism as a child might have done. It would require a Freudian expert to explain the silly childishness of this paragraph from *The State and Revolution*, published in September, 1917:

[31] *Soviets at Work*. I have quoted the passage as it appears in the English edition of Kautsky's *Dictatorship of the Proletariat*, p. 125. This rendering, which conforms to the French translations of the authorized text, is clearer and stronger than the version given in the confessedly "improved" version of Lenin's speech by Doctor Dubrovsky, published by the Rand School of Social Science.

> Capitalist culture has created industry on a large scale in the shape of factories, railways, posts, telephones, and so forth; and on this basis the great majority of the functions of the old state have become enormously simplified and reduced in practice to very simple operations, such as registration, filing, and checking. Hence they will be quite within the reach of every literate person, and it will be possible to perform them for the usual "working-man's wages."[32]

[32] The State and Revolution, *by N. Lenin, p. 12.*

Thus it was in September, before the overthrow of the Provisional Government. Then Lenin was at the head of a revolting faction and presented the task of reorganizing the state as very simple indeed. In April he was at the head of a government, confronted by realities, and emphasizing the enormous difficulty and complexity of the task of reorganization. *The Soviets at Work* and the later booklet, *The Chief Tasks of Our Times*, lay great emphasis upon the great difficulties to be overcome, the need of experienced and trained men, and the folly of expecting anything like immediate success. "We know all about Socialism," he said, "but we do not know how to organize on a large scale, how to manage distribution, and so on. The old Bolshevist leaders have not taught us these things, and this is not to the credit of our party."[33]

[33] The Chief Tasks of Our Times, *p. 12.*

The same man who had urged the workers to "take possession of the factories" now realized how utterly unfitted the mass of the workers must be for undertaking the management of modern industrial establishments:

> To every deputation of workers which has come to me complaining that a factory was stopping work, I have said, "If you desire the confiscation of your factory the decree forms are ready, and I can sign a decree at once. But tell me: Can you take over the management of the concern? Have you reckoned what you can produce? Do you know the relations of your work with Russian and foreign markets?" Then it has appeared that they are inexperienced in these matters; that there is nothing about them in the Bolshevist literature, in the Menshevist, either.[34]

[34] *Idem, p. 12.*

Lenin and his associates had been brought face to face with a condition which many Marxian Socialist writers had foreseen was likely to exist, not only in Russia, but in far more highly developed industrial nations, namely, a dangerous decline of production and of the average productivity of the workers, instead of the enormous increase which must be attained before any of the promises of Socialism could be redeemed. A few figures from official Bolshevist sources will serve to illustrate the seriousness of the decline in production. The great Soromovo Works had produced fifteen locomotives monthly, even during the last months of the Kerensky régime. By the end of April, 1918, it was pointed out, the output was barely two per month. At the Mytishchy Works in Moscow, the production, as compared with 1916, was only 40 per cent. At this time the Donetz Basin was held by the Bolsheviki. The average monthly output in the coal-fields of this important territory prior to the arrival of the Bolsheviki was 125,000,000 poods. The rule of the Bolsheviki was marked by a serious and continuous decline in production, dropping almost at once to 80,000,000 poods and then steadily declining, month by month, until in April-May, 1918, it reached the low level of 26,000,000 poods.[35] When the Bolsheviki were driven away, the production rose month by month, until, in December, 1918, it had reached 40,000,000 poods. Then the Bolsheviki won control once more and came back, and at once production declined with great swiftness, soon getting down to 24,000,000 poods.[36] These figures, be it remembered, are official Bolshevist figures.

[35] Economicheskaya Zhizn, *May 6, 1919.*

[36] *Idem.*

So serious was the decline of production in every department that a commission was appointed to investigate the matter. The commission reported in January, 1919, and from its report the following facts are quoted: in the Moscow railway workshops the number of workmen in 1916 was 1,192; in 1917 the number was 1,179; in 1918 it was 1,772—an increase of 50 per cent. The number of holidays and "off days" rose from 6 per cent. in 1916 to 12 per cent. in 1917 and 39.5 per cent. in 1918. At the same time, each car turned out per month represented the labor of 3.35 men in 1918 as against 1 in 1917 and .44 in 1916. In the Mytishchy Works, Moscow, the loss of production was enormous. Taking the eight-hour day as a basis, and counting as 100 the production of 1916, the production in 1917 amounted to 75, and only 40 in 1918. In the coal-mines of the Moscow region the fall of labor productivity was equally marked. The normal production per man is given as 750 poods per month. In 1916 the production was 614 poods; in 1917 it was 448 poods, and in 1918 it was only 242 poods. In the textile industries the decline in productivity was 35 per cent., including the flax industry, which does not depend upon the importation of raw materials.[37] In the Scherbatchev factory the per-capita production of calico was

68 per cent, lower than in 1917, according to the *Economicheskaya Zhizn* (No. 50).

37 For most of the statistical data in this chapter I am indebted to Prof. V. I. Issaiev, whose careful analyses of the statistical reports of the Soviet Government are of very great value to all students of the subject.—AUTHOR.

It is not necessary to quote additional statistics from the report of the investigating commission. The figures cited are entirely typical. The report as a whole reveals that there not only had been no arrest of the serious decline of the year 1917, but *an additional decline at an accelerated rate*, and that the condition was general throughout all branches of industry. The report attributes this serious condition partly to loss of efficiency in the workers due to under-nutrition, but more particularly to the mistaken conception of freedom held by the workers, their irresponsibility and indifference; to administrative chaos arising from inefficiency; and, finally, the enormous amount of time lost in holding meetings and elections and in endless committees. In general this report confirms the accounts furnished by the agent of the governments of Great Britain and the United States of America and published by them,[38] as well as reports made by well-known European Socialists.

38 See the British White Book and the Memorandum on Certain Aspects of the Bolshevist Movement in Russia, presented to the Foreign Relations Committee of the U. S. Senate by Secretary of State Lansing, January 5, 1920.

As early as April, 1918, Lenin and other Bolshevist leaders had taken cognizance of the enormous loss of time consumed by the innumerable meetings which Soviet control of industry involved. Lenin claimed, with much good reason, that much of this wasteful talking was the natural reaction of men who had been repressed too long, though his argument is somewhat weakened by the fact that there had been eight months of such talk before the Bolshevist régime began:

> The habit of holding meetings is ridiculed, and more often wrathfully hissed at by the bourgeoisie, Mensheviks, etc., who see only chaos, senseless bustle, and outbursts of petty bourgeoisie egoism. But without the "holding of meetings" the oppressed masses could never pass from the discipline forced by the exploiters to conscious and voluntary discipline. "Meeting-holding" is the real democracy of the toilers, their straightening out, their awakening to a new life, their first steps on the field which they themselves have cleared of reptiles (exploiters, imperialists, landed proprietors, capitalists), and which they want to learn to put in order themselves in their own way; for themselves, in accord with the principles of their, "Soviet," rule, and not the rule of the foreigners, of the nobility and bourgeoisie. The November victory of the toilers against the exploiters was necessary; it was necessary to have a whole period of elementary discussion by the toilers themselves of the new conditions of life and of the new problems to make possible *a secure transition to higher forms of labor discipline, to a conscious assimilation of the idea of the necessity of the dictatorship of the proletariat, to absolute submission to the personal orders of the representatives of the Soviet rule during work.*[39]

[39] The Soviets at Work, p. 37.

There is a very characteristic touch of Machiavellian artistry in this reference to "a secure transition to higher forms of labor discipline," in which there is to be "absolute submission to the personal orders of the representatives of the Soviet rule during work." The eloquent apologia for the Soviet system of industrial control by the workers carries the announcement of the liquidation of that system. It is to be replaced by some "higher forms of labor discipline," forms which will not attempt the impossible task of conducting factories on "debating-society lines." The "petty bourgeois tendency to turn the members of the Soviets into 'parliamentarians,' or, on the other hand, into bureaucrats," is to be combated. In many places the departments of the Soviets are turning "into organs which gradually merge with the commissariats" — in other words, are ceasing to function as governing bodies in the factories. There is a difficult transition to be made which alone will make possible "the definite realization of Socialism," and that is to put an end to the wastefulness arising from the attempt to combine the discussion and solution of political problems with work in the factories. There must be a return to the system of uninterrupted work for so many hours, with politics after working-hours. That is what is meant by the statement: "It is our object to obtain *the free performance of state obligations by every toiler after he is through with his eight-hour session of productive work.*"

Admirable wisdom! Saul among the prophets at last! The romancer turns realist! But this program cannot be carried out without making of the elaborate system of workers' control a wreck, a thing of shreds and patches. Away goes the Utopian combination of factory and forum, in which the dynamos are stilled when there are speeches to be made — pathetic travesty of industry and government both. The toiler must learn that his "state obligations" are to be performed after the day's work is done, and not in working-time at the expense of the pay-roll. More than this, it is necessary to place every factory under the absolute dictatorship of one person:

> Every large machine industry requires an absolute and strict unity of the will which directs the joint work of hundreds, thousands, and tens of thousands of people.... But how can we secure a strict unity of will? By subjecting the will of thousands to the will of one.[40]
>
> [40] The Soviets at Work.

If the workers are properly submissive, if they are "ideally conscious and disciplined," this dictatorship may be a very mild affair; otherwise it will be stern and harsh:

> There is a lack of appreciation of the simple and obvious fact that, if the chief misfortunes of Russia are famine and unemployment, these misfortunes cannot be overcome by any outbursts of enthusiasm, but only by thorough and universal organization of discipline, in order to increase the production of bread for men and fuel for industry, to transport it in time, and to distribute it in the right way. That, therefore, responsibility for the pangs of famine and unemployment falls on *every one who violates the labor discipline in any enterprise and in any business.* That those who are responsible should be discovered, tried, and *punished without mercy.*[41]

[41] *Idem.*

Not only must the workers abandon their crude conception of industrial democracy as requiring the abolition of individual authority, but they must also abandon the notion that in the management of industry one man is as good as another. They must learn that experts are necessary:[42] "Without the direction of specialists of different branches of knowledge, technique, and experience, the transformation toward Socialism is impossible." Although it is a defection from proletarian principles, a compromise, "a step backward by our Socialist Soviet state," it is necessary to "make use of the old bourgeois method and agree to a very high remuneration for the biggest of the bourgeois specialists." The proletarian principles must still further be compromised and the payment of time wages on the basis of equal remuneration for all workers must give place to payment according to performance; piece-work must be adopted. Finally, the Taylor system of scientific management must be introduced: "The possibility of Socialism will be determined by our success in combining the Soviet rule and Soviet organization of management with the latest progressive measures of capitalism. *We must introduce in*

Russia the study and the teaching of the Taylor system, and its systematic trial and adaptation."[43]

[42] *A much later statement of Lenin's view is contained in this paragraph from a speech by him on March 17, 1920. The quotation is from Soviet Russia, official organ of the Russian Soviet Government Bureau in the United States:*

"Every form of administrative work requires specific qualifications. One may be the best revolutionist and agitator and yet useless as an administrator. It is important that those who manage industries be completely competent, and be acquainted with all technical conditions within the industry. We are not opposed to the management of industries by the workers. *But we point out that the solution of the question must be subordinate to the interests of the industry.* Therefore the question of the management of industry must be regarded from a business standpoint. The industry must be managed with the least possible waste of energy, and the managers of the industry must be efficient men, whether they be specialists or workers."

[43] The Soviets at Work.

In all this there is much that is fine and admirable, but it is in direct and fundamental opposition to the whole conception of industrial control by factory Soviets. No thoughtful person can read and compare the elaborate provisions of the Instructions on Workers' Control, already summarized, and Lenin's *Soviets at Work* without reaching the conclusion that the adoption of the proposals contained in the latter absolutely destroys the former. The end of the Soviet as a proletarian industry-directing instrument was already in sight.

Bolshevism was about to enter upon a new phase. What the general character of that phase would be was quite clear. It had already been determined and Lenin's task was to justify what was in reality a reversal of policy. The essential characteristics of the Soviet system in industry, having proved to be useless impedimenta, were to be discarded, and, in like manner, anti-Statism was to be exchanged for an exaggerated Statism. In February, 1918, the Bolshevist rulers of Russia were confronted by a grave menace, an evil inherent in Syndicalism in all its variant forms, including Bolshevism—namely, the assertion of exorbitant demands by workers employed in performing services of immediate and vital importance in the so-called "key industries." Although the railway workers were only carrying the Bolshevist theories into practice, acquiescence in their demands would have placed the whole industrial life of Russia under their domination. Instead of a dictatorship of the proletariat, there would have been dictatorship by a single occupational group. Faced by this danger, the Bolshevist Government did not hesitate to nationalize the railways and place them under an absolute dictator, responsible, not to the railway workers, but to the central Soviet authority, the government. Wages, hours of labor, and working conditions were no longer subject to the decision of the railway workers' councils, but were determined by the dictators appointed by the state. The railway workers' unions were no longer recognized, and the right to strike was denied and strikes declared to be treason against the state. The railway workers' councils were not abolished at first, but were reduced to a nominal existence as "consultative bodies," which in practice were not consulted. Here was the apotheosis of the state: the new policy could not be restricted to railways; nationalization of industry, under state direction, was to take the place of the direction of industry by autonomous workers' councils.

In May, 1918, Commissar of Finances Gukovsky, staggered by the enormous loss incurred upon every hand, in his report to the Congress of Soviets called attention to the situation. He said that the railway system, the arterial system of the industrial life of the nation, was completely disorganized and demoralized. Freight-tonnage capacity had decreased by 70 per cent., while operating expenses had increased 150 per cent. Whereas before the war operating expenses were 11,579 rubles per verst, in May, 1918, *wages alone* amounted to 80,000 rubles per verst, the total working expenses being not less than 120,000 rubles per verst. A similar state of demoralization obtained, said Gukovsky, in the nationalized marine transportation service. In every department of industry, according to this highly competent authority, waste, inefficiency, idleness, and extravagance prevailed. He called attention to the swollen salary-list; the army of paid officials. Already the menace of what soon developed into a formidable bureaucracy was seen: "The machinery of the old régime has been preserved, the ministries remain, and parallel with them Soviets have arisen — provincial, district, volost, and so forth."

In June, 1918, after the railways had been nationalized for some time, Kobozev, Bolshevist Commissar of Communications, said: "The eight-hour workday and the payment per hour have definitely disorganized the whole politically ignorant masses, who understand these slogans, not as an appeal to the most productive efficiency of a free citizen, but as a right to idleness unjustified by any technical means. *Whole powerful railway workshops give a daily disgraceful exhibition of inactivity* on the principle of 'Why should I work when my neighbor is paid by time for doing no work at all?'"

Although nationalization of industry had been decided upon in February, and a comprehensive plan for the administration and regulation of nationalized enterprises had been published in March, promulgated as a decree, with instructions that it must be enforced by the end of May, it was not until July that the Soviet Government really decided upon its enforcement. It should be said, however, that a good many factories were nationalized between April and July. Many factories were actually abandoned by their owners and directors, and had to be taken over. Many others were just taken in an "irregular manner" by the workers, who continued their independent confiscations. For this there was indeed some sort of authority in the decree of March, 1918.[44] Transportation had broken down, and there was a lack of raw materials. It was officially reported that in May there were more than 250,000 unemployed workmen in Moscow alone. No less than 224 machine-shops, which had employed an aggregate of 120,000 men, were closed. Thirty-six textile factories, employing a total of 136,000 operatives, were likewise idle. To avert revolt, it was necessary to keep these unemployed workers upon the pay-roll. Under czarism the policy of subsidizing industrial establishments out of the government revenues had been very extensively developed. This policy was continued by the Provisional Government under Kerensky and by the Bolsheviki in their turn. Naturally, with industry so completely disorganized, this led toward bankruptcy at a rapid rate. The following extract from Gukovsky's report to the Central Executive Committee in May requires no elucidation:

[44] *See text of the decree—Appendix.*

> Our Budget has reached the astronomical figures of from 80 to 100 billions of rubles. No revenue can cover such expenditure. Our revenue for the half-year reaches approximately 3,294,000,000 rubles. It is exceedingly difficult to find a way of escape out of this situation. The repudiation of state loans played a very unfavorable part in this respect, as now it is impossible to borrow money—no one will lend. Formerly railways used to yield a revenue, and agriculture likewise. Now agriculturists refuse to export their produce, they are feeding better and hoarding money. The former apparatus—in the shape of a Government Spirit Monopoly and rural police officers—no longer exists. Only one thing remains to be done—to issue paper money *ad infinitum*. But soon we shall not be able to do even this.

At the Congress of the Soviets of People's Economy in May, Rykov, the president of the Superior Council of the National Board of Economy, reported, concerning the nationalization of industries, that so far it had been carried out without regard to industrial economy or efficiency, but exclusively from the point of view of successfully struggling against the bourgeoisie. It was, therefore, a war measure, and must not be judged by ordinary economic standards. Miliutin, another Bolshevist Commissar, declared that "nationalization bore a punitive character." It was pointed out by Gostev, another Bolshevist official, that it had been carried out against the wishes of many of the workers themselves quite as much as against the wishes of the bourgeoisie. "I must laugh when they speak of bourgeois sabotage," he said. "*We have a national people's and proletarian sabotage. We are met with enormous opposition from the labor masses when we start standardizing.*" For good or ill, however, and despite all opposition, Bolshevism had turned to nationalization and to the erection of a powerful and highly centralized state. What the results of that policy were we shall see.

IX

THE NATIONALIZATION OF INDUSTRY—I

To judge fairly and wisely the success or failure of an economic and political policy so fundamental and far-reaching as the nationalization of industry we must discard theories altogether and rely wholly upon facts. Nothing could be easier than to formulate theoretical arguments of great plausibility and force, either in support of the state ownership of industries and their direction by state agencies or in opposition to such a policy. Interesting such theorizing may be, but nothing can be conclusively determined by it. When we come to deal with the case of a country where, as in Russia, nationalization of industry has been tried upon quite a large scale, there is only one criterion to apply, namely, its relative success as compared with other methods of industrial organization and management in the same or like conditions. If nationalization and state direction can be shown to have brought about greater advantage than other forms of industrial ownership and control, then nationalization is justified by that result; if, on the other hand, its advantages are demonstrably less, it must be judged a failure.

Whether the nationalization of industry by the Bolshevist Government of Russia was a sound policy, wisely conceived and carried out with a reasonable degree of efficiency, can be determined with a fair approach to certainty and finality. Our opinions concerning Karl Marx's theory of the economic motivation of social evolution, or Lenin's ability and character, or the methods by which the Bolsheviki obtained power, are absolutely irrelevant and inconsequential. History will base its estimate of Bolshevism, not upon the evidence of the terrorism which attended it, ample and incontestable as that evidence may be, but upon its success or failure in solving the great economic problems which it set out to solve. Our judgment of the nationalization of industry must not be warped by our resentment of those features of Bolshevist rule which established its tyrannical character. The ample testimony furnished by the official journals published by the Bolshevist Government and the Communist Party enables us to visualize with great clearness the conditions prevailing in Russia before nationalization of industry was resorted to. We have seen that there was an alarming shortage of production, a ruinous excess of cost per unit of production, a great deal of inefficiency and waste, together with a marked increase in the number of salaried administrative officials. We have seen that during the period of industrial organization and direction by the autonomous organizations of the workers in the factories these evils grew to menacing proportions. It was to remedy these evils that nationalization was resorted to. If, therefore, we can obtain definite and authoritative answers to certain questions which inevitably suggest themselves, we shall be in a position to judge the merits of nationalization, not as a general policy, for all times and places, but as a policy for Russia in the circumstances and conditions prevailing when it was undertaken. The questions suggest themselves: Was there any increase in the total volume of production? Was the average per-capita production raised or lowered? Did the new methods result in lessening the excessive average cost per unit of production? Was there any perceptible marked increase in efficiency? Finally, did nationalization lessen the number of salaried administrative officials or did it have a contrary effect?

We are not concerned with opinions here, but only with such definite facts as are to be had. The replies to our questions are to be found in the mass of statistical data which the Bolsheviki have published. We are not compelled to rely upon anybody's opinions or observations; the numerous reports published by the responsible officials of the Bolshevist Government, and by their official press, contain an abundance of statistical evidence affording adequate and reliable answer to each of the questions we have asked.

Because the railways were nationalized first, and because of their vital importance to the general economic life of the nation, let us consider how the nationalization of railroad transportation worked out. The following table is taken from the report of the Commissar of Ways and Communications:

Year	Gross Receipts (rubles)	Working Expenses (rubles)	Working Expenses per Verst (rubles)	Wages and Salaries (rubles)	Profit and Loss (rubles)
1916	1,350,000,000	1,210,000,000	1,700	650,000,000	+140,000,000
1917	1,400,000,000	3,300,000,000	46,000	2,300,000,000	-1,900,000,000
1918	1,500,000,000	9,500,000,000	44,000	8,000,000,000	-8,000,000,000

These figures indicate that the nationalization of railways during the nine months of 1918 was characterized by a condition which no country in the world could stand for a very long time. This official table affords no scintilla of a suggestion that nationalization was succeeding any better than the anarcho-Syndicalist management which preceded it. The enormous increase in operating cost, the almost stationary receipts, and the resulting colossal deficit require no comment. At least on the financial side the nationalization policy cannot be said to have been a success, a fact which was frankly admitted by the *Severnaya Communa*, March 26, 1919. To see a profit of 140 million rubles transformed into a loss of 8 billion rubles is surely a serious matter.

Let us, however, adopt another test than that of finance, namely, the service test, and see whether that presents us with a more favorable result: According to the official report of the Commissar of Ways and Communications, there were in operation on October 1, 1917—that is, shortly before the Bolshevist *coup d'état*—52,597 versts[45] of railroad line in operation; on October 1, 1918, there were in operation 21,800 versts, a decrease of 30,797. On October 1, 1917, there were in working order 15,732 locomotives; on October 1, 1918, the number had dwindled to 5,037, a decrease of 10,695. On October 1, 1917, the number of freight cars in working condition was 521,591; on October 1, 1918, the number was 227,274, a decrease of 294,317.

[45] *One verst equals .663 mile, roughly, about two-thirds of a mile.*

The picture presented by these figures is, for one who knows the economic conditions in Russia, simply appalling. At its best the Russian railway system was wholly inadequate to serve the economic life of the nation. The foregoing official figures indicate an utter collapse of the railways at a time when the nation needed an efficient railroad transportation system more than at any time in its history. One of the reasons for the collapse of the railway system was the failure of the fuel supply. In northern and central Russia wood is generally used for fuel in the factories and on the railways. Difficult as it might be for them to maintain the supply of coal under the extraordinary conditions prevailing, it would seem that with enormous forests at their disposal, so near at hand, they would have found it relatively easy to supply the railways with wood for fuel purposes. Yet nowhere in the whole range of the industrial system of Russia was the failure more disastrous or more complete than here. According to an official estimate, the amount of wood fuel required for the railways from May 1, 1918, to May 1, 1919, estimated upon the basis of "famine rations," was 4,954,000 cubic sazhens,[46] of which 858,000 cubic sazhens was on hand, leaving 4,096,000 cubic sazhens as the amount to be provided. A report published in the *Economicheskaya Zhizn* (No. 41) stated that not more than 18 per cent. of the total amount of wood required was felled, and that not more than one-third of that amount was actually delivered to the railways. In other words, 82 per cent. of the wood fuel was not cut at all, at least so far as the particular economic body whose business it was to provide the wood was concerned. Extraordinary measures had to be taken to secure the fuel. From *Economicheskaya Zhizn*, February 22, 1919, we learn that the railway administration managed to secure fuel wood amounting to 70 per cent. of its requirements, and the People's Superior Economic Council another 2 per cent., a very large part of which had been secured by private enterprise. If this last statement seems astonishing and anomalous, it must be understood that as early as January 17, 1919, Lenin, as President of the Central Soviet Government, promulgated a decree which in a very large measure restored the right to private enterprise. Already nationalization was being pronounced a failure by Lenin. In an address announcing this remarkable modification of policy he said:

[46] *One sazhen equals seven feet.*

If each peasant would consent to reduce his consumption of products to a point a little less than his needs and turn over the remainder to the state, and if we were able to distribute that remainder regularly, we could go on, assuring the population a food-supply, insufficient, it is true, but enough to avoid famine.

This last is, however, beyond our strength, due to our disorganization. The people, exhausted by famine, show the most extreme impatience. Assuredly, we have our food policy, but the essential of it is that the decrees should be executed. *Although they were promulgated long ago, the decrees relative to the distribution of food products by the state never have been executed because the peasants will sell nothing for paper money.*

It is better to tell the truth. *The conditions require that we should pitilessly, relentlessly force our local organizations to obey the central power.* This, again, is difficult because millions of our inhabitants are accustomed to regard any central power as an organization of exploiters and brigands. They have no confidence in us and without confidence it is impossible to institute an economic régime.

The crisis in food-supplies, aggravated by the breakdown of transportation, explains the terrible situation that confronts us. At Petrograd the condition of the transportation service is desperate. The rolling-stock is unusable.

Another reason for the failure of the railways under nationalization during the first year's experimentation with that policy was the demoralization of the labor force. The low standard of efficiency, constant loafing, and idleness were factors in the problem. The interference by the workers' councils was even more serious. When the railways were nationalized the elected committees of workers, while shorn of much of their power, were retained as consultative bodies, as we have already seen. Toward the end of 1918 the officials responsible for the direction of the railroads found even that measure of authority which remained to these councils incompatible with efficient organization. Consequently, at the end of 1918 the abolition of the workers' committees of control was decreed and the dictatorial powers of the railroad directors made absolute. The system of paying wages by the day was replaced by a piece-work system, supplemented by cash bonuses for special efficiency. Later on, as we shall see, these changes were made applicable to all the nationalized industries. Thus, the principal features of the capitalist wage system were brought back to replace the communistic principles which had failed. When Lomov, president of the Chief Forest Committee, declared, as reported in *Izvestia*, June 4, 1919, that "proletarian principles must be set aside and the services of private capitalistic apparatus made use of," he simply gave expression to what was already a very generally accepted view.

The "return to capitalism," as it was commonly and justly described, had begun in earnest some months before Lomov made the declaration just quoted. The movement was attended by a great deal of internal conflict and dissension. In particular the trades-unions were incensed because they were practically suppressed as autonomous organs of the working-class. The dictatorship of the proletariat was already assuming the character of a dictatorship over the proletariat by a strongly centralized state. The rulers of this state, setting aside the written Constitution, were in fact not responsible to any electorate. They ruled by fiat and proclamation and ruthlessly suppressed all who sought to oppose them. They held that, industry having become nationalized, trades-unions were superfluous, and that strikes could not be tolerated because they became, *ipso facto*, acts of treason against the state. Such was the evolution of this anti-Statist movement.

The unions resisted the attempts to deprive them of their character as fighting organizations. They protested against the denial of the right to strike, the suppression of their meetings and their press. They resented the arbitrary fixing of their wages by officials of the central government. As a result, there was an epidemic of strikes, most of which were suppressed with great promptitude and brutality. At the Alexander Works, Moscow, eighty workers were killed by machine-gun fire. From March 6 to 26, 1919, the *Krasnaya Gazeta* published accounts of fifteen strikes in Petrograd, involving more than half the wage-workers of the city, some of the strikes being attended with violence which was suppressed by armed troops. At the beginning of March there was such a strike at the Tula Works, reported in *Izvestia*, March 2, 1919. On March 16, 1919, the *Severnaya Communa* gave an account of the strike at the famous Putilov Works, and of the means taken to "clear out the Social Revolutionary blackguards"—meaning thereby the striking workmen. *Pravda* published on March 23, 1919, accounts of serious strikes at the Putilov Works, the Arthur Koppel Works, the government car-building shops, and elsewhere. Despite a clearly defined policy on the part of the press to ignore labor struggles as far as possible, sufficient was published to show that there was an intense struggle by the Russian proletariat against its self-constituted masters. "The workers of Petrograd are in the throes of agitation, and strikes are occurring in some shops. The Bolsheviki have been making arrests," said *Izvestia* on March 2, 1919.

Of course it may be fairly said that the strikes did not of themselves indicate a condition of unrest and dissatisfaction peculiar to Russia. That is quite true. There were strikes in many countries in the early months of 1919. This fact does not, however, add anything to the strength of the defense of the Bolshevist régime. In the capitalist countries, where the struggle between the wage-earning and the employing classes is a normal condition, strikes are very ordinary phenomena. The Bolsheviki, in common with all other Socialists, pointed to these conflicts as evidence of the unfitness of capitalism to continue; and of the need for Socialism. It was the very essence of their faith that in the Socialist state strikes would be unknown, because no conflict of class interests would be possible. Yet here in the Utopia of the Bolsheviki the proletarian dictatorship was accompanied by strikes and lockouts precisely like those common to the capitalist system in all lands. *Moreover, while the nations which still retained the capitalist system had their strikes, there was not one of them in which such brutal methods of repression were resorted to.* Russia was at war, we are told, and strikes were a deadly menace to her very existence. But this argument, like the other, is of no avail. England, France, Italy, and America on the one side, and Germany and Austria upon the other side, all had strikes during the war, but in no one of them were strikers shot down with such savage recklessness as in Russia under the Bolsheviki.

Where and when in any of the great capitalist nations during the war was there such a butchery of striking workmen as that at the Alexander Works, already referred to? Where and when during the whole course of the war did any capitalist government suppress a strike of workmen with anything like the brutality with which the Bolshevist masters of Russia suppressed the strike at the Putilov Works in March, 1919? At first the marines in Petrograd were ordered to disperse the strikers and break the strike, but they refused to obey the order. At a meeting these marines decided that, rather than shoot down the striking workmen, they would join forces with them. Then the Bolsheviki called out detachments of coast guards, armed sailors from Kronstadt and Petrograd formerly belonging to the "disciplinary battalions," chiefly Letts. The strikers put up an armed resistance, being supported in this by a small body of soldiers. They were soon overcome, however, and the armed sailors took possession of the works and summarily executed many of the strikers, shooting them on the spot without even a drum-head court martial. The authorities issued a proclamation—published in *Severnaya*

Communa, March 16, 1919—forbidding the holding of meetings and "inviting" the strikers back to work:

> All honest workmen desirous of carrying out the decision of the Petrograd Soviet and ready to start work will be allowed to go into the factory on condition that they forthwith go to their places and take up their work. All those who begin work will receive an additional ration of one-half pound of bread. They who do not want to resume work will be at once discharged, without receiving any concessions. A special commission will be formed for the reorganization of the works. *No meetings will be allowed to be held....* For the last time the Petrograd Soviet invites the Putilov workmen to expiate their crime committed against the working-class and the peasantry of Russia, and to cease at once their foolish strike.

On the following day this "invitation" was followed up by a typical display of Bolshevist force. A detachment of armed sailors went to the homes of the striking workmen and at the point of the bayonet drove the men back into the works, about which a strong guard was placed. The men were kept at work by armed guards placed at strategic positions in the shops. All communication with the outside was strictly prohibited. Numerous arrests were made. With grim irony the Bolshevist officials posted in and around the shops placards explaining that, unlike imperialistic and capitalistic governments, the Soviet authority had no intention of suppressing strikes or insurrections by armed force. For the good of the Revolution, however, and to meet the war needs, the government would use every means at its command to force the workmen to remain at their tasks and to prevent all demonstrations.

A bitter struggle took place between the trades-unions and the Soviet Government. It was due, not to strikes merely, or even mainly, though these naturally brought out its bitterest manifestations. The real cause of the conflict was the fact that the government had thrown communism to the winds and adopted a policy of state capitalism. All the evils of capitalism in its relation to the workers reappeared, intensified and exaggerated as an inevitable result of being fundamental elements of the polity of an all-powerful state wholly free from democratic control. The abolition of the right to strike; the introduction of piece-work, augmented by a bonus system in place of day wages; the arbitrary fixing of wages and working conditions; the withdrawal of the powers which the workers' councils, led by the unions, had possessed since the beginning of the Revolution, and the substitution for the crude spirit of democracy which inspired the Soviet control of industry of the despotic principle of autocracy, "absolute submission to the will of a single individual"—these things inevitably evoked the active hostility of the organized workers. It was from the proletariat, and from its most "class-conscious" elements, that the Bolshevist régime received this determined resistance.

Many unions were suppressed altogether. This happened to the Teachers' Union, which was declared to be "counter-revolutionary."[47] It happened also to the Printers' Union. In this case the authorities simply declared that all membership cards were invalid and that the old officers were displaced. In order to work as a printer it was necessary to get a new card of membership, and such cards were only issued to those who signed declarations of loyalty to the Bolshevist authority.[48] The trades-unions were made to conform to the decisions of the Communist Party and subordinated to the rule of the Commissaries. Upon this point there is a good deal of evidence available, though most of it comes from non-Bolshevist sources. The references to this important matter in the official Bolshevist press are very meager and vague, and the Ransomes, Goodes, Malones, Coppings, and other apologists are practically silent upon the subject.

[47] *See Keeling, op. cit.*

[48] *Idem.*

The Socialist and trades-union leader, Oupovalov, from whom we have previously quoted, testifies that "Trades-unions, as working-class organizations independent of any political party, were transformed by the Bolsheviki into party organizations and subordinated to the Commissaries." Strumillo, equally competent as a witness, says: "Another claim of the Social Democrats—that trades-unions should be independent of political parties—likewise came to nothing. They were all to be under the control of the Bolsheviki. Alone the All-Russian Union of Printers succeeded in keeping its independence, *but eventually for that it was dispersed by the order of Lenin, and the members of its Executive Committee arrested.*" These statements are borne out by the testimony of the English trades-unionist, Keeling, who says:

> If a trades-union did not please the higher Soviet it was fined and suppressed and a new union was formed in its place by the Bolsheviks themselves. Entry to this new union was only open to members of the old union who signed a form declaring themselves entirely in agreement with, and prepared completely to support in every detail, the policy of the Soviet Government.
>
> Refusal to join on these terms meant the loss of the work and the salary, together with exclusion from both the first and second categories.[49] It will readily be understood how serious a matter it was to oppose any coercive measure.

[49] *I.e., the food categories entitling one to the highest and next highest food rations.*

> Every incentive was held out to the poorer people to spy and report on the others. A workman or a girl who gave information that any member of the trades-union was opposed in any way to the Soviet system was specially rewarded. He or she would be given extra food and promoted as soon as possible to a seat upon the executive of the union or a place on the factory committee.

Soon after the first Congress of the Railroad Workers' Unions, in February, 1918, the unions of railway workers were "merged with the state" — that is, they were forbidden to strike or to function as defensive or offensive organizations of the workers, and were compelled to accept the direction of the officials appointed by the central government and to carry out their orders. At the second Congress of the Railroad Workers' Unions, February, 1919, according to *Economicheskaya Zhizn* (No. 42), this policy was "sharply and categorically opposed" by Platonov, himself a Bolshevik and one of the most influential of the leaders of the railway men's unions. At the Moscow Conference of Shop Committees and Trades-Unions, March, 1919, it was reported, according to *Economicheskaya Zhizn* (No. 51), the unions "having given up their neutrality and independence, completely merged their lot with that of the Soviet Government.... Their work came to be closely interwoven with the state activities of the Soviet Government.... Only practical utilitarian considerations prevent us from completely merging the trades-unions with the administrative apparatus of the state."

At the ninth Congress of the Communist Party, held in Moscow, Bucharin proposed the adoption of certain "basic principles" governing the status of trades-unions and these were accepted by the Congress: "In the Soviet state economic and political issues are indivisible, therefore the economic organs of the Labor movement — the unions — have to be completely merged with the political — the Soviets — and not to continue as independent organizations as is the case in a capitalistic state. Being more limited in their scope, they have to be subordinate to the Soviets, which are more universal institutions. But merging with the Soviet apparatus the unions by no means become organs of the state power; they only take upon themselves the economic functions of this power." In his speech Bucharin contended that "such an intimate connection of the trades-unions with the Soviet power will present an ideal network of economic administrative organization covering the whole of Russia." It is quite clear that the unions must cease to exist as fighting organizations in the Bolshevist state, and become merely subordinate agencies carrying out the will of the central power.

Even if this testimony, official and otherwise, were lacking, it would be evident from the numerous strikes of a serious character among the best organized workers, and from their violence, that Bolshevism at this stage of its development found itself in opposition to the trades-unions. And if the evidence upon that point were not overwhelming and conclusive, it would only be necessary to read carefully the numerous laws and decrees of the Bolshevist Government, and to observe the development of its industrial policy, in order to understand that trades-unions, as independent and militant working-class organizations, fighting always to advance the interests of their class, could not exist under such a system.

The direct and immediate reason for the policy that was adopted toward the unions was, of course, the state of the industries, which made it impossible to meet the ever-growing demands made by the unions. There was, however, a far deeper and profounder reason, namely, the character of the unions themselves. The Bolsheviki had been forced to recognize the fundamental weakness of every form of Syndicalism, including Sovietism. They had found that the Soviets were not qualified to carry on industry efficiently; that narrow group interests were permitted to dominate, instead of the larger interests of society as a whole. The same thing was true of the trades-unions. By its very nature the trades-union movement is limited to a critical purpose and attitude; it makes demands and evades responsibilities. The trades-union does not and cannot, as a trades-union, possess the capacity for constructive functioning that a co-operative society possesses, for instance.

This fact was very clearly and frankly stated in March, 1919, by L. B. Krassin, in a criticism which was published in the *Economicheskaya Zhizn* (No. 52). He pointed out that, apart from the struggle for higher wages, "the labor control on the part of the trades-unions confined itself the whole time to perfunctory supervision of the activities of the plants, and completely ignored the general work of production. A scientific technical control, the only kind that is indispensable, is altogether beyond the capacities of the trades-unions." The same issue of this authoritative Bolshevist organ stated that at the Conference of Electrical Workers it was reported that "In the course of last year everybody admitted the failure of workers' control," and that the conference had adopted a resolution "to replace the working-men's control by one of inspection—*i.e.*, by the engineers of the Council of National Economy."

Instead of the expected idyllic peace and satisfaction, there was profound unrest in the Utopia of the Bolsheviki. There was not even the inspiration of enthusiastic struggle and sacrifice to attain the goal. The organized workers were disillusioned. They found that the Bolshevist state, in its relations to them as employer, differed from the capitalist employers they had known mainly in the fact that it had all the coercive forces of the state at its command, and a will to use them without any hesitation or any mercy. One view of the social and industrial unrest of the period is set forth in the following extract from the *Severnaya Communa*, March 30, 1919:

> At the present moment a tremendous struggle is going on within the ranks of the proletariat between two diametrically opposed currents. Part of the proletariat, numerically in the great majority, still tied to the village, both in a material as well as an ideological respect, is in an economic sense inclined to anarchism. It is not connected in production and in interest in its development. The other part is the industrial, highly skilled mechanics, who fight for new methods of production.
>
> *By the equalization of pay, and by the introduction of majority rule in the management of the factories, supposed to be a policy of democracy, we are only sawing off the limb on which we are sitting*, for the flower of our proletariat, the most efficient workers, prefer to go to the villages, or to engage in home trades, or to do anything else but to remain within those demolished and dusty fortresses we call factories. Why, this means in its truest sense *a dictatorship of unskilled laborers*!

This outcry from one of the principal official organs of the Bolsheviki is interesting from several points of view. The struggle within the proletariat itself is recognized. This alone could only mean the complete abandonment of faith in the original Bolshevist ideal, which was based upon the solidarity of interest of the working-class as a whole. The denunciation of the equalitarian principle of uniform wages for all workers, and of majority rule in the factories, could only come from a conviction that Bolshevism and Sovietism were alike unsuited to Russia and undesirable. The scornful reference to a "dictatorship of unskilled laborers" might have come from any bourgeois employer.

From the official Bolshevist press of this period pages of quotations might easily be given to show that the transformation to familiar capitalist conditions was proceeding at a rapid rate. Thus, the Bolshevist official, Glebov, reported at the Conference of Factory Committees, in March, 1919: "The fight against economic disintegration demanded the reintroduction of the premium system. This system has produced splendid results in many instances, having increased the productivity of labor 100 to 200 per cent." The Bolshevist journal, *Novy Put*, declared, "The most effective means for raising the efficiency of labor is the introduction of the premium and piece-work system as against daily wages." The *Economicheskaya Zhizn* (No. 46) declared, "An investigation undertaken last month by the trades-unions has shown that in 75 per cent. of the plants the old system of wages has been reintroduced and that nearly everywhere this has been followed by satisfactory and even splendid results." The same issue of this important official organ showed that there had been large increases in production wherever the old system of wages and premiums had been restored. At the Marx Printing Works the increase was 20 per cent.; at the Nobel Factory 35 per cent.; at the Aviation Plant 150 per cent.; and at Seminov's Lumber Mill 243 per cent.

The *Severnaya Communa* reported that "In the Nevski Works the substitution of the premium system for the monthly wage system increased the productivity of the working-men three and one-half times, and the cost of labor for one locomotive dropped from 1,400,000 rubles to 807,000 rubles—*i.e.*, to almost one-half." Rykov, president of the Superior Council of National Economy, one of the ablest of the Bolshevist officials, reported, according to *Izvestia*, that "in the Tula Munition Works, after the old 'premium' system of wages had been restored, the productivity of the works and of labor rose to 70 per cent. of what it was in 1916."

These are only a few of the many similar statements appearing in the official Bolshevist press pointing to a reversal of policy and a return to capitalist methods. On March 1, 1919, a decree of the People's Commissaries was promulgated which introduced a new wage scale, based upon the principle of extra pay for skill. The greater the skill the higher the rate of wages was the new rule. As published in *Severnaya Communa*, the scale provided for twenty-seven classes of workers. The lowest, unskilled class of laborers, domestics, and so forth, receive 600 rubles per month (1st class), 660 rubles (2d class), and so on. Higher employees, specialists, are put in classes 20 to 27, and receive from 1,370 to 2,200 rubles a month. Skilled mechanics in chemical plants, for example, receive 1,051-1,160 rubles. Unskilled laborers, 600 rubles, and chemical engineers more than 2,000 rubles a month.

Nationalization of industry meant, and could only mean, state capitalism. Communism was as far away as it was under czarism. And many of the old complaints so familiar in capitalist countries were heard. The workers were discontented and restless; production, while it was better than under Soviet control, was still far below the normal level; there was an enormous growth of bureaucracy and an appalling amount of corruption. Profiteering and speculation were rampant and inefficiency was the order of the day. The following extract from an article in *Pravda*, March 15, 1919, is a confession of failure most abject:

> Last year the people of Russia were suffering from lack of bread. To-day they are in distress because there is plenty of foodstuffs which cannot be brought out from the country and which will, no doubt, decay to a great extent when hot weather arrives.
>
> The misery of bread scarcity is replaced by another calamity—the plentifulness of breadstuffs. That the situation is really such is attested by these figures:
>
> The Food Commission and its subsidiary organs have stored up from August, 1918, to February 20, 1919, grain and forage products amounting to 82,633,582 poods. There remained on the last-mentioned date in railroad stations and other collection centers not less than 22,245,072 poods of grain and fodder. Of these stocks, according to the incomplete information by the

Transport Branch of the Food Commission, there are stalled on the Moscow-Kazan and Syzran-Viazma Railroads alone not less than 2,000,000 poods of grain in 2,382 cars. There are, moreover, according to the same source, on the Kazanburgsk and Samara-Zlatoostovsk Line, at least 1,300 more carloads of breadstuffs that cannot be moved.

All this grain is stalled because there are no locomotives to haul the rolling-stock. Thus the starving population does not receive the bread which is provided for it and which is, in part, even loaded up in cars.

In a hungry land there must be no misery while there is a surplus of bread. Such a misfortune would be truly unbearable!

On April 15, 1919, *Izvestia* published an article by Zinoviev, in which the famous Bolshevist leader confessed that the Soviet Government had not materially benefited the average working-man:

Has the Soviet Government, has our party done everything that can be done for the direct improvement of the daily life of the average working-man and his family? Alas! we hesitate to answer this question in the affirmative.

Let us look the truth in the face. We have committed quite a number of blunders in this realm. *We have to confess that we are unable to improve the nutrition of the average worker to any serious extent.* But do the wages correspond with the actually stupendous rise of prices for unrationed foodstuffs? Nobody will undertake to answer this question entirely in the affirmative, while the figures given by Comrade Strumilin show that in spite of a threefold raise of the wage scale, the real purchasing power of these wages had shrunk, on the average, more than 30 per cent. by March of the current year, as compared with May of last year.

The *Economicheskaya Zhizn*, May 6, 1919, gave a despondent account of the coal industry and the low production, accompanied by this alarming picture: "The starving, ill-clad miners are running away from the pits in a panic, and it is to be feared that in two or three weeks not only the whole production of coal will be stopped, but most of the mines will be flooded."

Nationalization of industry was not a new thing in Russia. It was, indeed, quite common under czarism. The railways were largely state owned and operated by the government. Most of the factories engaged in the manufacture of guns and munitions were also nationalized under czarism. It is interesting, therefore, to compare the old régime with the new in this connection. Under czarism nationalization had always led to the creation of an immense bureaucracy, politically powerful by reason of its numbers, extravagant, inefficient, and corrupt. That nationalization under the new régime was attended by the same evils, in an exaggerated form, the only difference being that the new bureaucracy was drawn from a different class, is written so plainly in the records that he who runs may read. No country in the world, it is safe to say, has ever known such a bureaucracy as the Bolshevist régime produced.

At the eighth All-Russian Congress of the Communist Party, held in March, 1919, Lenin said: "You imagine that you have abolished private property, but instead of the old bourgeoisie that has been crushed you are faced by a new one. The places of the former bourgeoisie have already been filled up by the newly born bourgeoisie." The backbone of this new bourgeoisie was the vast army of government officials and employees. These and the food speculators and profiteers, many of whom have amassed great wealth—real wealth, not worthless paper rubles—make up a formidable bourgeoisie. Professor Miliukov tells of a statistical department in Moscow with twenty-one thousand employees; and of eighteen offices having to be visited to get permission to buy a pair of shoes from the government store. Alexander Berkenheim, vice-chairman of the Moscow Central Union of Russian Consumers' Co-operative Societies, said: "The experiment in socialization has resulted in the building up of an enormous bureaucratic machine. To buy a pencil one has to call at eighteen official places." These men are competent witnesses, notwithstanding their opposition to Bolshevism. Let us put it aside, however, and consider only a small part of the immense mass of official Bolshevist testimony to the same general effect.

On February 21, 1919, the Bolshevist official, Nemensky, presented to the Supreme Council of National Economy the report of the official inspection and audit of the Centro-Textile, the central state organization having charge of the production and distribution of textiles. There are some sixty of these organizations, such as Centro-Sugar, Centro-Tea, Centro-Coal, and so on, the entire number being federated into the Supreme Council of National Economy. From the report referred to, as published in *Economicheskaya Zhizn*, February 25, 1919, the following paragraphs are quoted:

> An enormous staff of employees (about 6,000), for the most part loafing about, doing nothing; it was discovered that 125 employees were actually not serving at all, but receiving a salary the same as the others. There have been cases where some have been paid twice for the same period of time. *The efficiency of the officials is negligible to a striking degree....*

> The following figures may partially serve as an illustration of what was the work of the collaborators: For four months—from August 25 to November 21, 1918—the number of letters received amounted to 59,959 (making an average of 500 a day), and the number of letters sent was 25,781 (an average of 207 per day). Each secretary had to deal with 10 letters received and 4 sent, each typist with 2 letters sent, and each clerk with 1 letter received and 0.5 sent. Together with chairs, tables, etc., the inventory-book contained entries of dinners, rent, etc. When checking the inventory of the department it was established that the following were missing—142 tables, 500 chairs,

39 cupboards, 14 typewriters, etc. On the whole, the entries in the book exceeded by 50 per cent, the number of articles found on the spot.

Commenting upon this report the *Izvestia*[50] said: "An enormous staff of employees in most cases lounge about in idleness. An inquiry showed that *the staff of the Centro-Textile included 125 employees who were practically not in its service, though drawing their pay. There were cases where one and the same person drew his pay twice over for one and the same period of time.* The working capacity of the employees is ridiculously low; the average correspondence per typist was one letter outward and one inward per day; the average per male clerk was a half a letter outward and one inward." We do not wonder, at Nemensky's own comment, "Such Soviet institutions are a beautiful example of deadening bureaucracy and must be liquidated."

50 *No. 63, 1919.*

The disclosures made in the Centro-Textile were repeated in other state economic institutions. Thus the *Izvestia* of the State Control, commenting upon the Budget for 1919, said:

> The Audit Department sees in the increase of expenditure for the payment of work a series of negative causes. Among these is that it leads to a double working on parallel lines—*viz.*, the same work is done by two and even more sections, resulting in mutual friction and disorder and bringing the number of employees beyond all necessary requirements. We noticed on more than one occasion that an institution with many auxiliary branches had been opened before any operations to be carried on by them were even started.
>
> Furthermore, the work is mostly very slovenly and inefficiently conducted. It leads to an increase of the number of employees and workmen without benefit to the work.

In the *Bulletin of the Central Executive Committee of the Soviets* (No. 15) we find this confession: "We have created extraordinary commissaries and Extraordinary Commissions without number. All of these are, to a lesser or greater degree, only mischief-makers." Lunacharsky, the Bolshevist Commissary of Education, is reported by the *Severnaya Communa* of May 23, 1919, as saying: "The upper stratum of the Soviet rule is becoming detached from the masses and the blunders of the communist workers are becoming more and more frequent. These latter, according to statements made by workmen, treat the masses in a high-handed manner and are very generous with threats and repressions." In *Pravda*, May 14, 1919, the Bolshevik, Monastyrev, wrote: "Such a wholesale loafing as is taking place in our Soviet institutions and such a tremendous number of officials the history of the world has never known and does not know. All the Soviet papers have written about it, and we have felt it on our backs, too." *Izvestia* of the Central Executive Committee (No. 15), 1919, said:

"Besides Soviets and committees, many commissaries and committees have been instituted here. Almost every commissariat has an extraordinary organ peculiar to its own department. As a result we have numberless commissaries of all kinds. All of them are more or less highly arbitrary in their behavior and by their actions undermine Soviet authority."

These are only a few of the many statements of a like character published in the official Bolshevist press. In a country which had long been accustomed to an immense bureaucracy, the horde of officials was regarded with astonishment and alarm. Like the old bureaucracy, the new bureaucracy was at once brutal and corrupt. No one can read the reports published by the Bolsheviki themselves and fail to be impressed by the entire absence of idealism so far as the great majority of the officials are concerned, a fact which Lenin himself has commented upon more than once. That there were and are exceptions to the rule we may well believe, just as there were such exceptions under the old régime of Nicholas II. Upon the whole, however, it is difficult to see wherein the bureaucracy of the Bolsheviki was less brutal, less coarse, or less corrupt than that of czarism. But again let the Bolsheviki speak through their own recognized spokesmen:

According to *Izvestia* of the Central Executive Committee, November 1, 1918, a commission of five which had been appointed to discover and distribute metal among the factories in proportion to their needs was found to have been bribed to distribute the metal, not in proportion to the needs of the industries, but according to the value of the bribe.

From the *Weekly Report of the Extraordinary Commission*, No. 1, page 28, we learn that the administration of the combined Moscow nationalized factories was convicted of a whole series of abuses and speculations, resulting in the embezzlement of many millions of rubles. It was said that members of the administrative board and practically all the employees took part in this graft.

From *Izvestia* of the Central Executive Committee, November 3, 1918, we learn that the Soviet of National Economy of Kursk, connected with the Supreme Council of National Economy, was found guilty of speculative dealings in sugar and hemp.

In the same important official journal, January 22, 1919, the well-known Bolshevik, Kerzhentzev, in a terrible exposure from which we have already quoted in an earlier chapter, says: "The abundant testimony, verified by the Soviet Commission, portrays a very striking picture of violence. When these members of the Executive Committee [he names Glakhov, Morev, and Makhov] arrived at the township of Sadomovo they commenced to assault the population and to rob them of foodstuffs and of their household belongings, such as quilts, clothing, harness, etc. No receipts for the requisitioned goods were given and no money paid. *They even resold to others on the spot some of the breadstuffs which they had requisitioned.*" Again, the same journal published, on March 9, 1919, a report by a prominent Bolshevik, Sosnovsky, on conditions in the Tver Province, saying: "The local Communist Soviet workers behave themselves, with rare exceptions, in a disgusting manner. *Misuse of power is going on constantly.*"

A cursory examination of the files of the *Bulletin of the Central Executive Committee of the Soviets*, for the first few months of 1919, reveals a great deal of such evidence as the foregoing. In No. 12 we read: "The toiling population see in the squandering of money right and left by the commissaries and in their indecent loudness and profanity during their trips through the district, the complete absence of party discipline." In No. 13 of the same organ there is an account of the case of Commissary Odintzov, a member of the peace delegation to the Ukraine, who was "found speculating in breadstuffs." In No. 20 we read that "members of the Extraordinary Commission, Unger and Lebedev, were found guilty of embezzlement." No. 25 says that "a case has been started against the commissaries, O. K. Bogdanov and Zaitzev, accused of misappropriating part of the requisitioned gold and silver articles."

Let us hear from some of the leading Bolsheviki who participated in the debate on the subject of the relation of the central Soviet authority to local self-government at the eighth Congress of the Communist Party, March, 1919. Nogin, former president of the Moscow Soviet, said: "The time has come to state openly before this meeting how low our party has fallen. We have to confess that the representatives both of the central and the local authorities disgrace the name of the party by their conduct. *Their drunkenness and immorality, the robberies and other crimes committed by them, are so terrible as scarcely to be believed.*" Commissar Volin said: "Some of the local authorities give themselves over to outrageous abominations. How can they be put a stop to? The word 'communist' rouses deep hatred, not only among the bourgeoisie, but even among the poorer and the middle classes which we are ruining. What can we do for our own salvation?" Pakhomoff said: "I sent several comrades to the villages. *They had barely reached their destination when they turned bandits.*" Ossinsky said, "The revolts now taking place are not White Guard risings, as formerly, but rebellions caused by famine *and the outrageous behavior of our own commissaries.*"

Zinoviev was equally emphatic in his declaration: "It cannot be concealed from this meeting that in certain localities the word 'communist' has become a term of abuse. The people are beginning to hate the 'men in leather jackets,' as the commissaries were nicknamed in Perm. The fact cannot be denied, and we must look the truth in the face. Every one knows that both in the provinces and in the large towns the housing reform has been carried out imperfectly. True, the bourgeoisie has been driven out of its houses, *but the workmen have gained nothing thereby. The houses are taken possession of by Bolshevist state employees*, and sometimes they have been occupied, not even by the 'Soviet bureaucrat,' but by his mother-in-law or grandmother."

Not only has the bribery of officials grown, as revealed by the reports of the Extraordinary Commissions, but many of the Bolshevist officials have engaged in food speculation. That the greatest buyers of the food illegally sold at the Sukharevka market are the highly paid Soviet officials is a charge frequently made in the Bolshevist press. In November, 1919, Tsurupa, People's Commissary for Supplies, published an article in *Izvestia* (No. 207), exposing the speculation in foodstuffs at the Sukharevka market, formerly the largest market for second-hand goods in Moscow, now the center of illicit speculation. Tsurupa said:

> At the present moment a number of measures are being drawn up to begin war on "Sukharevka." The struggle must be carried on in two directions: first, the strengthening of the organs of supply and the control over the work of Soviet machinery; secondly, the destruction of speculators. The measures of the second kind are, of course, merely palliative, and it is impossible to overcome "Sukharevka" without insuring the population a certain supply of the rationed foodstuffs.
>
> Even among our respected comrades there are some who consider "Sukharevaka" as an almost normal thing, or, at any rate, as supplementing the gaps in food-supply.

Many defects in our organization are directly conducive to speculation. Thus many head commissariats, centers, factories, and works pay their workmen and employees in foodstuffs exceeding their personal requirements, and, as a rule, these articles find their way to "Sukharevka" for purposes of speculation.

The foodstuffs which find their way to "Sukharevka" are sold at such high prices that *only the upper circles of Soviet employees can afford to buy them, the masses of consumers being totally unable to do so.* These foodstuffs are at the disposal of the—so to speak—*Soviet bourgeoisie*, who can afford to squander thousands of rubles. "Sukharevka" gives nothing to the masses.

The Moscow Extraordinary Commission is carrying on an active campaign against "Sukharevka" speculation. As a result of a fortnight's work, 437 persons have been arrested, and a series of transactions have been discovered. The most important cases were as follows:

(1) Sale of 19 million rubles' worth of textiles.

(2) Sale of three wagon-loads of sugar. (At the price of even 200 rubles, and not 400 rubles, a wagon of 36,000 pounds of sugar works out at 8,000,000 rubles, and the whole deal amounts to 24,000,000 rubles.)

(3) Seventeen wagon-loads of herrings.

(4) 15,000,000 rubles' worth of rubber goods, etc.

In the course of the campaign of the Moscow Extraordinary Commission above referred to it was discovered that the state textile stores in Moscow had been looted by the "Communists" in charge of them. Millions of yards of textiles, instead of being placed on sale in the nationalized stores, had been sold to speculators and found their way into the Sukharevka. During the summer of 1919 the Bolshevist official press literally teemed with revelations of graft, spoliation, and robbery by officials. The report of the Smolensk Extraordinary Commission showed that hundreds of complaints had been made and investigated. In general the financial accounts were kept with almost unbelievable carelessness and laxity. Large sums of money were paid out on the order of single individuals without the knowledge of any other officials, and without check of any sort. Out of a total expenditure of three and a half million rubles for food rations to soldiers' families there were no vouchers or receipts for 1,161,670 rubles, according to the report. Commenting upon the reign of corruption in all parts of Soviet Russia, the *Krasnaya Gazeta*, in an article entitled, "When Is This to End?" said:

> In the Commissariat of the Boards for the various municipalities thefts of goods and money are almost of daily occurrence. Quite recently representatives of the State Control found that silk and other goods for over a million rubles had been stolen within a short space of time from the goods listed as nationalized. Furthermore, it has come out during the inspection of the nationalized houses that thefts and embezzlements of the people's money have become an ordinary occurrence. It is remarkable how light-fingered gentry who are put to manage the confiscated houses succeed in getting away after pocketing the money belonging to the Soviet, and all that with impunity, *and yet the money stolen by them is estimated not at hundreds of rubles, but at tens of thousands of rubles.* Will there ever be an end to these proceedings? Or is complete liberty to be given to the thieves in Soviet Russia to do as they like?

> Why does the Extraordinary Commission not see to the affairs of the Commissariat of the Municipality? It is high time all these Augean stables were cleaned up. This must stop at last. The Soviet authorities are sufficiently strong to have some scores of these thieves of the people's property hanged. To close one's eyes to all this is the same as encouraging the thieves.

Here, then, is a part of the evidence of the brutality and corruption of the vast bureaucracy which Bolshevism has developed to replace the old bureaucracy of the Czars. It is only a small part of the total mass of such evidence.[51] Every word of it comes from Bolshevist officials and journals of standing and authority. It will not do to seek to evade the issue by setting up the plea that corruption and brutality are found in other lands. That plea not only "begs the question," but it destroys the only foundation upon which an honest attempt to justify Bolshevism can be made, namely, the claim that it represents a higher stage of civilization, of culture, and morality than the old. Only a profound belief in the righteousness of that claim could justify the recourse to such a terrible method of bringing about a change in the social organization of a great nation. There is not the faintest shadow of a reason for believing that Bolshevism has been one whit less corrupt than the czarist bureaucracy.

51 *In Les Bolsheviks à l'œuvre, Paris, 1920, A. Lockerman gives a list of many similar cases of looting and graft by commissars.*

What of efficiency? Does the available evidence tend to show that this bureaucratic system managed to secure a degree of efficiency in production and distribution commensurate, in part, at least, with its enormous cost? On the contrary, while there was a marked increase in output after nationalization was introduced, due to the restoration of capitalist methods of management, the enormous cost at which the improvement was effected, for which the bureaucracy was responsible, left matters in a deplorable condition. This can be well understood in view of the fact, cited by Professor Issaiev, that in one of the largest metal works in Moscow the overhead charges, cost of administration, accounting, and so on, which in 1916, the last year of the old régime, amounted to 15 per cent. of the total cost, rose to over 65 per cent. in 1918-19. This was not an unusual case, but fairly typical. Once again, however, let us resist the temptation to quote such figures, based upon the calculations and researches of hostile critics, and confine ourselves strictly to Bolshevist testimony.

At the end of December, 1918, Rykov, president of the Supreme Council of National Economy, reported to the Central Executive Committee, according to *Economicheskaya Zhizn*, "Now almost all the large and medium-sized establishments are nationalized." A few days later an article by Miliutin, published in the same paper, said: "A year ago there were about 36 per cent. of nationalized establishments throughout Soviet Russia. At the present time 90 per cent. of industrial establishments are nationalized." On January 12, 1919, the same journal reported that nationalization had become general throughout Russian industry, embracing the textile and metallurgical industries, glass-making, printing, publishing, practically all commerce, and even barber shops. We are, therefore, in a fair position to judge the effects of nationalization upon the basis of subsequent reports.

It is not as well known as it ought to be that the Bolsheviki, even under nationalization, continued the practice, established under czarism and maintained by the Provisional Government under Kerensky, of subsidizing factories from the central treasury of the government. Bad as this practice was under capitalism, it was immeasurably worse when applied to industry under Soviet control and to nationalized industry. It was not only conducive to laxity and bad management, but it invited these as well as being destructive of enterprise and energy. The sums spent for this purpose were enormous, staggering in their total. A few illustrations must suffice to show this. According to *Economicheskaya Zhizn* (No. 50), in the month of January, 1919, the Metal Department of the Supreme Council of National Economy distributed among the various nationalized metallurgical works 1,167,295,000 rubles, and the central organization of the copper industry received 1,193,990,000 rubles. According to a report of the Section of Polygraphic Trades, published in *Pravda*, May 17, 1919, nineteen nationalized printing-establishments lost 13,500,000 rubles during 1918, the deficit having to be made up by subsidies from the central treasury. At the Conference of Tobacco Workers, held on April 25, 1919, it was reported, according to *Severnaya Communa*, that the Petrograd factories alone were being operated at a loss approaching two million rubles a month. It was further stated that "the condition of the tobacco industry is bad. The number of plants has been decreased by more than half, and the output is only one-third." In the report of Nemensky on the audit of the Centro-Textile, from which we have already quoted, we read:

> The Finance Credit Division of the Centrotekstil received up to February 1, 1919, 3,400,000,000 rubles. There was no control of the expenditure of moneys. *Money was advanced to factories immediately upon demand, and there were cases when money was forwarded to factories which did not exist.* From July 1 to December 31, 1918, the Centrotekstil advanced on account of products to be received 1,348,619,000 rubles. The value of the goods securing these advances received up to January 1, 1919, was only 143,716,000 rubles. The Centrotekstil's negligent way of doing business may be particularly observed from the way it purchased supplies of raw wool. Up to January 1, 1919, only 129,803 poods of wool was acquired, whereas the annual requirement is figured at 3,500,000 poods.

The value of the goods actually received was, according to this authority, only 10 per cent. of the money advanced. We are told that "money was forwarded to factories which did not exist." That this practice was not confined to the Centro-Textile we infer from the account given in the *Izvestia* of State Control (No. 2) of a firm which obtained a large sum of money in advance for Westinghouse brakes to be manufactured and supplied by it, though investigation proved that the firm did not even own a foundry and was unable to furnish any brakes at all. How much of this represents inefficiency, and how much of it graft, the reader must judge for himself. The

Bolshevist newspaper, *Trud*, organ of the trades-unions, in an article dealing with the closing down of nineteen textile factories, said, April 28, 1919:

> In our textile crisis a prominent part is played also by the bad utilization of that which we do have. Thus the efficiency of labor has dropped to almost nothing, of labor discipline there is not even a trace left, the machinery, on account of careless handling, has deteriorated and its productive capacity has been lowered.

In *Izvestia* of the Central Executive Committee, March 21, 1919, Bucharin said: "Our position is such that, together with the deterioration of the material production—machinery, railways, and other things—*there is a destruction of the fundamental productive force, the labor class, as such*. Here in Russia, as in western Europe,[52] the working-class is dissolving, factories are closing, and the working-class is reabsorbed into the villages."

[52] Sic!

From the report of the Supreme Council of National Economy, March, 1919, we learn that in the vast majority of the branches of Russia's industry the labor required for production had increased from 400 to 500 per cent. The Congress of Salesmen's Unions, held at the end of April, 1919, adopted a resolution, published in *Izvestia* (No. 97), which said, "The nationalization of commerce, owing to the pell-mell speed of the methods employed in carrying it out, has assumed with us extremely ugly forms, and has only aggravated the bad state of affairs in the circulation of goods in the country, which was poor enough as it was."

These statements show that in the early part of last year the Bolshevist régime was in a very critical condition. Demands for the "liquidation" of the system were heard on every hand.

Instead of this, the resourceful rulers of Soviet Russia once more revolutionized their methods. The period of nationalization we have been considering may be described as the first phase, the period of the rule of industry by the professional politicians of the Communist Party. When, in March, 1919, Leonid B. Krassin[53] undertook the reorganization of the industrial life of the nation, Bolshevism entered upon a new phase.

[53] Krassin's first name is usually given as "Gregory," but this is an error. His full name is Leonid Borisovitch Krassin. He is a Siberian of bourgeois extraction.

X
THE NATIONALIZATION OF INDUSTRY—II

The second phase of nationalization may be characterized as the adoption by a political state of the purest capitalist methods. Krassin was not a Bolshevik or a Socialist of any kind, so far as can be learned. He severed his rather nominal connection with the Socialist movement in 1906, it is said, and, thoroughly disillusioned, devoted himself to his profession and to the management of the Petrograd establishment of the great German firm of Siemens-Schuckart. He is said to have maintained very cordial relations with Lenin and was asked by the latter to accept three portfolios, namely, Commerce and

Industry, Transports, and War and Munitions. He agreed to take the appointment, provided the Soviet Government would accept his conditions. He demanded (1) the right to appoint specialists of his own choosing to manage all the departments under his control, regardless of their political or social views; (2) that all remaining workers' committees of control be abolished and that he be given the power to replace them by responsible directors, with full powers; (3) that piece-work payments and premiums take the place of day-work payment, with the right to insist upon overtime regardless of any existing rules or laws.

Of course, acceptance of these conditions was virtually an abandonment of every distinctive principle and ideal the Bolsheviki had ever advanced. Krassin immediately set to work to bring some semblance of order out of the chaos. The "iron discipline" that was introduced and the brutal suppression of strikes already described were due to his powerful energy. A martinet, with no sort of use for the Utopian visions of his associates, Krassin is a typical industrial despot. The attitude of the workers toward him was tersely stated by the *Proletarskoe Echo* in these words: "How Comrade Krassin has organized the traffic we have all seen and now know. We do not know whether Comrade Krassin has improved the traffic, but one thing is certain, that his autocratic ways as a Commissary greatly remind us of the autocratic policy of a Czar."[54]

[54] Quoted by H. W. Lee, The Dictatorship of the Proletariat, p. 7.

Yet Krassin failed to do more or better than prolong the hopeless struggle against utter ruin and disastrous failure. He was, after all, an engineer, not a miracle-worker. Trades-unions were deprived of power and made mere agencies for transmitting autocratic orders; tens of thousands of useless politicians were ousted from the factories and the railways; the workers' control was so thoroughly broken that there were not left in Soviet Russia a dozen workers' committees possessing the power of the printers' "chapel" in the average large American newspaper plant, or anything like the power possessed by hundreds, and perhaps thousands, of shop committees in our industrial centers.[55] But Krassin and his stern capitalist methods had come too late. The demoralization had gone too far.

[55] *In view of the denials of the dissolution of workers' control, circulated by Soviet Russia and the whole body of pro-Bolshevist propagandists, it may be well to clinch the statements made on this point by quoting from an indisputable authority. In the issue of Economicheskaya Zhizn, November 13, 1919, appears the following paragraph:*

"Schliapnikoff, Commissar of Labor in the Soviet Republic, writes: 'The principal cause of the deplorable situation of the Russian industry is a total absence of order and discipline in the factories. The Working Men's Councils and the Shop Committees, created with the purpose of establishing order in the factories, exercised an injurious influence on the general course of affairs by destroying the last traces of discipline and by squandering away the property of the factories. All those circumstances put together have compelled us to abolish the Working Men's Councils and to place at the head of the most important concerns special "dictators," with unlimited powers and entitled to dispose of the life and death of the workmen.'"

Only a brief summary of the most important statistical data illustrating the results attained during the remainder of the year 1919, that is to say, the second phase of nationalization, can be given here. To attempt anything like a detailed presentation of the immense mass of available official statistical data covering this period would of itself require a large volume. If we take the *Economicheskaya Zhizn* for the months of October and November, 1919, we shall be able to get a fairly good measure of the results attained during the half-year following the reorganization of the system by

Krassin. It must always be borne in mind that the *Economicheskaya Zhizn* is the official organ of the Supreme Economic Council and of the Ministries of Finance, Commerce and Trade, and Food. To avoid having to use the name of the journal in almost every other line, the statements of fact made upon its authority are followed by numbers inclosed in brackets; these numbers indicate the issues from which the statements are taken.[56]

[56] For the mass of translations covering this period the author is indebted to Mr. Alexander Kerensky.

Turning our attention first to the important subject of transportation, to which Krassin naturally devoted special attention, we find that on the entire railway system of Soviet Russia the number of freight-cars and trucks in daily service during August and September averaged between 7,000 and 7,500. Of this number from 45 to 50 per cent.—that is, from 3,500 to 3,750 cars—were used for carrying fuel for the railway service itself; transportation of military supplies took 25 per cent., from 1,750 to 1,850 cars; 10 per cent., from 700 to 750 cars, were used for "evacuation purposes," and only 15 to 20 per cent., 1,050 to 1,150 cars, for general transportation (*215*). It is worthy of note that of this absurdly inadequate service for the transportation of general supplies for the civilian population, 95 per cent. was used for the transportation of wood fuel for the cities and towns (*229*). Not less than 50 per cent. of all the locomotives in the country were out of order at the beginning of November, 1919, and it was stated that to increase the percentage of usable engines to the normal level would require, under the most favorable circumstances, a period of at least five years (*228*). Despite this deplorable condition there was still a great deal of bureaucratic red tape and waste. At the meeting of the directors of the Supreme Council of National Economy, in September, Markov, a member, argued in favor of eliminating the red tape and waste. He pointed out that wood was being transported to Moscow *from* the West and at the same time *to* the West from the North. The Main Fuel Committee had rejected a proposal to exchange the supplies of wood and thus save transportation (*214*). River transportation was in just as bad a condition, to judge from the fact that the freight tonnage on the river Volga was only 11 per cent. of the pre-war volume (*228*).

To prove the humanitarian character of the Bolshevist régime its apologists in this country and in England have cited the fact that the Soviet authorities offered a prize for the invention of a hand-cart which would permit a maximum load to be pushed or drawn with a minimum expenditure of human strength. Quite another light is thrown upon this action by the data concerning the breakdown of mechanical transportation and the rapid disappearance of horses from Moscow and Petrograd. The number of horses in September, 1919, was only 8 per cent. of the number in November, 1917—that is to say, under Bolshevism the number of horses had declined 92 per cent. (*207*). Of course the decline was not so enormous throughout the whole of Soviet Russia, but it was, nevertheless, so serious as to prohibit any hope of making up the loss of mechanical power by the use of horses. Accordingly, we find arrangements for the organization of a rope haulage system for the transportation of coal and food. In the Bazulk and Aktiubin districts provision was made for the use of 6,000 carts to transport wood fuel, and 10,000 carts for corn (*228*). Similar arrangements were under way in other districts. From locomotives and steamers to transport food and fuel there was a return to the most primitive of methods, such as were used to transport the Great Pyramid in Egypt, as shown by the hieroglyphs. For this purpose the peasants were mobilized (*228*). The bodies of masses of men were substituted for horses and mechanical traction. *Thus was reintroduced into*

Russian life in the twentieth century the form of labor most hated in the old days of serfdom.

The fuel situation was exceedingly bad. Not more than 55 per cent. of the fuel oil required could be obtained, the deficiency amounting to over four million poods of oil (*221*). Only 33 per cent. of the fuel wood required was obtained (*221*). The production of coal in the Moscow region was 45 per cent. lower than in 1917 (*224*). To overcome the shortage of fuel in Petrograd a large number of houses and boats were ordered to be wrecked for the sake of the wood (*227*). To save the country from perishing for lack of fuel, it was proposed that the modest fir cones which dropped from the trees be collected and saved. It was proposed to mobilize school-children, disabled soldiers, and old and sick persons to collect these fir cones (*202*).

In the nationalized cotton-factories there were 6,900,962 spindles and 169,226 looms, but only 300,000 spindles and 18,182 looms were actually working on September 1st (*207*). On January 1, 1919, there were 48,490 textile-workers in the Moscow District; six months later there were 33,200, a reduction of 15,290 — that is, 35 per cent. (*220*). In the same period the number of workers engaged in preparing raw cotton was reduced by 47.2 per cent. (*220*). In the metal works of Petrograd there were nominally employed a total of 12,141 workers, of which number only 7,585 — that is, 62.4 per cent. — were actually working. Of 7,500 workmen registered at the Putilov Works only 2,800, or 37.3 per cent., were actually working on August 15th. At the Nevsky Shipbuilding and Engineering Works not less than 56 per cent. of the employees were classed as absentees for the first half of July, 70 per cent. for the second half, and 84 per cent. for the first half of August. That is to say, of those nominally employed at this important works the actual daily attendance was 44 per cent.

during the first half of July, 30 per cent. for the second half, and only 16 per cent. for the first half of August (*209*). Since then the Nevsky Shipbuilding and Engineering Works have been entirely closed. It must be remembered that even during the Kerensky régime the metallurgical establishments in Petrograd District, which included some of the finest plants in the world, gave employment to more than 100,000 workmen as against 12,141 registered employees in September, 1919.

In the nationalized leather-factories of the Moscow District the output of large hides was 43 per cent. less than the output of 1918, which was itself far below the normal average (*227*). In the factories which were not nationalized the output of large hides was 60 per cent. less than in 1918. The apparent superiority of the nationalized factories indicated by these figures is explained by the fact that the Centrokaja, the central administration of the leather industry, gave preference to the nationalized factories in the supply of tanning acids, fuel, and other necessities of production (*227*). Just as in the metallurgical industry smaller undertakings had a better chance of surviving than larger ones (*211*), so in the leather industry[57] (*227*). In both cases the establishments not nationalized are far more successful than the nationalized. The output of small hides in nationalized undertakings fell by 60 per cent., and in the establishments not nationalized by 18 per cent. (*227*).

[57] *Yet we find the Bolshevik, Bazhenov, writing in the Economicheskaya Zhizn (No. 50), in March, 1919, the following nonsense: "The only salvation for Russia's industry lies in the nationalization of large enterprises and the closing of small and medium-sized ones." Bazhenov is evidently a doctrinaire Marxist of the school to whom one ounce of theory is of more worth than a ton of facts.*

The four nationalized match-factories in the northern region employed 2,000 persons. The output in October, 1919, was 50 per cent. of the normal output, the explanation being given that the falling off was due to the fact that large numbers of workmen had to be sent off into the villages to search for bread, while others had to be assigned to work in the fields and to loading wood for fuel (*225*). The manufacture of electric lamps was practically at a standstill. The Petrograd factories were closed down because of a shortage of skilled workmen and technical directors; the Moscow factories, because of the complete absence of gas (*210*). The sugar industry was almost completely liquidated (*207*).

In the report of the People's Commissariat for Finance we get a graphic and impressive picture of the manner in which this ill-working nationalization was, and is, bolstered up. For financing the nationalized industries appropriations were made as follows:

First six months of 1918   762,895,100   rubles

Second six months of 1918   5,141,073,179   "

First six months of 1919   15,439,115,828   "

The report calls attention to the fact that whereas it had been estimated that there would be paid into the treasury during the first six months of 1919 for goods issued for consumption 1,503,516,945 rubles, the sum actually received was 54,564,677 rubles — that is, only 3.5 per cent.

Some idea of the conditions prevailing can be gathered from the desperate attempts to produce substitutes for much-needed articles. The *ersatz* experiments and achievements of the Germans during the war may have had something to do with this. At all events, we find attempts made in the cotton-factories to use "cottonized" flax as a substitute for cotton

(*207*). These attempts did not afford any satisfactory or encouraging results. In consequence of the almost complete stoppage of the sugar industry we find the Soviet authorities resorting to attempts to produce sugar from sawdust (*207*). Even more pathetic is the manner in which attempts were made to supply salt. This necessary commodity had, for all practical purposes, completely disappeared from the market, though on October 3d, in Petrograd, it was quoted at 140 to 150 rubles per pound (*221*). As a result of this condition, in several districts old herring-barrels, saturated with salt, were cut up into small pieces and used in cooking instead of salt (*205*). A considerable market for these pieces of salted wood was found.

We may profitably close this summary of the economic situation in Soviet Russia in October and November, 1919, by quoting from the report of the Chief Administration of Engineering Works:

> If we had reason to fear last year for the working of our transport, the complaints of its inefficiency being well grounded, matters have become considerably worse during the period under report. Water transport is by no means in a better position, whilst of haulage transport there is no need to speak.... The consuming needs of the workmen have not been even remotely satisfied, either in the last year or in the current year, by the Commissariat of Food Supply, *the main source of food-supply of the workmen being speculation and free market*. But even the latter source of food-supply of the workmen in manufacturing districts is becoming more and more inaccessible. Besides the fact that prices have soared up to a much greater extent than the controlled rates of wages, we see the almost complete disappearance of food articles from working-center markets. *Of recent times, even pilgrimage to villages is of no avail. The villages will not part with food for money even at high prices.* What they demand is articles of which the workers are no less in need. Hence the workers' escape from the factories (*220*).

Unfortunately, a good many of the concerns enumerated [in the Tula District] do not work or work only with half the output, in spite of the fact that 20 of the shafts working yield considerable quantities of coal, 10 mines supply much raw material (15 milliard poods of minerals are estimated to be lying in this district), whilst there is also a large number of broken lathes and machinery which can, however, be repaired. Bread for the workers could also be found, if all efforts were strained (the district used to export corn in peace-time). All these possibilities are not carried into life, as there are no people who could by their intense will and sincere desire restore the iron discipline of labor. Our institutions are filled with "Sovburs" and "Speks," who only think of their own welfare and not of the welfare of the state and of making use of the revolutionary possibilities of the "toilers in revolt."

In the light of this terrible evidence we can readily believe what Zinoviev wrote in an article contributed to the *Severnaya Communa* in January of this year. In that article he said: "King Famine seems to be putting out his tongue at the proletariat of Petrograd and their families.... Of late I have been receiving, one after another, starving delegations from working men and women. They do not protest, nor do they make any demands; they merely point out, with silent reproach, the present intolerable state of affairs."

We are not dependent upon general statements such as Zinoviev's for our information concerning the state of affairs in Soviet Russia in January, 1920. We have an abundance of precise and authoritative data. In the first place, Gregor Alexinsky has published, in admirable translation, the text of the most important parts of the reports made to the Joint Congress of the Councils of National Economy, Trades-Unions and the Central Soviet Power. This congress opened in Moscow on January 25, 1920, and lasted for several days. Important reports were made to it by A. Rykov, president of the Supreme Council of National Economy; M. Tomsky, chairman of the Central Council of Trades-Unions; Kamenev, president of the Moscow Soviet; Lenin, Trotsky, and others. Alexinsky was fortunate enough to secure copies of the stenographic reports of the speeches made at this joint congress. In addition to this material the present writer has had placed at his disposal several issues of *Izvestia* containing elaborate reports of the congress. At the outset Rykov dealt with the effects of the World War and the Civil War upon the economic situation:

> During the past few years of Imperialistic (World) and Civil Wars the exhaustion of the countries of Europe, and in particular of Russia, has reached unheard-of proportions. This exhaustion has affected the whole territory of the Imperialistic war, but *the Civil war has been, as regards dissipation of the national wealth and waste of material and human resources, much more detrimental than the Imperialistic war*, for it spread across the greater part of the territory of Soviet Russia, involving not only the clashing of armies, but also devastation, fires, and destruction of objects of greatest value and of structures.

> The Civil War, having caused an unparalleled waste of the human and material resources of the Republic, has engendered an economic and productive crisis. In its main features this crisis is one of transportation, fuel, and human labor power.

Truly these are interesting admissions—here is "a very Daniel come to judgment." The civil war, we are told, has been "much more detrimental than the Imperialistic war," it has "caused an unparalleled waste of the human and material resources of the republic." Is it not pertinent to remind ourselves that for bringing on the civil war the Bolsheviki were solely responsible? There was no civil war in Russia until they began it. The whole of the democratic forces of Russia were unitedly working for the reconstruction of the nation upon a sound basis of free democracy. They began the civil war in the face of the most solemn warnings and despite the fact that every thoughtful person could foresee its inevitable disastrous results. By Rykov's confession the Bolsheviki are condemned for having brought upon Russia evils greater than those which the World War brought in its train. Of the transportation problem Rykov has this to say:

> Before the war, the percentage of disabled locomotives, even in the worst of times, never rose above 15 per cent. At the present time, however, we have 59.5 per cent. of disabled locomotives—*i.e.*, out of every 100 locomotives in Soviet Russia 60 are disabled, and only 40 capable of working. The repair of disabled locomotives also keeps on declining with extraordinary rapidity; before the war we used to repair up to 8 per cent.; this percentage, after the October revolution, sometimes dropped to 1 per cent.; now we have gone up, but only 1 per cent., and we are now repairing 2 per cent. of our locomotives. Under present conditions of railway transportation the repairs do not keep abreast of the deterioration of our locomotives, and *every month we have, in absolute figures, 200 locomotives less than the preceding month*. It is indispensable that we raise the repair of locomotives from 2 per cent. up to 10 per cent., in order to stop the decline and further disintegration of railway transportation, in order to maintain it at least on the level on which it stands at the present time. As for the broad masses of the population, the workers and peasants of Soviet Russia, *these figures simply mean that there is no possibility of utilizing any one of those grain-producing regions, nor those which have raw material and fuel, that have been added to Soviet Russia as a result of the victory of the Red Army.*

According to Trotsky, Rykov's figures, depressing enough in all conscience, did not disclose the full gravity of the situation. The real number of disabled locomotives was greater than the figures given, he said, for the reason that "we frequently call 'sound' half-disabled locomotives which threaten to drop out completely on the morrow." Rykov's statements do more than merely confirm those previously quoted from the *Economicheskaya Zhizn*: they show that from October to January there had been a steady increase of deterioration; that conditions had gone from bad to worse. The report proceeds to illustrate the seriousness of the situation by concrete examples of the actual conditions confronting the government:

> We have a metallurgical region in the Ural mountains; but we have had at our disposal until now but *one single special train a month to carry metals from the Urals to central Russia*. In order to transport 10 million poods[58] of metal by one single train per month several decades would be required, should we be able to utilize those scanty supplies of metal which are ready in the Urals.

_58_ *One pood equals thirty-six pounds.*

In order to deliver cotton from Turkestan to the textile factories in Moscow, we have to carry more than one-half million poods per month—up to 600,000 poods. But at this time we have only about two trains a month; that is, scores of years will be required for transporting under present conditions from Turkestan those 8 million poods of cotton which we could convert, but are unable to deliver to the factories.

The disorganized and demoralized state of the transportation system was only partly responsible for the shortage of raw materials, however. It was only one of several causes: "On account of the disorganized state of transportation we are unable to obtain cotton now, as the railroads are unable to carry it here. But even as regards those raw materials which are produced in the central parts of Soviet Russia, such as flax, wool, hemp, hides, even in these raw stuffs Soviet Russia is experiencing a severe crisis." Attention is called to the enormous decline in the production of flax, the acreage devoted to this crop being only 30 per cent. of that formerly devoted to it and the yield very much poorer. Rykov offers as an explanation of this condition the fact that, as the Soviet Government had not been able to deliver to the peasants in the flax-producing districts "any considerable quantity of foodstuffs," the peasants grew foodstuffs instead of flax. He adds, "Another reason why the peasants began to cultivate grains instead of flax was that the speculative prices of bread are higher than the fixed prices of flax at which the state is purchasing it." He pours the cold water of realism upon the silly talk of huge exports of flax from Russia as soon as trade with foreign nations is opened up, and says, "*But we shall not be able to export large quantities of flax abroad, and the catastrophic decline in flax production as compared with 1919 raises the question whether the flax industry shall not experience in 1920 a flax shortage similar to the one experienced by the textile industry in cotton.*"

Rykov calls attention to the decline in the production of hides for leather and of wool. During the first six months of 1919 the hides collected amounted to about one million pieces, but the total for the whole of 1920 was not expected to exceed 650,000 pieces. "The number of hides delivered to the government decreases with every succeeding month." There was also to be observed "a decline in the quantity of live stock, especially those kinds which furnish wool for our woolen mills." But perhaps the most impressive part of his report is that dealing with the fuel shortage. Though adjacent to large coal-fields, as well as to vast forests, Moscow in the winter of 1919-20 lacked fuel "even for heating the infirmaries and hospitals." For the winter of 1919-20 the Council of People's Commissaries had fixed the necessary quantity of wood for fuel to be produced at 12,000,000 to 14,000,000 cubic sagenes (one cubic sagene being equal to two cubic meters). But the Administrations which were charged with the work forwarded to the railroads and to the rivers less than 2,500,000 sagenes. It must be added that of these same 2,500,000 sagenes the Soviet Administrations were not able to transport to the cities and industrial centers more than a very small quantity, and "even the minimum program of supply of fuel for the factories of Moscow could not be carried out because of the lack of means of transport."

Bad as this is, the coal-supply is in a worse condition yet. "Things are going badly for the production of coal and petroleum" we are told. Upon their reoccupation of the Donetz Basin the Bolsheviki found coal on the surface, ready to be shipped, which was estimated at 100,000,000 poods. "But until the reconstruction of bridges and re-establishment of railroad communications in the Donetz territory these coal-supplies cannot be utilized." Of course the havoc wrought by war in the Donetz Basin must be taken into account and full allowance made for it. But what is the explanation of conditions in the coal-fields of the Moscow region, which from the very first has been under Bolshevist rule, and never included in the territory of war, civil or otherwise? Says Rykov:

> The fields of Moscow not only have not given what they ought to have given for the fuel-supply of Soviet Russia, but the production of coal remained in 1919 at the same level as in 1918 and it did not reach the figure of 30,000,000 poods; whereas, under the Czar at the time of the Imperialist War, the Czar's officials, with the aid of prisoners of war, knew how to increase the production of coal in the Moscow fields to the extent of 40,000,000 poods and even more.

This brings us face to face with the most vitally important fact of all, namely, the relatively low productivity of labor under nationalization of industry as practised in the sorry Utopia of the Bolsheviki. This is evident in every branch of industry. "When we speak, in the factories and mills, of the increase of the productivity of labor, the workmen always answer us," says Rykov, "with the same demand and always present us with the same complaint, *Give us bread and then we will work.*" But the demand for bread could not be met, despite the fact that there was a considerable store of wheat and other flour grains. Whereas at the beginning of 1919 there was a wheat reserve of 60,000,000 poods, on January 1, 1920, the reserve was 90,000,000 poods. Rykov admits that this is really not a great deal, and explains that in 1919 the government had only been able to collect about half the wheat demanded from the peasants, despite the vigorous policy pursued. He says that "in the grain elevators there are reserves which assure the supply for workmen and peasants for three months." This calculation is based upon the near-famine rationing, for Rykov is careful to add the words, "according to the official food rations."

So, the whole reserve, if fairly distributed, would last until April. But again the problem of transportation comes in: "If the workers and peasants have until now received no bread, and if up to this time a food shortage exists in the greater part of the starving consuming localities, the cause does not lie in inadequate preparations, but in the fact that we are unable to ship and distribute the grain already carted and stored in the granaries." As a result of these conditions the workers in the factories at mass-meetings "demand the breach of the economic front of Bolshevism," that is to say, the re-establishment of free and unrestricted commerce. In other words, their demand is for the abolition of the nationalization policy. It is from the *proletariat* that this cry comes, be it observed; and it is addressed to rulers who claim to represent the "dictatorship of the proletariat"! Could there be more conclusive evidence that Bolshevism in practice is the dictatorship of a few men *over* the proletariat?

What remedial measures does this important official, upon whom the organization of the work of economic reconstruction chiefly depends, propose to his colleagues? All that we get by way of specific and definite plans is summed up in the following paragraph:

> The Council of People's Commissaries has already decided to call upon individual workmen as well as groups of them to repair the rolling-stock, granting them the right to use the equipment which they shall have repaired with their own forces for the transportation of food to those factories and mills which repair the locomotives and cars. Recently this decision has been also extended to the fuel-supply. Each factory and each mill now has the opportunity to carry its own fuel, provided they repair with their own forces the disabled locomotives and cars they obtain from the commissariat of ways and communications.

Was ever such madness as this let loose upon a suffering people? Let those who have dilated upon the "statesmanship" and the "organizing genius" of these men contemplate the picture presented by the decision of the Council of People's Commissaries. Each factory to repair with its own forces the disabled locomotives and cars it needs to transport fuel and raw materials. Textile-workers, for instance, must repair locomotives and freight-cars or go without bread. Individual workmen and groups of workmen and individual factories are thus to be turned loose upon what remains of an organized transportation system. Not only must this result in the completion of the destruction of railway transportation, but it must inevitably cripple the factories. Take workers from unrelated industries, unused to the job, and set them to repairing locomotives and freight-cars; every man who has ever had anything to do with the actual organization and direction of working forces knows that such men, especially when the special equipment and tools are lacking, cannot perform, man for man, one-tenth as much as men used to the work and equipped with the proper tools and equipment. And then to tell these factory workers that they have "the right to use the equipment which they shall have repaired" means, if it means anything at all, that from the factories are to be diverted further forces to operate railway trains and collect food, fuel, and raw materials. What that means we have already noted in the case of the decline of production in the match-factories, "owing to the wholesale dispersing of workmen in the search for bread, to field work and unloading of wood."[59] Of all the lunacy that has come out of Bolshevist Russia, even, this is perhaps the worst.

[59] Economicheskaya Zhizn, *No. 225.*

Rykov tells us that at the end of 1919 4,000 industrial establishments had been nationalized. "That means," he says, "that nearly the whole industry has been transferred to the state, to the Soviet organizations, and that the industry of private owners, of manufacturers, has been done away with, for the old statistics estimated the total number of industrial establishments, including peasants' homework places, to be around 10,000. The peasants' industry is not subject to nationalization, and 4,000 nationalized industrial establishments include not only the largest, but also the greater part of the middle-sized, industrial enterprises of Soviet Russia."

What is the state of these nationalized factories, and are the results obtained satisfactory? Again Rykov's report gives the answer in very clear terms: "Of these 4,000 establishments only 2,000 are working at present. All the rest are closed and idle. The number of workers, by a rough estimate, is about 1,000,000. Thus you can see that both in point of number of the working-men employed as well as in point of numbers of still working establishments, the manufacturing industry is also in the throes of a crisis." The explanation offered by Trotsky, that the industrial failure was due to the destruction of technical equipment, Rykov sweeps aside. "*The Soviet state, the Workers' and Peasants' Power, could not utilize even those lathes, machines, and factory equipment which were still at its disposal.* And a considerable part of manufacturing enterprises was shut down, while part is still working only in a few departments and workshops." On every hand it is evident that shortage of raw materials and of skilled labor are the really important causes, not lack of machinery. Of 1,191 metallurgical plants 614 had been nationalized. The government had undertaken to provide these with about 30 per cent. of the metals required, but had been able to supply only 15 per cent., "less than one-quarter of the need that must be satisfied in order to sustain a minimum of our industrial life."

Take the textile industry as another example: Russia was the third country in Europe in textile manufacture, England and Germany alone leading her, the latter by no large margin. No lack of machinery accounts for the failure here, for of the available looms only 11 per cent. were used in 1919, and of the spindles only 7 per cent. The decline of production in 1919 was enormous, so that at the end of that year it was only 10 per cent. of the normal production. We are told that: "During the period of January-March, 1919, 100,000 to 200,000 poods of textile fabrics were produced per month; during the period of September-November only 25,000 to 68,000 poods were produced per month. Therefore we have to face an almost complete stoppage of all textile production in central Russia, which dominated all the other textile regions in Russia."

Rykov seems to have no illusions left concerning the prospects for the immediate future. He realizes that Bolshevism has nothing to offer the working-people of Russia in the way of immediate improvement. He confesses "that in regard to industry the supplying of the population with footwear, clothing, metals, and so on, Soviet Russia is living only one-third of the life which Russia lived in times of peace." As to the future he has only this to say: "Such a condition might last one or two years, during which we might live on former reserves, thanks to that which remained from the preceding period of Russian history. But these reserves are being exhausted and from one day to another, from one hour to another, we are approaching a complete crisis in these branches of industry."

But what of the human element in industry, the workers themselves, that class whose interests and aspirations Bolshevism is supposed to represent? We have already noted Rykov's admission that the workers and peasants lack bread and his explanation. Upon this same matter, Tomsky, president of the Central Council of the Trades-Unions, says:

> So far as food-supplies are concerned it is evident that under the present condition of transport we will not be able to accumulate reserves of provisions sufficiently great so that each workman may have a sufficient ration. We must renounce the principle of equality in rationing and reduce the latter to two or three categories of workman's ration. We must recognize that making our first steps upon the road of ameliorating the situation of industrial workers, we must introduce a system of so-called "supply of essential occupation." "Above all, we will have to supply those groups of workmen who are especially necessary to production."

Two and a quarter years after the forcible seizure of power by the Bolsheviki one of their "statesmen" prates to his colleagues about making the "first steps" toward "ameliorating the situation of industrial workers." The leading speakers who addressed the congress discussed at length the bearing of these conditions upon what Trotsky called "the dissipation of the working-class"—that is, the disappearance of the proletariat from the industrial centers. Rykov explained that:

> The crisis of skilled labor has a special importance for our industry, because even in those industrial branches which work for our army we make vain efforts because of the lack of qualified workmen. Sometimes for weeks and even entire months we could not find the necessary number of workmen skilled and knowing the trade of which the factories and mills had such need, in order to give to the Red Army rifles, machine-guns, and cannon and thereby save Moscow. We experienced enormous difficulties to find even as few as twenty or thirty workmen. We hunted for them everywhere, at the employment bureaus, among trades-unions, in the regiments, and in the villages. The wastage of the most precious element which production calls for—that is to say, skilled labor—is one of the most dangerous phenomena of our present economic life. This wastage has reached to-day colossal and unheard-of dimensions and *there are industrial enterprises which we cannot*

> operate even if we had fuel and raw materials, because competent skilled labor is lacking.

That Rykov is not an alarmist, that his statements are not exaggerated, we may be quite assured. Even Trotsky protested that conditions were worse than Rykov had described them, and not better. While Rykov claimed that there were 1,000,000 workmen engaged in the nationalized factories, Trotsky said that in reality there were not more than 850,000. But how is this serious decrease in the number of workmen to be accounted for? An insatiable hunger, idle factories, unused raw materials, a government eagerly seeking workmen, and yet the workmen are not forthcoming. Trotsky offers this explanation: "Hunger, bad living conditions, and cold drive the Russian workmen from industrial centers to the rural districts, and not only to those districts, but also *into the ranks of profiteers and parasites.*" Kamenev agrees with Trotsky and says that "profiteering is the enemy whom the Moscow proletariat has felt already for some time to be present, but who has succeeded in growing up to full height and is now *eating up the entire fabric of the new socialistic economic structure.*" Tomsky answers the question in a very similar manner. He says:

> If in capitalistic society a shortage of labor power marks the most intensive activity of industry, in our own case this has been caused by conditions which are unique and unprecedented in capitalist economic experience. Only part of our industry is at work, and yet there is a shortage of labor power felt in the cities and industrial centers. We observe an exodus of laborers from industrial centers, caused by poor living conditions. Those hundreds of skilled laborers whom we are at present lacking for the most elementary and minimal requirements of industry have gone partly to the country, to labor communes, Soviet farms, producers' associations, while another part, a very considerable one, serves in the army. *But the proletariat also leaks away to join the ranks of petty profiteers and barter-traders, we are ashamed and sorry*

to confess. This fact is being observed and there is no use concealing or denying it. There is also another cause which hurts the industrial life and hinders a systematic organization of work. This is the migration of the workers from place to place in search of better living conditions. All of this, again, is the result of the one fundamental cause—the very critical food situation in the cities and, in general, the hard conditions of life for the industrial proletariat.

Finally, some attention must be given to the speech of Lenin, reported in *Izvestia*, January 29, 1920. Discussing the question whether industry should be administered by a "collegium" or by a single individual clothed with absolute authority, Lenin defended the latter as the only practical method, illustrating his case by reference to the Red Army. The Soviet organization in the army was well enough at first, as a start, but the system of administration has now become "administration by a single individual as the only proper method of work." He explains this point in the following words:

Administration by "colleges" as the basic type of the organization of the Soviet administration presents in itself something fundamental and necessary for the first stage when it is necessary to build anew. But with the establishing of more stable forms, a transition to practical work is bound up with administration by a single individual, a system which, most of all, assures the best use of human powers and a real and not verbal control of work.

Thus the master pronounces the doom of industrial Sovietism. No cry of, "All power to the Soviets!" comes from his lips now, but only a demand that the individual must be made all-powerful. Lenin the ruler pours scorn upon the vision of Lenin the leader of revolt. His ideal now is that of every industrial despot everywhere. He has no pity for the toiler, but tells his followers that they must "replace the machines which are lacking and those which are being destroyed by the strength of the living laborer." That means rope haulage instead of railway transportation; it means that, instead of being masters of great machines, the Russian toilers must replace the machines.

What a picture of "the dictatorship of the proletariat" these utterances of the leading exponents of Bolshevism make! Proletarians starving in a land of infinite abundance; forced by hunger, cold, and oppression to leave homes and jobs and go back to village life, or, much worse, to become either vagabonds or petty profiteers trafficking in the misery of their fellows. Their tragic condition, worse than anything they had to endure under czarism, suggests the lines:

> The hungry sheep look up and are not fed,
>
> But, swollen with wind and the rank mist they draw,
>
> Rot inwardly, and foul contagion spread.

We do not wonder at Krassin's confession, published early this year in the *Economicheskaya Zhizn*, urging "a friendly liquidation of Bolshevism in Russia" and declaring that: "The Communistic régime cannot restore the life of the country, and the fall of Bolshevism is inevitable. The people are beginning to recognize that the Bolshevist experiment has plunged them into a sea of blood and torment and aroused no more than a feeling of fatigue and disappointment."

Here, then, is a picture of nationalized industry under Bolshevism, drawn by no unfriendly or malicious critic, but by its own stout upholders, its ablest champions. It is a self-portrait, an autobiographical sketch. In it we can see Bolshevism as it is, a repellent and terrifying thing of malefic might and purpose. Possessed of every vice and every weakness of capitalism, with none of its virtues, Bolshevism is abhorrent to all who love liberty and hold faith in mankind. Promising plenty, it gives only famine; promising freedom, it gives only fetters; promising love, it gives only hate; promising order, it gives only chaos; promising righteous and just government, it gives only corrupt despotism; promising fraternity, it gives only fratricide.

Yet, despite the overwhelming mass of evidence, there will still be defenders and apologists of this monstrous perversion of the democratic Socialist ideal. We shall be told that the Bolsheviki have had to contend against insurmountable obstacles; that when they entered into power they found the industrial system already greatly demoralized; that they have been compelled to devote themselves to war instead of to reconstruction; that they have been isolated and deprived of those things with which other nations hitherto supplied Russia.

All these things are true, but in what way do they excuse or palliate the crimes of the Bolsheviki? When they overthrew the Provisional Government and by brute force usurped its place they knew that the industrial life of the nation, including the transportation system, had been gravely injured. They knew, moreover, that it was recovering and that its complete restoration could only be brought about by the united effort of all the freedom-loving elements in the land. They knew, or ought to have known, just as every sane person in and out of Russia knew, that if they deserted the Allies in the time of their gravest peril, and, by making peace with Germany, aided her upon the western front, the Allies would not—could not and dare not—continue to maintain their friendly and cooperative relations with Russia. They knew, or ought to have known, as every sane person in and out of Russia did, that if they tried to impose their rule upon the nation by force of arms, they would be resisted and there would be civil war. All these things Lenin and his followers had pointed out to them by clear-visioned Socialists. All of them are written large upon history's pages.

No defense of Bolshevism has yet been made which is not itself an accusation.

XI

FREEDOM OF PRESS AND ASSEMBLY

I

n

1903, after the split of the Russian Social Democratic Party into two factions—the Bolsheviki and the Mensheviki—the late Rosa Luxemburg, in an article which she contributed to *Iskra* (*Spark*), gave a keen analysis of Lenin. She charged that he was an autocrat at heart, that he despised the workers and their rights. In burning words she protested that Lenin wanted to rule Russia with an iron fist, to replace one czarism by another. Now, Rosa Luxemburg was no "mere bourgeois reformer," no "sentimental opportunist"; even at that time she was known in the international Socialist movement as "Red Rosa," a revolutionist among revolutionists, one of the reddest of them all. Hating despotism and autocracy as such, and not merely the particular manifestation of it in the Romanov régime, she saw quite clearly, and protested against, the contempt for democracy and all its ways which, even at that time, she recognized as underlying Lenin's whole conception of the revolutionary struggle.

A very similar estimate of Lenin was made ten years later, in 1913, by one of his associates, P. Rappaport. When we remember that it was written a year before the World War began, and five years before the outbreak of the Russian Revolution in March, 1917, this estimate of Lenin, written by Rappaport in 1913, is remarkable: "No party in the world could live under the régime of the Czar Social Democrat, who calls himself a liberal Marxist, and who is only a political adventurer on a grand scale."

These estimates of Lenin by fellow-Socialists who knew him well, and who were thoroughly familiar with his thought, possess no small amount of interest to-day. Of course, we are concerned with the individual and with the motivation of his thought and actions only in so far as the individual asserts an influence upon contemporary developments, either directly, by deeds of his own, or indirectly through others. There is much significance in the fact that "Bolshevism" and "Leninism" are already in use as synonyms, indicating that a movement which has spread with great rapidity over a large part of the world is currently regarded as exemplifying the thought and the purpose of the man, Ulianov, whom posterity, like his contemporaries, will know best by his pseudonym. Nicolai Lenin's contempt for democratic ways, and his admiration for autocratic and despotic ways, are thus of historical importance.

There was much that was infamous in the régime of the last of the Romanovs, Nicholas II, but by comparison with that of his successor, "Nicholas III," it was a régime of benignity, benevolence, and freedom. No government that has been set up in modern times, among civilized peoples, has been so thoroughly tyrannical, so intolerant and hostile to essential freedom, as the government which the Bolsheviki established in Russia by usurpation of power and have maintained thus far by a relentless and conscienceless use of every instrumentality of oppression and suppression known to the hated Romanovs. Without mandate of authority from the people, or even any considerable part of the people, this brutal power dissolved the Constituent Assembly and annulled all its acts; chose its own agents and conferred upon them the title of representatives of the people; disbanded the courts of law and substituted therefor arbitrary tribunals, clothed with unlimited power; without semblance of lawful trial, sentenced men and women to death, many of them not even accused of any crime whatsoever; seized innocent men, women, and children as hostages for the conduct of others; shot and otherwise executed innocent persons, including women and children, for crimes and offenses of others, of which they admittedly knew nothing; deprived citizens of freedom, and imprisoned them in vile dungeons, for no crime save written or spoken appeal in defense of lawful rights; arbitrarily suppressed the existing freedom of assemblage and of publication; based civic rights upon the acceptance of particular beliefs; by arbitrary decree levied unjust, unequal, and discriminatory taxes; filled the land with hireling secret spies and informers; imposed a constitution and laws upon the people without their consent, binding upon the people, but not upon itself; placed the public revenues at the disposal of a political faction representing only a minority of the people; and, finally, by a decree restored involuntary servitude.

This formidable indictment is no more than a mere outline sketch of the despotism under which Russia has suffered since November, 1917. There is not a clause in the indictment which is not fully sustained by the evidence given in these pages. Lenin is fond of quoting a saying of Marx that, "The domination of the proletariat can most easily be accomplished in a war-weary country—*i.e.*, in a worn-out, will-less, and weakened land." He and his associates found Russia war weary, worn out, and weakened indeed, but not "will-less." On the contrary, the great giant, staggering from the weakness and weariness arising from years of terrible struggle, urged by a mighty will to make secure the newly conquered freedom, was already turning again to labor, to restore industry and build a prosperous nation. By resorting to the methods and instrumentalities which tyrants in all ages have used to crush the peoples rightly struggling to be free, the Bolsheviki have imposed upon Russia a tyranny greater than the old. That they have done this in the name of liberty in no wise mitigates their crime, but, on the contrary, adds to it. The classic words of the English seventeenth-century pamphleteer come to mind: "Almost all tyrants have been first captains and generals for the people, under pretense of vindicating or defending their liberties.... Tyrants accomplish their ends much more by fraud than force ... with cunning, plausible pretenses to impose upon men's understandings, and in the end they master those that had so little wit as to rely upon their faith and integrity."

The greatest liberty of all, that liberty upon which all other liberties must rest, and without which men are slaves, no matter by what high-sounding names they may be designated, is the liberty of discussion. Perhaps no people in the world have realized this to the same extent as the great Anglo-Saxon peoples, or have been so solicitous in maintaining it. Only the French have approached us in this respect. The immortal words of a still greater seventeenth-century pamphleteer constitute a part of the moral and political heritage of our race. Who does not thrill at Milton's words, "Give me the liberty to know, to utter, and to argue freely according to conscience, above all liberties." That fine declaration was the inspiration of Patrick Henry's sublime demand, "Give me liberty or give me death." Upon that rock, and that rock alone, was built "government of the people, by the people, and for the people."

The manner in which the Bolsheviki have stifled protest, discussion, and appeal through the suppression of the opposition newspapers constitutes one of the worst chapters in their infamous history. Yet, strangely enough, of such perversity is the human mind capable, they have found their chief defenders, outside of Russia, among individuals and groups devoted to the upholding of popular liberties. Let us take, for example, the case of Mr. William Hard and his laborious and ingenious—though disingenuous—articles in defense of the Bolsheviki, published in the *New Republic* and elsewhere:

In an earlier volume,[60] written at the close of 1918, and published in March, 1919, the present writer said of the Bolsheviki, "When they came into power they suppressed all non-Bolshevist papers in a manner differing not at all from that of the Czar's régime, forcing the other Socialist partizan groups to resort to pre-Revolution underground methods." The statement that the "other Socialist partizan groups" were forced to "resort to pre-Revolution underground methods," made in the connection it was, conveyed to every person reading that paragraph who knew anything at all of the history of the Russian revolutionary struggle the information that the statement that the Bolsheviki "suppressed all non-Bolshevist papers" was not to be interpreted as meaning the suppression was absolute. Even if it had not been pointed out elsewhere—as it was, upon the authority of a famous Socialist-Revolutionist—that in some instances suppressed papers managed to appear in spite of the authorities, simply changing their names, *precisely as they had done under czarism,* the statement quoted above would have been justified as a substantially correct statement of the facts, particularly in view of the boast of responsible Bolsheviki themselves that they had suppressed the entire opposition press and that only the Bolshevist press remained. Certainly when one speaks or writes of the suppression of newspapers under czarism one does not deny that the revolutionists from time to time found ways and means of circumventing the authorities, and that it was more or less common for such suppressed newspapers to reappear under new names. The whole point of the paragraph in question was that the characteristic conditions of czarism had been restored.

<u>60</u> *Bolshevism, by John Spargo, New York, 1919.*

With a mental agility more admirable than either his controversial manners or his political morals, by a distortion of facts worthy of his mentors, but not of himself or of his reputation, Mr. Hard makes it appear that the Bolsheviki only suppressed the opposition newspapers after the middle of 1918, when, as he alleges, the opposition to the Bolsheviki assumed the character of "open acute civil war." Mr. Hard admits that prior to this time there were suppressions and that "if any paper tried not merely to criticize the Lenin administration, but to utterly destroy the Bolshevik Soviet idea of the state, its editor was likely to find his publishing life quite frequently interrupted."

Now the facts in the case are as different from Mr. Hard's presentation as a normal mind can well conceive. Mr. David N. Shub, a competent authority, made an exhaustive reply to Mr. Hard's article, a reply that was an exposure, in the columns of *Struggling Russia*. Before reproducing Mr. Shub's reply it may be well to set forth a few facts of record which are of fundamental importance: *On the very day on which the Bolsheviki published the decree on the establishment of the Soviet power, November 10, 1917, they published also a decree directed against the freedom of the press.* The decree proper was accompanied by a characteristic explanatory statement. This statement recited that it had been necessary for the Temporary Revolutionary Committee to "adopt a series of measures against the counter-revolutionary press of various shades"; that protests had been made on all sides against this as a violation of the program which provided for the freedom of the press; repressive measures were temporary and precautionary, and that they would cease and complete freedom be given to the press, in accordance with the widest and most progressive law, "as soon as the new régime takes firm root." The decree proper read:

I. Only those organs of the press will be suspended

(a) Which appeal for open resistance to the government of workmen and peasants.

(b) Which foment disorders by slanderously falsifying facts.

(c) Which incite to criminal acts—*i.e.*, acts within the jurisdiction of the police courts.

II. Provisional or definitive suspension can be executed only by order of the Council of People's Commissaries.

III. These regulations are only of a provisional nature and shall be abrogated by a special ukase when life has returned to normal conditions.

If Mr. Hard or any of the numerous journalistic apologists of the Bolsheviki in this country will look the matter up he or they will find that this decree copied the forms usually used by the Czar's government. It is noteworthy that the restoration of freedom of the press was already made dependent upon that czaristic instrument, the *ukase*. On the 16th of November the Central Executive Committee of the Soviets adopted a resolution which read:

> The closure of the bourgeois papers was caused not only by the purely fighting requirements in the period of the rising and the suppression of counter-revolutionary attempts, but likewise as a necessary temporary measure for the establishment of a new régime in the sphere of the press, under which the capital proprietors of printing-works and paper would not be able to become autocratic beguilers of public opinion.... The re-establishment of the so-called freedom of the press, *viz.*, the simple return of printing-offices and paper to capitalists, poisoners of the people's conscience, would be an unpermissible surrender to the will of capital—*i.e.*, a counter-revolutionary measure.

At the meeting when this resolution was adopted, and speaking in its support, Trotsky made a speech remarkable for its cynical dishonesty and its sinister menace. He said, according to the report in *Pravda* two days later:

> *Those measures which are employed to frighten individuals must be applied to the press also....* All the resources of the press must be handed over to the Soviet Power. You say that formerly we demanded freedom of the press for the *Pravda*? But then we were in a position to demand a minimum program; now we insist on the maximum program. *When the power was in the hands of the bourgeoisie we demanded juridical freedom of the press.* When the power is held by the workmen and peasants—we must create conditions for the freedom of the press.

Quite obviously, as shown by their own official reports, Mr. Hard and gentlemen of the *New Republic*, Mr. Oswald Villard and gentlemen of *The Nation*, and you, too, Mr. Norman Thomas, who find Mr. Hard's disingenuous pleading so convincing,[61] the hostility of the Bolsheviki to freedom of the press was manifest from the very beginning of their rule. On the night of November 30th ten important newspapers were suppressed and their offices closed, among them being six Socialist newspapers. Their offense lay in the fact that they urged their readers to stand by the Constituent Assembly. Not only were the papers suppressed and their offices closed, but the best equipped of them all was "requisitioned" for the use of a Bolshevist paper, the *Soldatskaia Pravda*. The names of the newspapers were: *Nasha Rech, Sovremennoie Delo, Utro, Rabochaia Gazeta, Volia Naroda, Trudovoe Slovo, Edinstvo,* and *Rabotcheie Delo*. The suppression of the *Rabochaia Gazeta*, official organ of the Central Committee of the Social Democratic Party, caused a vigorous protest and the Central Committee of the party decided "to bring to the knowledge of all the members of the party that the central organ of the party, the *Rabochaia Gazeta,* is closed by the Military Revolutionary Committee. While branding this as an arbitrary act in defiance of the Russian and international proletariat, committed by so-called Socialists on a Social-Democrat paper and the Labor Party, whose organ it is, the Central Committee has decided to call upon the party to organize a movement of protest against this act in order to open the eyes of the labor masses to the character of the régime which governs the country."

[61] See The World Tomorrow, February, 1920, p. 61.

In consequence of the tremendous volume of protest and through the general adoption of the devices familiar to the revolutionaries under czarism—using new names, changing printing-offices, and the like—most of the papers reappeared for a brief while in one form or another. But in February, 1918, all the anti-Bolshevist papers were again suppressed, save one, the principal organ of the Cadets, formerly the *Rech*, but later appearing as the *Nash Viek*. This paper was suffered to appear for reasons which have never been satisfactorily explained. Mr. Shub's article contains a detailed, though by no means full, account of the further suppressions:

> A few days after the Bolshevist coup, in November, 1917, the Bolsheviki closed down, among others, the organ of the Mensheviki-Internationalists, *Rabochaya Gazeta*; the central organ of the Party of Socialists-Revolutionists, *Dyelo Naroda*; the *Volia Naroda*, published by Catherine Breshkovsky; the *Yedinstvo*, published by George Plechanov; the *Russkaya Volia*, published by Leonid Andreiev; the *Narodnoye Slovo*, the organ of the People's Socialists, and the *Dien*, published by the well-known Social-Democrat, Alexander Potresov.
>
> The printing-presses which belonged to Andreiev were confiscated and his paper, *Russkaya Volia, never again appeared under any other name*. The editor-in-chief of the *Volia Naroda*—the newspaper published by Catherine Breshkovsky—A. Agunov, was incarcerated by the Bolsheviki in the Fortress of Saints Peter and Paul and this paper was *never able to appear again, even under a changed name*. The offices of the *Dyelo Naroda* were for a time guarded by groups of armed soldiers in sympathy with the Party of Socialists-Revolutionists, and notwithstanding all orders by the Commissary of the Press to cease publication, the Socialists-Revolutionists managed from time to time to issue their newspapers, in irregular form, under one name or another. But the copies of the paper would be confiscated from the newsdealers immediately upon their appearance, and the newsboys who risked the selling of it were subjected to unbelievable persecutions. There were even cases when the sellers of these "seditious" Socialist papers were shot by the Bolsheviki. These facts were recorded by every newspaper which appeared from time to time in those days in Petrograd and Moscow.
>
> The *Dien* (*Day*) did not appear at all for some time after its suppression. Later there appeared in its place the *Polnotch* (*Midnight*), which was immediately suppressed for publishing an exposé of the Bolshevist Commissary, Lieutenant Schneuer, an ex-provocateur of the Tzar's government and a

German spy, the same Schneuer who conducted negotiations with the German command for an armistice, and who later, together with Krylenko, led the orgy called "the capture of the General Headquarters," in the course of which General Dukhonine, the Commander-in-Chief of the Russian Army, was brutally murdered and mutilated for his refusal to conclude an armistice with the Germans.

A few days after the *Polnotch* was closed another paper appeared in its place, called *Notch* (*Night*), but this one was just as rapidly suppressed. Again *V Glookhooyou Notch* (*In the Thick of Night*) appeared for a brief period, and still later *V Temnooyou Notch* (*In the Dark of Night*). The paper was thus appearing once a week, and sometimes once every other week, under different names. I have all these papers in my possession, and their contents and fate would readily convince the reader how "tolerantly" the Bolsheviki, in the early days of their "rule," treated the adverse opinions of even such leading Socialists as Alexander Potresov, one of the founders of the Russian Social-Democratic Labor Party, who, for decades, was one of the editors of the central organs of the party.

The publication of G. V. Plechanov's—Russia's greatest Socialist writer and leader—the *Yedinstvo*, after it was suppressed, appeared in the end of December, 1917, under the name *Nashe Yedinstvo*, but was closed down in January, 1918, and the Bolsheviki *confiscated its funds kept in a bank and ordered the confiscation of all moneys coming in by mail to its office*. This information was even cabled to New York by the Petrograd correspondent of the New York Jewish pro-Bolshevist newspaper, the *Daily Forward*. The *Nashe Yedinstvo*, at the head of which, besides George Plechanov, there were such widely known Russian revolutionists and Socialists as Leo Deutsch, Vera Zasulitch, Dr. N. Vassilyev, L. Axelrod-Orthodox, and Gregory Alexinsky, was thus permanently destroyed by the Bolsheviki in January, or early in February, 1918, and never appeared again under any other name.

The newspapers *Dien*, *Dyelo Naroda*, the Menshevist *Novy Looch*, and a few others did make an attempt to appear later, but on the eve of the conclusion of the Brest-Litovsk Treaty *all* oppositional Socialist newspapers were again suppressed wholesale. In the underground Socialist bulletins, which were at that time being published by the Socialists-Revolutionists and Social

Democrats, it was stated that this move was carried out by order of the German General Staff. The prominent Social Democrat and Internationalist, L. Martov, later, at an open meeting of the Soviet, flung this accusation in the face of Lenin, *who never replied to it by either word or pen.*

When the Germans, after the Brest-Litovsk Treaty, still continued their offensive movement, occupying one Russian city after another, and the Bolsheviki had reasons to believe that they were nearing their end, they somewhat relaxed their régime and some newspapers obtained the possibility of appearing again, *on condition that all such newspapers, under threat of fine and confiscation, were to print on their first pages all the Bolshevist decrees and all distorted information and explanations by the Bolshevist commissaries.* Aside from that, the press was subject to huge fines for every bit of news that did not please the eye of the Bolshevist censor. Thus, for instance, *Novaya Zhizn*, Gorky's organ, was fined 35,000 rubles for a certain piece of "unfavorable" news which it printed.

However, early in May, 1918—*i.e., before the beginning of the so-called "intervention" by the Allies*—even this measure of "freedom" of the press appeared too frivolous for the Bolshevist commissaries, and they permanently closed down *Dyelo Naroda*, *Dien*, and *Novy Looch*, and, somewhat later, all the remaining opposition papers, including Gorky's *Novaya Zhizn*, and since that time none of them have reappeared. In spite of endless attempts, Maxim Gorky did not succeed in obtaining permission to establish his paper even six months afterward, when he had officially made peace with the Soviet régime. The Bolsheviki are afraid of the free speech of even their official "friends," and that is the true reason why there is not in Soviet Russia to-day a single independent organ of the press.[62]

62 April, 1919.

With one kick of the Red Army boot was thus destroyed Russia's greatest treasure, her independent press. The oldest and greatest founts of Russian culture and social justice, such as the monthly magazine, *Russkoye Bogatstvo,* and the daily *Russkya Viedomosti,* which even the Czar's government never dared to suppress permanently, were brutally strangled. These organs have raised entire generations of Russian radicals and Socialists and had among their contributors and editors the greatest savants, publicists, and journalists of Russia, such as Nicholas Chernishevsky, Glieb Uspensky, Nicholas Mikhailovsky, N. Zlatovratsky, Ilya Metchnikov, Professor N. Kareiev, Vladimir Korolenko, Peter Kropotkin, and numerous others.

Let us look at the subject from a slightly different angle: one of the first things they did was to declare the "nationalization" of the printing-establishments of certain newspapers, which they immediately turned over to their own press. In this manner the printing-establishment of the *Novoye Vremia* was seized and used for the publication of *Izvestia* and *Pravda,* the latter being an organ of the party and not of the government. Here was a new form of political nepotism which a Tweed might well envy and only a Nash could portray. We are at the beginning of the nepotism, however. On November 20, 1917, the advertising monopoly was decreed, and on December 10th following it went into effect. This measure forbade the printing of advertisements in any except the official journals, thereby cutting off the revenue from advertising, upon which newspapers depend, from all except official journals. This measure alone had the effect of limiting the possibility of publication practically to the official papers and those which were heavily subsidized. Moreover, the Bolsheviki used the public revenues to subsidize their own newspapers. They raised the postal rates for sending newspapers by mail to a prohibitive height, and then carried the newspapers of their own partizans free of charge at the public expense. They "nationalized" the sale of newspapers, which made it unlawful for unauthorized persons to obtain and offer for sale any save the official Bolshevist newspapers and those newspapers published by its partizans which supported the government. The decree forbade taking subscriptions for the "unauthorized" papers at the post-offices, in accordance with custom, forbade their circulation through the mails, and imposed a special tax upon such as were permitted to appear. Article III of this wonderful decree reads:

> Subscriptions to the bourgeois and pseudo-Socialist newspapers are suppressed and will not hereafter be accepted at the post-office. Issues of these journals that may be mailed will not be delivered at their destination.
>
> Newspapers of the bourgeoisie will be subject to a tax which may be as great as three rubles for each number. Pseudo-Socialist journals such as the *V period* and the *Troud Vlast Naroda*[63] will be subject to the same tax.

[63] *These were organs of the Mensheviki and the Social Revolutionists.*

Is it any wonder that by the latter part of May, 1918, the anti-Bolshevist press had been almost entirely exterminated except for the fitful and irregular appearance of papers published surreptitiously, and the few others whose appearance was due to the venality of some Bolshevist officials? Was there ever, in the history of any nation, since Gutenberg's invention of movable type made newspapers possible, such organized political nepotism? Was there ever, since men organized governments, anything more subversive of freedom and political morality? Yet there is worse to come; as time went on, new devices suggested themselves to these perverters of democracy and corrupters of government. On July 27, 1918, *Izvestia* published the information that the press department would grant permits for periodical publications, *provided they accepted the Soviet platform*. In carrying out this arrangement, so essentially despotic, the press department reserved to itself the right to determine *whether or not the population was in need of the proposed publication*, whether it was advisable to permit the use of any of the available paper-supply for the purpose, and so forth and so on. Under this arrangement permission was given to publish a paper called the *Mir*. Ostensibly a pacifist paper, the *Mir* was very cordially welcomed by the Bolshevist papers to the confraternity of privileged journals. That the *Mir* was subsidized by the German Government for the propaganda of international pacificism (this was in the summer of 1918) seems to have been established.[64] The closing chapter of the history of this paper is told in the following extract from *Izvestia*, October 17, 1918, which is more interesting for its disclosures of Bolshevist mentality than anything else:

[64] See Dumas, op. cit., p. 80.

> The suppression of the paper *Mir* (*Peace*).—In accordance with the decision published in the *Izvestia* on the 27th July, No. 159, the Press Department granted permits to issue *to periodical publications which accepted the Soviet platform*. When granting permission the Press Department took into consideration the available supplies of paper, *whether the population was in need of the proposed periodical publication*, and also the necessity of providing employment for printers and pressmen. Thus permission was granted to issue the paper *Mir*, especially in view of the publisher's declaration that the paper was intended to propagate pacifist ideas. At the present moment *the requirements of the population of the Federal Socialist Republic for means of daily information are adequately met by the Soviet publications*; employment for those engaged in journalistic work is secured in the Soviet papers; a paper crisis is approaching. The Press Department, therefore, considers it impossible to permit the further publication of the *Mir* and has decided to *suppress this paper forever*.

Another device which the Bolsheviki resorted to was the compulsion of people to purchase the official newspapers, whether they wanted them or not. On July 20, 1918, there was published "Obligatory Regulation No. 27," which provided for the compulsory purchase by all householders of the *Severnaya Communa*. This unique regulation read as follows:

Obligatory Regulation No. 27

Every house committee in the city of Petrograd and other towns included in the Union of Communes of the Northern Region is under obligation to subscribe to, paying for same, one copy of the newspaper, the *Severnaya Communa*, the official organ of the Soviets of the Northern Region.

The newspaper should be given to every resident in the house on the first demand.

Chairman of the Union of the Communes of the Northern region, Gr. Zinoviev.

Commissary of printing, N. Kuzmin.

The *Severnaya Communa*, on November 10, 1918, published the following with reference to this beautiful scheme:

To the Notice of the House Committees of the Poor:

On 20th July of the present year there was published obligatory regulation No. 27, to the following effect:

"Every house committee in the city of Petrograd and other towns included in the Union of Communes of the Northern Region is under obligation to subscribe to, paying for same, one copy of the newspaper, the *Severnaya Communa*, the official organ of the Soviets of the Northern Region.

"The newspaper should be given to every resident in the house on the first demand.

"Chairman of the Union of the Communes of the Northern region, Gr. Zinoviev.

"Commissary of printing, N. Kuzmin."

However, until now the majority of houses inhabited mainly by the bourgeoisie do not fulfil the above-expressed obligatory regulation, and the working population of such houses is deprived of the possibility of receiving the *Severnaya Communa* in its house committees.

Therefore, the publishing office of the *Severnaya Communa* brings to the notice of all house committees that it has undertaken, through the medium of especial emissaries, the control of the fulfilment by house committees of the obligatory regulation No. 27, and all house committees which cannot show a receipt for a subscription to the newspaper, the *Severnaya Communa*, will be immediately called to the most severe account for the breaking of the obligatory regulation.

Subscriptions will be received in the main office and branches of the *Severnaya Communa* daily, except Sundays and holidays, from 10 to 4.

After this it is something of an anticlimax to even take note of the tremendous power wielded by the Revolutionary Tribunal of the Press, Section of Political Crimes, which was created in March, 1918. The decree relating to this body and outlining its functions, dated December 18, 1917, read as follows:

The Revolutionary Tribunal of the Press

1. Under the Revolutionary Tribunal is created a Revolutionary Tribunal of the Press. This Tribunal will have jurisdiction of crimes and offenses against the people committed by means of the press.

2. Crimes and offenses by means of the press are the publication and circulation of any false or perverted reports and information about events of public life, in so far as they constitute an attempt upon the rights and interests of the revolutionary people.

3. The Revolutionary Tribunal of the Press consists of three members, elected for a period not longer than three months by the Soviet of Workmen's, Soldiers',

and Peasants' Deputies. These members are charged with the conduct of the preliminary investigation as well as the trial of the case.

4. The following serve as grounds for instituting proceedings: reports of legal or administrative institutions, public organizations, or private persons.

5. The prosecution and defense are conducted on the principles laid down in the instructions to the general Revolutionary Tribunal.

6. The sessions of the Revolutionary Tribunal of the Press are public.

7. The decisions of the Revolutionary Tribunal of the Press are final and are not subject to appeal.

8. The Revolutionary Tribunal imposes the following penalties: (1) fine; (2) expression of public censure, which the convicted organ of the Press brings to the general knowledge in a way indicated by the Tribunal; (3) the publication in a prominent place or in a special edition of a denial of the false report; (4) temporary or permanent suppression of the publication or its exclusion from circulation; (5) confiscation to national ownership of the printing-shop or property of the organ of the Press if it belongs to the convicted parties.

9. The trial of an organ of the Press by the Revolutionary Tribunal of the Press does not absolve the guilty persons from general criminal responsibility.

Under the provisions of this body the newspapers which were appearing found themselves subject to a new terror. An offensive reference to Trotsky caused the *Outre Rossii* to be mulcted to the extent of 10,000 rubles. Even the redoubtable Martov was punished and the *Vperiod*, organ of the Social Democratic Party, suppressed. The *Nache Slovo* was fined 25,000 rubles and the *Ranee Outre* was mulcted in a like amount for printing a news article concerning some use of the Lettish sharp-shooters by the Bolsheviki, though there was no denial that the facts were as stated. It was a common practice to impose fines of anywhere from 10,000 to 50,000 rubles upon papers which had indulged in criticism of the government or anything that could be construed as "an offense against the people" or "an attempt upon the rights and interests of the revolutionary people."

Here, then, is a summary of the manner in which the Bolsheviki have suppressed the freedom of the press. It is a record which cannot be equaled, nor approached, in all the history of Russia during the reign of Nicholas Romanov II. Mr. Hard attempts to cover the issue with confusion by asking, "Is there any government in the world that permits pro-enemy papers to be printed within its territory during a civil war?" and he is applauded by the entire claque of so-called "Liberal" and "Radical" pro-Bolshevist journals. It was done in this country during the War of the Rebellion, Mr. Hard; it has been done in Ireland under "British tyranny." The Bolshevist records show, first, that the suppression of non-Bolshevist journals was carried out upon a wholesale scale when there was no state of civil war, no armed resistance to the Bolsheviki; that it was, in fact, carried out upon a large scale during the period when preparations were being made for holding the Constituent Assembly which the Bolsheviki themselves, in repeated official declarations, had sworn to uphold and defend. The records show, furthermore, that the Bolsheviki sought not merely to suppress those journals which were urging civil war, but that, as a matter of fact, they suppressed the papers which urged the contrary—that is, that the civil war be brought to an end. The *Vsiegda Vperiod* is a case in point. In February, 1919, the Central Executive Committee of the Soviets announced that it had confirmed the decision to close this newspaper, *"as its appeals for the cessation of civil war appear to be a betrayal of the working-class."*

No, Mr. Hard. No, Mr. Oswald Villard. No, Mr. Norman Thomas. No, gentlemen of the *New Republic*. No, gentlemen of *The Nation*. There can be no escape through the channels of such juggling with facts. When you defend the Bolshevist régime you defend a monstrous organized oppression, and you thereby disqualify yourselves to set up as champions and defenders of Freedom. When you protest against restrictions of popular liberties here the red ironic laughter of the tyrants you have defended drowns the sound of your voices. When you speak fair words for Freedom in America your fellow-men hear only the echoes of your louder words spoken for tyranny in Russia. You do not approach the bar with clean hands and clean consciences. You are forsworn. By what right shall you who have defended Bolshevism in Russia, with all its brutal tyranny, its loathsome corruption, its unrestrained reign of hatred, presume to protest when Liberty is assailed in America? Those among us who have protested against every invasion of popular liberties at home, and have at the same time been loyal to our comrades in Russia who have so bravely resisted tyranny, have the right to enter the lists in defense of Freedom in America, and to raise our voices when that Freedom is assailed. You have not that right, gentlemen; you cannot speak for Freedom, in America or anywhere else, without bringing shame upon her.

In all the platforms and programs of the Socialist parties of the world, without a single exception, the demand for freedom of the press has held a prominent place. No accredited spokesmen of the Socialist movement, anywhere, at any time, has suggested that this demand was made with mental reservations of any kind, or that when Socialists came into power they would suppress the publication of views hostile to their own, or the views of parties struggling to introduce other changes. Yet we find Lenin at the meeting of the Central Executive Committee of the Soviets held on November 18, 1917, saying: "We, the Bolsheviki, have always said that when we came into power we would shut down the bourgeois newspapers. To tolerate bourgeois newspapers is to quit being

Socialists." And Trotsky supported this position and affirmed it as his own.

We have here only the beginnings of a confession of moral bankruptcy, of long-continued, systematic, studied misrepresentation of their purpose and deception of their comrades and of all who believed the words they said, unsuspecting the serious reservations back of the words. *Theses Respecting the Social Revolution and the Tasks of the Proletariat During Its Dictatorship in Russia* is, as might be inferred from its title, a characteristic piece of Lenin's medieval scholasticism, in which, with ponderous verbosity, he explains and interprets Bolshevism. Let us consider *Theses* Nos. 17, 18, 19, and 20:

(17) The former demands for a democratic republic, and general freedom (that is freedom for the middle classes as well), were quite correct in the epoch that is now past, the epoch of preparation and gathering of strength. *The worker needed freedom for his press, while the middle-class press was noxious to him, but he could not at this time put forward a demand for the suppression of the middle-class press.* Consequently, the proletariat demanded general freedom, even freedom for reactionary assemblies, for black labor organizations.

(18) Now we are in the period of the direct attack on capital, the direct overthrow and destruction of the imperialist robber state, and the direct suppression of the middle class. It is, therefore, absolutely clear that in the present epoch the principle of defending general freedom (that is also for the counter-revolutionary middle class) is not only superfluous, but directly dangerous.

(19) This also holds good for the press, and the leading organizations of the social traitors. The latter have been unmasked as the active elements of the counter-revolution. They even attack with weapons the proletarian government. Supported by former officers and the money-bags of the defeated finance capital, they appear on the scene as the most energetic organizations for various conspiracies. The proletariat dictatorship is their deadly enemy. Therefore, they must be dealt with in a corresponding manner.

(20) As regards the working-class and the poor peasants, these possess the fullest freedom.

What have we here? One reads these paragraphs and is stunned by them; repeated readings are necessary. We are told, in fact, that all the demands for freedom of the press, including the bourgeois press, made by Socialists out of office, during the period of their struggle, were hypocritical; that the demand for freedom for all was made for no other reason than the inability of those making it to secure their freedom by themselves and apart from the general freedom; that there was always an unconfessed desire and intention to use the power gained through the freedom thus acquired to suppress the freedom already possessed by others. What a monstrous confession of duplicity and deceit long practised, and what a burden of suspicion and doubt it imposes upon all who hereafter in the name of Socialism urge the freedom of the press.[65]

[65] *See Kautsky*, The Dictatorship of the Proletariat.

Let us hear from another leading Bolshevist luminary, Bucharin, who shares with Lenin the heaviest tasks of expounding Bolshevist theories and who is in some respects a rival theologian. In July, 1918, Bucharin published his pamphlet, *The Program of the Communists*, authorized by the Communist Party, of whose organ, *Pravda*, he is the editor. A revolutionary organization in this country published the greater part of this pamphlet, and it is significant that it omitted Chapter VII, in which Bucharin reveals precisely the same attitude as Lenin. He goes farther in that he admits the same insincerity of attitude toward equal suffrage and the Constituent Assembly based on the will of the majority. He says:

If we have a dictatorship of the proletariat, the object of which is to stifle the bourgeoisie, to compel it to give up its attempts for the restoration of the bourgeois authority, then it is obvious that there can be no talk of allowing the bourgeoisie electoral rights or of a change from soviet authority to a bourgeois-republican parliament.

The Communist (Bolshevik) party receives from all sides accusations and even threats like the following: "You close newspapers, you arrest people, you forbid meetings, you trample underfoot freedom of speech and of the press, you reconstruct autocracy, you are oppressors and murderers."

It is necessary to discuss in detail this question of "liberties" in a Soviet republic.

At present the following is clear for the working-men and the peasants. The Communist party not only does not demand any liberty of the press, speech, meetings, unions, etc., for the bourgeois enemies of the people, but, on the contrary, it demands that the government should be always in readiness to close the bourgeois press; to disperse the meetings of the enemies of the people; to forbid them to lie, slander, and spread panic; to crush ruthlessly all attempts at a restoration of the bourgeois régime. This is precisely the meaning of the dictatorship of the proletariat.

Another question may be put to us: "Why did the Bolsheviki not speak formerly of the abrogation of full liberty for the bourgeoisie? Why did they formerly support the idea of a *bourgeois-democratic republic? Why did they support the idea of the Constituent Assembly and did not speak of depriving the bourgeoisie of the right of suffrage?* Why have they changed their program so far as these questions are concerned?"

The answer to this question is very simple. The working-class formerly did not have strength enough to storm the bulwarks of the bourgeoisie. It needed preparation, accumulation of strength, enlightenment of the masses, organization. It needed, for example, the freedom of its own labor press. But it could not come to the capitalists and to their governments and demand that they shut down their own newspapers and give full freedom to the labor papers. Everybody would merely laugh at the working-men. Such demands can be made only at the time of a storming attack. And there had never been such a time before. This is why the working-men

> demanded (and our party, too) "Freedom of the press." (Of the whole press, including the bourgeois press.)

A more immoral doctrine than that contained in these utterances by the foremost intellectual leaders of Russian Bolshevism can hardly be conceived of. How admirably their attitude and their method is summed up in the well-known words of Frederick II of Prussia: "I understand by the word 'policy' that one must make it his study to deceive others; that is the way to get the better of them." And these are the men and this the policy which have found so many champions among us! When or where in all the history of a hundred years was such a weapon as this placed in the hands of the reactionists? Here are the spokesmen of what purports to be a Socialist republic, and of the political party which claims to present Socialism in its purest and undiluted form, saying to the world, "Socialists do not believe in freedom of the press; they find it convenient to say they do while they are weak, in order to gain protection and aid for their own press, but whenever and wherever they obtain the power to do so they will suppress the press of all who disagree with them or in any way oppose them." That, and not less than that, is the meaning of these declarations.

The Socialist Party of America has always declared for the fullest freedom of the press, without any expressed qualifications or reservations. Tens of thousands of honest men and women have accepted the party's declarations upon this subject in good faith, and found satisfaction and joy in upholding them. No doubt of the sincerity of the professions of loyalty to the principle of freedom and equality for all ever entered their minds; no thought or suspicion of sinister secret reservations or understandings ever disturbed their faith. Not once, but hundreds of times, when unjust discrimination by government officials and others seemed to imperil the safety of some Socialist paper, men and women who were not Socialists at all, but who were believers in freedom of the press, rushed to their aid. This hundreds of thousands of Americans have done, because they believed the Socialists were sincere in their professions that they wanted only justice, not domination; that they sought only that measure of freedom they themselves would aid others in securing and maintaining.

If at any time some one had challenged the good faith of the Socialists, and charged that in the event of their obtaining control of the government they would use its powers to cripple and suppress the opposition press, he would have been denounced as a malignant libeler of honest men and women. Yet here come Lenin and Bucharin, and others of the same school, affirming that this has always been a Socialist principle; that the Bolsheviki at least have always said they would act in precisely that manner. What say American Socialists? The Socialist Party has declared its support of the party of Lenin and Trotsky and Bucharin; its national standard-bearer has declared himself to be a Bolshevik; the party has joined the party of the Russian Bolsheviki in the Third International, forsaking for that purpose association with the non-Bolshevist Socialist parties and the Second International.

Unless and until they unequivocally and unreservedly repudiate the vicious doctrine set forth by the leading theorists of Bolshevism, the spokesmen of American Socialism will be properly and justly open to the suspicion that they cherish in their hearts the intention to use the powers of government whensoever, and in whatsoever manner, these shall fall under their control, to abolish the principle of equal freedom for all, and to suppress by force the organs of publicity of all who do not agree with them.

If they are not willing to repudiate this doctrine, and to deny the purpose imputed to them, let them be honest and admit the belief and the purpose. Silence cannot save them in the face of the words of Lenin and Bucharin. Silence is eloquent confession henceforth. Behind every Socialist speaker who seeks to obscure this issue with rhetoric, or to remain silent upon it, every American who believes in and loves Freedom—thousands of Socialists among the number—will see the menacing specter of Bolshevism, nursling of intriguing hate and lying treason. America will laugh such men to scorn when they invoke Freedom's name. Against the masked spirit of despotism which resides in the Bolshevist propaganda America will set her own traditional ideal, so well expressed in Lincoln's fine saying, "As I would not be a slave, so I would not be a master," and Whitman's line, so worthy to accompany it—"By God! I want nothing for myself that all others may not have upon equal terms."

That is the essence of democracy and of liberty; that is the sense in which these great words live in the heart of America. And that, too, be it said, is the sense in which they live in the Socialism of Marx—of which Bolshevism is a grotesque and indecent caricature. That is the central idea of Marx's vision of a world free from class divisions and class strife—a world where none is master and none is slave; where all good things are accessible to all upon equal terms, and where burdens are shared with the equality that is fraternal.

With the freedom of the press freedom of assemblage and of speech is closely interwoven. The foes of the freedom of the press are always and everywhere equally the foes of the right to assemble for discussion and argument. And the Bolsheviki are no exception to the rule. From the beginning, as soon as they had consolidated their power sufficiently to do so, they have repressed by all the force at their command the meetings, both public and private, of all who were opposed to them, even meetings of Socialists called for no purpose other than to demand government by equal suffrage and meetings of workmen's unions called for the purpose of explaining their grievances in such matters as wages, hours of labor, and shop management. Hundreds of pages of evidence in support of this statement could be given if that were necessary. Here, for example, is the testimony of V. M. Zenzinov, member of the Central Committee of the Socialists-Revolutionists Party:

> The Bolsheviki are the only ones who are able to hold political meetings in present-day Russia; everybody else is deprived of the right to voice his political opinions, for "undesirable" speakers are promptly arrested on the spot by the Bolshevist police. All the Socialist, non-Bolshevist members of the Soviets were ejected by force of arms; many leaders of Socialist parties have been arrested. The delegates to the Moscow Congress of the Party of Socialists-Revolutionists scheduled for May, 1918, were arrested by the Bolsheviki, yet nobody will attempt to claim that this party, which has participated in every International Socialist Congress, is not a Socialist Party.
>
> It was during my stay in Petrograd in April, 1918, that a conference of factory and industrial plants employees of Petrograd and vicinity was held, to which 100,000 Petrograd working-men (out of a total of 132,000) sent delegates. The conference adopted a resolution sharply denouncing the Bolshevist régime. Following this conference an attempt was made in May to call together an All-Russian Congress of workmen's deputies in Moscow, but all the delegates were arrested by the Bolsheviki, and to this day I am ignorant of the fate that befell my comrades. For all I know they may have been put to death, as a number of other Socialists have been.

Here is the testimony of Oupovalov, Social Democrat and trades-unionist, who once more speaks only of matters of which he has personal knowledge:

On June 22, 1918, the Social Democratic Committee at Sormovo called a Provincial Non-Party Labor Conference for the purpose of discussing current events; 350 delegates were present, representing 350,000 workmen. The afternoon meeting passed off safely, but before the opening of the evening meeting a large crowd of local workmen who had gathered in front of the conference premises were fired upon by a Lettish detachment by order of the commissaries. The result was that several peaceful workmen were killed and wounded. The conference was dispersed, and I, being one of the speakers, was arrested. After a fortnight's confinement in a damp cellar, with daily threats of execution, I was released, owing to energetic protests on the part of my fellow-workmen, but not for long.

A Labor meeting was convoked at Sormovo by a commissar of the People's Economic Soviet from Moscow for the purpose of discussing the question of food-supply. I was delegated by the Social Democratic Party to speak at this meeting and criticize the Bolsheviks' food policy. *The resolution proposed by me demanded the cessation of civil war, the summoning of the Constituent Assembly, the right for co-operatives to purchase foodstuffs freely.* Out of the 18,000 persons present only 350 voted against the resolution.

That same night I was arrested and sentenced to be shot. The workmen declared a strike, demanding my release. The Bolsheviks sent a detachment of Letts, who fired on the unarmed workmen and many were killed. Nevertheless, the workmen would not give in, and the Bolsheviki mitigated their sentence and deported me to the Perm Province.

But what is the use of citing any number of such instances? When a score, a hundred, or a thousand have been cited we shall hear from the truculent defenders of Bolshevism that no testimony offered by Russian revolutionists of the highest standing is worth anything as compared to the testimony of the Ransomes, Goodes, Coppings, Lansburys, *et al.*, the human phonograph records who repeat with such mechanical precision the words which the Bolsheviki desire the world outside of Russia to hear. Against this logic of unreason no amount of testimony can prevail. It is not so easy, however, to dispose of a "decree" of the Soviet Government—for is not a "decree" a thing to be regarded as the Mohammedan regards the Koran? Here, then, is a Bolshevist decree—not, it need hardly be said, to be found included in any of the collections of Bolshevist laws and decrees issued to impress the public of America in favor of the Bolsheviki. Read, mark, and learn, and inwardly digest it, Mr. Oswald Villard, Mr. Norman Thomas, Mr. William Hard, gentlemen of the Civil Liberties Bureau, and you others who find America so reactionary and tyrannical. It is taken from the *Severnaya Communa*, September 13, 1919, and is signed by Zinoviev:

Decree Regulating Right of Public Associations and Meetings

(1) All societies, unions, and associations—political, economic, artistic, religious, etc.—formed on the territory of the Union of the Commune of the Northern Region must be registered at the corresponding Soviets or Committees of the Village Poor.

(2) The constitution of the union or society, a list of founders and members of the committee, with names and addresses, and a list of all members, with their names and addresses, must be submitted at registration.

(3) All books, minutes, etc., must always be kept at the disposal of representatives of the Soviet Power for purposes of revision.

(4) Three days' notice must be given to the Soviet or to the Committee of the Village Poor, of all public and private meetings.

(5) All meetings must be open to the representatives of the Soviet Power, *viz.*, the representatives of the Central and District Soviet, the Committee of the Poor, and the Kommandantur of the Revolutionary Secret Police Force.

(6) Unions and societies which do not comply with those regulations will be regarded as counter-revolutionary organizations and prosecuted.

This document, like so many others issued by the Bolsheviki, bears a striking resemblance to the regulations which were issued under Czar Nicholas II. There is not the slightest suggestion of a spirit and purpose more generous in its regard for freedom. Nowhere is there any evidence of a different psychology. Of course, it may be said in defense, or extenuation if not defense, of the remarkable decree just quoted that it was a military measure; that it was due to the conditions of civil warfare prevailing. That defense might be seriously considered but for the fact that similar regulations have been imposed in places far removed from any military activity, where there was no civil warfare, where the Bolsheviki ruled a passive people. More important than this fact, however, is the evidence of the attitude of the Bolsheviki, as revealed by their accredited spokesmen. From this it is quite clear that, regardless of this or that particular decree or proclamation, *the Bolsheviki look upon the continuous and permanent suppression of their opponents' right to hold meetings as a fundamental policy*. The decree under consideration, with its stringent provisions requiring registration of all societies and associations of every kind, the list and addresses of all members, and of all who attend the meetings, and the arrangement for the attendance of the "Kommandantur of the Revolutionary Secret-Police Force" at meetings of every kind, trades-union meetings and religious gatherings no less than political meetings, is fully in harmony with the declaration of fundamental policy made by the intellectual leaders of Bolshevism. *Pravda*, December 7, 1919, quotes Baranov as saying at the seventh All-Russian Congress: "We do not allow meetings of Mensheviki and Cadets, who in these meetings would speak of counter-revolution within the country. The Soviet Power will not allow such meetings, of course, just as it will not allow freedom of the press, as there are appearing sufficient White Guardists' leaflets." But let us listen once more to the chief sophist:

7. "Freedom of meeting" may be taken as an example of the demands for "pure democracy." Any conscious workman who has not broken with his own class will understand immediately that it would be stupid to permit freedom of

meetings to exploiters at this period, and under the present circumstances, when the exploiters are resisting their overthrow, and are fighting for their privileges. When the bourgeoisie was revolutionary, in England in 1649, and in France in 1793, it did not give "freedom of meetings" to monarchists and nobles who were calling in foreign troops and who were "meeting" to organize attempts at restoration. *If the present bourgeoisie, which has been reactionary for a long time now, demands of the proletariat that the latter guarantee in advance freedom of meetings for exploiters no matter what resistance the capitalists may show to the measures of expropriation directed against them, the workmen will only laugh at the hypocrisy of the bourgeoisie.*

On the other hand, the workmen know very well that "freedom of meetings," even in the most democratic bourgeois republic, is an empty phrase, for the rich have all the best public and private buildings at their disposal, and also sufficient leisure time for meetings and for the protection of these meetings by the bourgeois apparatus of authority. The proletarians of the city and of the village and the poor peasants—that is, the overwhelming majority of the population, have none of these three things. So long as the situation is such, "equality"—that is, "pure democracy"—is sheer fraud. In order to secure genuine equality, in order to realize in fact democracy for the toilers, one must first take away from the exploiters all public and luxurious private dwellings, one must give leisure time to the toilers, *one must protect the freedom of their meetings by armed workmen, and not by noble or capitalist officers with browbeaten soldiers.*

Only after such a change can one speak of freedom of meetings and of equality, without scoffing at workmen, toilers, and the poor. And no one can bring about this change except the advance-guard of the toilers—that is, the proletariat—by overthrowing the exploiters, the bourgeoisie.

8. "Freedom of press" is also one of the main arguments of "pure democracy," but again the workmen know that the Socialists of all countries have asserted millions of times that *this freedom is a fraud so long as the best printing machinery and the largest supplies of paper have been seized by the capitalists, and so long as the power of capital over the press continues, which power in the whole world is clearly more harsh and more cynical in proportion to the development of democratism and the republican principle, as, for example, in*

America. In order to secure actual equality and actual democracy for the toilers, for workmen and peasants, *one must first take from capitalists the possibility of hiring writers, of buying up publishing houses, of buying up newspapers, and to this end one must overthrow the yoke of capital, overthrow the exploiters, and put down all resistance on their part.* The capitalists have always called "freedom" the freedom to make money for the rich and the freedom to die of hunger for workmen. The capitalists call "freedom" the freedom of the rich, freedom to buy up the press, freedom to use wealth, to manufacture and support so-called public opinion. The defenders of "pure democracy" again in actual fact turn out to be the defenders of the most dirty and corrupt system of the rule of the rich over the means of education of the masses. They deceive the people by attractive, fine-sounding, beautiful, but absolutely false phrases, trying to dissuade the masses from the concrete historic task of freeing the press from the capitalists who have gotten control of it. Actual freedom and equality will exist only in the order established by the Communists, in which it will be impossible to become rich at the expense of another, where it will be impossible, either directly or indirectly, to subject the press to the power of money, where there will be no obstacle to prevent any toiler (or any large group of such) from enjoying and actually realizing the equal right to the use of public printing-presses and of the public fund of paper.

These are "theses" from the report of Lenin on "Bourgeois and Proletarian Democracies," published in *Pravda,* March 8, 1919. That the very term "proletarian democracy" is an absurd self-contradiction, just as "capitalist democracy" would be, since democracy is inherently incompatible with class domination of any kind, is worthy of remark only in so far as the use of the phrase shows the mentality of the man. Was ever such a farrago of nonsense put forward with such solemnly pretentious pedantry? The unreasoning hatred and shallow ignorance of the most demagogic soap-box Socialist propaganda are covered with the verbiage of scholasticism, and the result is given to the world as profound philosophy. If there is any disposition to question the justice of this summary judgment a candid consideration of the two "theses" just quoted should suffice to settle all doubts.

In the first place, the dominant note is hatred and retaliation: In 1649 the bourgeoisie of England suppressed the right of assemblage, and in 1793 the bourgeoisie of France did likewise. Therefore, if the present bourgeoisie, "which has been reactionary for a long time," now demands that the workers guarantee freedom of meetings, the workers will only laugh at their hypocrisy. One is reminded of the ignorant pogrom-makers who gave the crucifixion of Jesus as their reason for persecuting Jews in the twentieth century. Upon what higher level is Lenin's justification than the ignorant feeling of hostility toward England, still found in some dark corners of American life, because of the misgovernment of the Colonies by the England of George the Third? Is there to be no allowance for the advance made, even by the bourgeoisie, since the struggles of 1649 and 1793; no consideration of the fact that the bourgeoisie of England and France in later years have gone far beyond the standards set by their forerunners in 1649 and 1793; *that they have granted freedom of assemblage, even to those struggling to overthrow them*? Is twentieth-century Socialism to have no higher ideal than capitalism already had in the seventeenth and eighteenth centuries? Waiving the greater question of whether or not the claim of any class to succeed to power is worthy of attention unless its ideals are measurably higher than those of the class it would displace, is it not quite clear that Lenin's appeal to "history" is arrant demagoguery?

Consider the argument further: There is no freedom of meetings, "even in the most democratic bourgeois republic," we are told, because "the rich" have the halls in which to meet, the leisure for meeting and the "bourgeois apparatus of authority" for the protection of their meetings. This absurd travesty of facts which are well known to all who know life in democratic nations is put forward by a man who is hailed as a philosopher-statesman, though his ponderous "theses" show him to be among the most blatant demagogues of modern history, his greatest mental gift being unscrupulous cunning. The workers lack leisure for meetings, we are told, therefore no freedom of meeting exists—in the bourgeois democracies. Well, what of the Utopia of the Bolsheviki, the Utopia of Lenin's own fashioning? Is there greater leisure for the worker there? By its own journals we are informed that the Russian worker now works *twelve hours a day*, but let us not take advantage of that fact, which is admittedly due to a desperate economic condition—for which, however, the Bolsheviki are mainly responsible. But in the very much praised labor laws of the Russian Socialist Federal Soviet Republic an eight-hour workday is provided for. Are we to assume that this leaves sufficient leisure to the workers to make freedom of meeting possible for them? Very well. To a very large extent the eight-hour day prevails in this poor despised "bourgeois democracy," either as a result of legislation or of trades-union organization. Nay, more, the forty-four-hour week is with us, and even the *six-hour day*, in some trades. The unattained ideal of Sovdepia's labor legislation is thus actually below what is rapidly coming to be our common practice. Anybody who knows anything at all of the facts knows that the conditions here set forth are true of this country and, to a very large degree, of England.

Is it true that freedom of assemblage is impossible in this poor old "bourgeois democracy," because, forsooth, the workers lack the halls in which to meet? Is that the condition in England, or in any of the western nations in which the much-despised "bourgeois democracy" prevails? How many communities are there in America where meeting-halls are accessible only to "the rich," where they cannot be had by the workers upon equal terms with all other people? Over the greater part of America—wherever "bourgeois democracy" exists—our publicly owned auditoriums, the city halls, and school halls, are open to all citizens upon equal terms. Even where private halls have to be hired, and stiff rents paid, it is common for the collections to cover expenses and even leave a profit. In many of the cities the organized workers own their own auditoriums. In England, Belgium, Denmark, and other European countries—"bourgeois democracies" all—a great many of the finest auditoriums are those owned and controlled by the workmen's organizations, and they are frequently hired by "the rich." Finally, wherever the government of any city has come under the control of Socialist or Labor movements, auditoriums freely accessible to the workers have been provided, and this obstacle to freedom of assemblage which gives Lenin such concern has been removed. This has been done, moreover, without descending to the level of old oppressors, and it has not been necessary to resort to "armed workmen," any more than to "browbeaten soldiers" with capitalist officers to protect the freedom of assemblage.

So, too, with the freedom of the press. In the nations where democratic laws prevail *the workers' press is just as strong and powerful as the interest and will of the workers themselves decree.* If the Socialist press in our cities is weak and uninfluential, that fact is the natural and inevitable corollary of the weakness of the Socialist movement itself. Was *L'Humanité*, when it was still a great and powerful newspaper, or were the Berlin *Vorwärts*, *Le Peuple* of Brussels, and *L'Avanti* of Rome, less "free" than other newspapers? Were they less "free" than *Pravda*, even, to say nothing of the anti-Bolshevist papers opposed to Bolshevism? True, they had not the privilege of looting the public treasuries; they could not force an oppressive, discriminatory, and confiscatory tax upon the other newspapers; they could not utilize the forces of the state to seize and use the plants belonging to their rivals; they could not rely upon the power of the state to compel people against their will to "subscribe" to them. In other words, the freedom they possessed was the freedom to publish their views and to gain as many readers as possible by lawful methods; the only "freedom" they lacked was the freedom of brigandage, the right to despoil and oppress others.

So much, then, for the labored sophistry of the chief Talmudist of Bolshevism and his tiresome "theses" with their demagogic cant and their appeals to the lowest instincts and passions of his followers. The record herein set forth proves beyond shadow of a doubt that neither in the régime Lenin and his co-conspirators have thus far maintained nor in the ideal they set for themselves is there any place for that freedom of speech and thought and conscience without which all other liberties are unavailing. These men prate of freedom, but they are tyrants. If they be not tyrants, "we then extremely wrong Caligula and Nero in calling them tyrants, and they were rebels that conspired against them." If Lenin, Trotsky, Zinoviev, and Bucharin are not tyrants, but liberators, so were the Grand Inquisitors of Spain.

XII
"THE DICTATORSHIP OF THE PROLETARIAT"

I

n

a pamphlet entitled *Two Tactics*, published in Geneva, in 1905, at the time of the first Russian Revolution, Lenin wrote:

> Whoever wants to try any path to Socialism other than political democracy *will inevitably come to absurd and reactionary conclusions, both in an economic and a political sense.* If some workmen ask us, "Why not achieve the maximum program?" we shall answer them by pointing out how alien to Socialism the democratic masses are, how undeveloped are the class contradictions, how unorganized are the proletarians.... The largest possible realization of democratic reform is necessary and requisite for the spreading of socialistic enlightenment and for introducing appropriate organization.

These words are worth remembering. In the light of the tragic results of Bolshevism they seem singularly prophetic, for certainly by attempting to achieve Socialism through other methods than those of political democracy Lenin and his followers have "come to absurd and reactionary conclusions, both in an economic and a political sense." They profess, for example, to have established in Russia a "dictatorship of the proletariat." In reality they have set up a tyrannical rule over the proletariat, together with the rest of the population, by an almost infinitesimal part of the population of Russia. Lenin and his followers claim to be the logical exemplars of the teachings of Karl Marx, whereas their whole theory is no more than a grotesque travesty of Marx's teachings.

More than seventy years have elapsed since the publication of Marx's *Communist Manifesto*, in which he set forth his theory of the historic rôle of the proletariat. Thirty-seven years — more than a full generation — have elapsed since his death in 1883. Even if it were true that during the period spanned by these two dates Karl Marx believed in and advocated the dictatorship of the proletariat in the sense in which that term is used by the Bolsheviki, that fact would possess little more than historical interest. Much has happened since the death of

Marx, and still more since the early 'seventies, when his life-work virtually ended, which the political realist needs must take into account. Marx did not utter the last word of human wisdom upon the laws and methods of social progress and so render new and fresh judgments unnecessary and wrong. No one can study the evolution of Marx himself and doubt that if he were alive to-day he would hold very different views from those which he held in 1847 and subsequently. Our only justification for considering the relation of Leninism to Marxism lies in the fact that in this and other countries outside of Russia a considerable element in the Socialist movement, deceived by Lenin's use of certain Marxian phrases, gives its support to Leninism in the belief that it is identical with Marxism. Nothing could be farther from the teachings of Marx than the oppressive bureaucratic dictatorship by an infinitesimal minority set up by Lenin and his disciples.

In the *Communist Manifesto* Marx used the term "proletariat" in the sense in which it was used by Barnave and other Intellectuals of the French Revolution, not as it is commonly used to-day, as a synonym for the wage-earning class. The term as used by Marx connoted not merely an absence of property, not merely poverty, but a peculiar state of degradation. Just as in Roman society the term was applied to a large class, including peasants, wage laborers, and others without capital, property, or assured means of support, unfit and unworthy to exercise political rights, so the term was used by Marx, as it had been by his predecessors, to designate a class in modern society similarly denied the rights of citizenship. When Marx wrote in 1847 this was the condition of the wage-earning class in every European country. In no one of these countries did the working-class enjoy the right of suffrage. Marx saw no hope of any amelioration of the lot of this class. On the contrary, he believed that the evolution of society would take the form of a relentless, brutal process, unrestrained by any humane consciousness or legislation, which would culminate in a division of society into two classes, on the one hand a very small ruling and owning class, on the other hand the overwhelming majority of the population. He specifically rejected the idea of minority rule: "All previous historical movements were movements of minorities, or in the interest of minorities. *The proletarian movement is the self-conscious independent movement of the immense majority, in the interest of the immense majority.* The proletariat, the lowest stratum of our present society, cannot stir, cannot raise itself up, without the whole superincumbent strata of official society being sprung into the air."

Not only does Marx here present the proletarian uprising as the culmination of a historical process which has made proletarians of "the immense majority," but, what is more significant, perhaps, he presents this movement, not as a conscious *ideal*, but as an inevitable and inescapable *condition*. In 1875, in a famous letter criticizing the Gotha program of the German Social Democrats, he wrote: "Between capitalist and communist society lies the period of the revolutionary transformation of the one into the other. This requires a political transition stage, which can be nothing less than the revolutionary dictatorship of the proletariat." It is mainly upon this single quotation that Lenin and his followers rely in claiming Marxian authority for the régime set up in Russia under the title the Dictatorship of the Proletariat. The passage cited cannot honestly and fairly be so interpreted. We are bound to bear in mind that Marx still held to the belief that the revolution from capitalist to communist society could only take place when the proletariat had become "the immense majority."

Moreover, it is quite clear that he was still thinking, in 1875, of dictatorship by this *immense majority* as a temporary measure.

Of course, the word "dictatorship" is a misnomer when it is so used, but not more so than when used to describe rule by any class. Strictly speaking, dictatorship refers to a rule by a single individual who is bound by no laws, the absolute supremacy of an individual dictator. Friedrich Engels, who collaborated with Marx in writing the *Communist Manifesto* and in much of his subsequent work, and who became his literary executor and finished *Das Kapital*, certainly knew the mind of Marx as no other human being did or could. Engels has, fortunately, made quite clear the sense in which Marx used the term "dictatorship of the proletariat." In his *Civil War in France*, Marx described the Paris Commune as "essentially a government of the working-class, the result of the struggle of the producing class against the appropriating class, the political form under which the freedom of labor could be attained being at length revealed." He described with glowing enthusiasm the Commune with its town councilors chosen by universal suffrage, and not by the votes of a single class. As Kautsky remarks, "the dictatorship of the proletariat was for him a condition which necessarily arose in a real democracy, because of the overwhelming numbers of the proletariat."[66] That this is a correct interpretation of Marx's thought is attested by the fact that in his introduction to the *Civil War in France* Engels describes the Commune, based on the general suffrage of the whole people, as "the Dictatorship of the Proletariat."

66 *Kautsky*, The Dictatorship of the Proletariat, *p. 45.*

Of course, the evolution of modern industrial nations has proceeded upon very different lines from those forecasted by Marx. The middle class has not been exterminated and shows no signs of being submerged in the wage-earning class; the workers are no longer disfranchised and outside the pale of citizenship; on the contrary, they have acquired full political rights and are becoming increasingly powerful in the parliaments. In other words, the wage-earning class is, for the most part, no longer "proletarian" in the narrow sense in which Marx used the term. Quite apart from these considerations, however, it is very obvious that the theory of Lenin and his followers that the whole political power of Russia should be centered in the so-called industrial proletariat, which even the Bolsheviki themselves have not estimated at more than 3 per cent. of the entire population, bears no sort of relation to the process Marx always had in mind when he referred to "proletarian dictatorship." Not only is there no sanction for the Leninist view in Marxian theory, but the two are irreconcilably opposed.

The Bolshevist régime does not even represent the proletariat, however. The fact is thoroughly well established that the political power rests in the Communist Party, which represents only a minority of the proletariat. What we have before us in Russia is not even a dictatorship of the proletariat, but a dictatorship over an entire people, including the proletariat, by the Communist Party. The testimony of the Bolsheviki themselves upon this point is abundant and conclusive. If any good purpose were served thereby, pages of statements to this effect by responsible Bolshevist leaders could be cited; for our present purpose, however, the following quotations will suffice:

In a letter to workmen and peasants issued in July, 1918, Lenin said, "The dictatorship of the proletariat *is carried out by the party of the Bolsheviki*, which, as early as 1905, and earlier, became one with the entire revolutionary proletariat." In an article entitled, "The Party and the Soviets," published in *Pravda*, February 13, 1919, Bucharin, editor-in-chief of that important official organ of the Communist Party, said: "It is no secret for any one that in a country where the working-class and the poorest peasantry are in power, that party is the directing party which expresses the interests of these groups of the population—the Communist Party. All the work in the Soviet goes on under the influence and the political leadership of our party. It is the forms which this leadership should assume that are the subject of disagreement." In *Pravda*, November 5, 1919, the leading editorial says of the "adventure of Yudenich" that in the last analysis "this ordeal has strengthened the cause of revolution and has *strengthened the hegemony of the Communist Party.*" In the *Samara Kommuna*, April 11, 1919, we read that "The Communist Party as a whole is responsible for the future of the young Soviet Socialist Republic, for the whole course of the world Communist revolution. In the country *the highest organ of authority, to which all Soviet institutions and officials are subordinate, is again the Communist Party.*"

Not only do we find that the Bolshevist régime rests upon the theory of the hegemony of the Communist Party, but in practice the party functions as a part of the state machinery, as the directing machinery, in point of fact, placing the Soviets in a subordinate position. At times the Communist Party has exercised the entire power of government, as, for example, from July, 1918, to January, 1919. Thus we read in *Izvestia*, November 6, 1919, "From October, 1917, up to July, 1918, is the first period of Soviet construction; from July, 1918, up to January, 1919, the second period, *when the Soviet work was conducted exclusively by the power of the Russian Communist Party;* and the third period from January this year, when in the work of Soviet construction broad non-partizan masses participated."

This condition was, of course, made possible by the predominance of Communist Party members in the Soviet Government, a predominance due to the measures taken to exclude the anti-Bolshevist parties. Thus 88 per cent. of the members of the Executive Committees of the Provincial Soviets were members of the Communist Party, according to *Izvestia*, November 6, 1919. In the army, while their number was relatively small, not more than 10,000 in the entire army, members of the Communist Party held almost all the responsible posts. Trotsky, as Commander-in-Chief, reported to the seventh Congress, according to the *Red Baltic Fleet*, December 11, 1919, "our Army consists of peasants and workmen. *Workmen represent scarcely more than 15 to 18 per cent., but they maintain the same directing position as throughout Soviet Russia.* This is a privilege secured to them because of their greater consciousness, compactness, and revolutionary zeal. The army is the reflection of our whole social order. It is based on the rule of the working-class, in which latter the party of Communists plays the leading rôle." Trotsky further said: "The number of members of this party in the army is about ten thousand. The responsible posts of commissaries are occupied by them in the overwhelming majority of instances. In each regiment there is a Communist group. The significance of the Communists in the army is shown by the fact that when conditions become unfavorable in a given division the commanding staff appeals to the Revolutionary Military Soviet with a request that a group of Communists be sent down." Accordingly, it is not surprising to find the party itself exercising the functions of government and issuing orders. In *Izvestia* and *Pravda*, during April, 1919, numerous paragraphs were published relating to the mobilization of regiments by the Communist Party.

From figures published by the Bolsheviki themselves it is possible to obtain a tolerably accurate idea of the actual numerical strength of the Communist Party. During the second half of 1918, when, as stated in the paragraph already quoted from *Izvestia*, "the Soviet work was conducted exclusively by the power of the Russian Communist Party," there was naturally a considerable increase in the party membership, for very obvious reasons. In *Severnaya Communa*, February 22, 1919, appeared the following:

> At the session of the Moscow Committee of the Russian Communist Party, on February 15, 1919, the following resolutions were carried: Taking into account—(1) That the uninterrupted growth of our party during the year of dictatorship has inevitably meant *that there have entered its ranks elements having absolutely nothing in common with Communism*, joining in order to use the authority of the Russian Communist Party for their own personal, selfish aims; (2) That these elements, taking cover under the flag of Communism, are by their acts discrediting in the eyes of the people the prestige and glorious name of our Proletarian Party; (3) That *the so-called "Communists of our days" by their outrageous behavior are arousing discontent and bitter feeling in the people*, thus creating a favorable soil for counter-revolutionary agitation—taking all this into account, the Moscow Committee of the Russian Communist Party declares:
>
> (*a*) That the party congress about to be held should call on all party organizations to check up in the strictest manner all members of the party and cleanse its ranks of elements foreign to the party; (*b*) that one must carry on a decisive struggle against those elements whose acts create a counter-revolutionary state of mind; (*c*) that one must make every effort to raise the moral level of members of the Russian Communist Party and educate them in the spirit of true Proletarian Communism; (*d*) that one must direct all efforts toward strengthening party discipline and establishing strict control by the party over all its members in all fields of Party-Soviet activity.

Yet, notwithstanding the inflation of party membership here referred to, we find *Izvestia* reporting in that same month, February, 1919, as follows: "The secretary of the Communist Party of the Moscow Province states that the total number of party members throughout the whole province is 2,881." At the eighth Congress of the Communist Party, March, 1919, serious attention was given to the inflation of the party membership by the admission of Soviet employees and others who were not Communists at heart, and it was decided to cleanse the party of such elements and, after that was done, to undertake a recruiting campaign for new members. Yet, according to the official minutes of this Congress, *"the sum total of the Communist Party throughout Soviet Russia represents about one-half of one per cent. of the entire population."* We find in *Izvestia*, May 8, 1919, that out of a total of more than two million inhabitants in the Province of Kaluga the membership of the Communist Party amounted to less than one-fifth of one per cent. of the population: "According to the data of the Communist Congress of the Province of Kaluga there are 3,861 registered members of the party throughout the whole province." On the following day, May 9, 1919, *Izvestia* reported: "At the Communist Congress of the Riazan Province 181 organizations were represented, numbering 5,994 members." As the population of the Riazan Province was well over 3,000,000 it will be seen that here again the Communist Party membership was less than one-fifth of one per cent. of the population.

At this time various Bolshevist journals gave the Communist Party membership at 20,000 for the city of Moscow and 12,000 for Petrograd. Then took place the so-called "re-registration," to "relieve the party of this ballast," as *Pravda* said later on, "those careerists of the petty bourgeois groups of the population." In Petrograd the membership was reduced by nearly one-third and in some provincial towns by from 50 to

75 per cent. The result was that in September, 1919, *Pravda* reported the number of Communist Party members in Petrograd as 9,000, "with at least 50,000 ardent supporters of the anti-Bolshevist movement." This official journal did not regard the 9,000 as a united body of genuine and sincere Communists: "Are the 9,000 upholding the cause of Bolshevism acting according to their convictions? No. Most of them are in ignorance of the principles of the Communists, *which at heart they do not believe in*, but all the employees of the Soviets study these principles much the same as under the rule of the Czar they turned their attention to police rules *in order to get ahead*."

On October 1, 1919, *Pravda* published two significant circular letters from the Central Committee of the Communist Party to the district and local organizations of the party. The first of these called for "a campaign to recruit new members into the party" and to induce old members to rejoin. To make joining the party easier "entry into the party is not to be conditioned by the presentation of two written recommendations as before." The appeal to the party workers says, "During 'party-week' *we ought to increase the membership of our party to half a million*." The second circular is of interest because of the following sentences: "The principle of administration by 'colleges' must be reduced to a minimum. Discussions and considerations must be given up. *The party must be as soon as possible rebuilt on military lines*, and there must be created a military revolutionary apparatus which would work solidly and accurately. In this apparatus there must be clearly distributed privileges and duties."

The frenzied efforts to increase the party membership by "drives" in which every device and every method of persuasion and pressure was used brought into the party many who were not Communists at all. Thus we find *Pravda* saying, December 12, 1919: "The influx of many members to the collectives (Soviet Management groups) comes not only from the working-class, *but also from the middle bourgeoisie* which formerly considered Communists as its enemies. One of the new collectives is a collective at the estate of Kurakin (a children's colony). Here entered the collective not only loyal employees, *but also representatives of the teaching staff.*" *Pravda* adds that "this inrush of the bourgeoisie, the bourgeoisie that formerly considered the Communists as its enemies, is not at all to our interest. Of course, there may be honest Soviet officials who have in fact shown their loyalty to the great ideas of Communism, and such can find their place in our ranks." Other Bolshevist journals wrote in the same spirit deploring the admission of so many "bourgeois" Soviet officials into the party.

In spite of this abnormal and much-feared inflation of the party membership, *Pravda* reported on March 18, 1920, that with more than 300,000 workmen in Petrograd the total membership of the Communist Party in that city was only 30,000. That is to say, including all the Soviet officials and "bourgeois elements," the party membership amounted to rather less than 10 per cent. of the industrial proletariat, and that in the principal center of the party, the first of the two great cities. Surely this is proof that the Communist Party really represents only a minority of the industrial proletariat. If even with all its bourgeois elements it amounts in the principal industrial city, its stronghold, to less than 10 per cent. of the number of working-men, we may be quite certain that in the country as a whole the percentage is very much smaller.

Even if we take into account only the militant portion of the organized proletariat, the Communist Party is shown to represent only a minority of it. *Economicheskaya Zhizn*, October

15, 1919, published an elaborate statistical analysis of the First Trades-Union Conference of the Moscow Government. We learn that in the Union of Textile Workers, the largest union represented, of 131 delegates present only 27, or 20.6 per cent., declared themselves to be Communists; while 94, or 71.7 per cent., declared themselves to be non-party, and 3 declared that they were Mensheviki. Of the 21 delegates of the Union of Compositors 13, or 62.3 per cent., declared themselves to be Mensheviki; 7, or 33 per cent., to be non-party, and only 1 registered as a Communist. The Union of Soviet employees naturally sent a majority of delegates who registered as Communists, 45 out of 67 delegates, or 67 per cent., so registering themselves. The unions were divided into four classes or categories, as follows:

Category	No. of Delegates	No. of Members Represented
First: Workers employed in large industries	287	266,660
Second: Workers employed in small industries	113	806,200
Third: "Mixed unions" of Soviet employees, etc	197	204,100
Fourth: Intellectual workers' unions	183	132,800

If we take the first two categories as representing the industrial proletariat as a whole we get 1,072,860 proletarians represented by 400 delegates; in the third and fourth categories, representing Soviet officials, Intellectuals, and "petty bourgeois elements," we get 380 delegates representing 336,900 members. Thus the industrial proletariat secured only about one-third of the representation in proportion to membership secured by the other elements. Representation was upon this basis:

Category	One Delegate for Every
First: Workers in large industries	610 workers
Second: Workers in small industries	1,427 "
Third: "Mixed unions"—Soviet employees, city employees, etc	247 "
Fourth: Intellectuals	237 "

With all this juggling and gerrymandering the Bolsheviki did not manage to get a majority of out-and-out Communists, and only by having a separate classification for "sympathizers" did they manage to attain such a majority, namely, 52 per cent. of all delegates. If we take the delegates of workers engaged in the large industries, the element which Lenin has so often called "the kernel of the proletariat," we find that only 28 per cent. declared themselves as belonging to the Communist Party. At the All-Russian Conference of Engineering Workers, reported in *Economicheskaya Zhizn* (No. 219), we find that of the delegates present those declaring themselves to be Communists were 40 per cent., those belonging to no party 46 per cent., and Mensheviki 8 per cent.

In considering these figures we must bear in mind these facts: First, delegates to such bodies are drawn from the most active men in the organizations; second, persecution of all active in opposition to the Bolsheviki inevitably lessened the number of active opponents among the delegates; third, for two years there had been no freedom of press, speech, or assemblage for any but the Communists; fourth, by enrolling as a Communist, or even by declaring himself to be a "sympathizer," a man could obtain a certain amount of protection and a privileged position in the matter of food distribution. When all these things are duly taken into account the weakness of the hold of the Bolsheviki upon the minds of even the militant part of the proletariat is evident.

What an absurdity it is to call the Bolshevist régime a dictatorship of the proletariat, even if we accept the narrow use of this term upon which the Bolsheviki insist and omit all except about 5 per cent. of the peasantry, a class which comprises 85 per cent. of the entire population. It is a dictatorship by the Communist Party, a political faction which, according to its own figures, had in its membership in March, 1919, about one-half of one per cent. of the population—or, roughly, one and a half per cent. of the adult population entitled to vote under the universal franchise introduced by the Provisional Government; a party which, after a period of confessedly dangerous inflation by the inclusion of non-proletarian elements in exceedingly large numbers, had in March of this year, in the greatest industrial center, a membership amounting to less than 10 per cent. of the number of working-men. To say that Soviet Russia is governed by the proletariat is, in the face of these figures, a grotesque and stupid misstatement.

XIII
STATE COMMUNISM AND LABOR CONSCRIPTION

Many

of the most influential critics of modern Socialism have argued that the realization of its program must inevitably require a complete and intolerable subjection of the individual to an all-powerful, bureaucratic state. They have contended that Socialism in practice would require the organization of the labor forces of the nation upon military lines; that the right of the citizen to select his or her own occupation subject only to economic laws, and to leave one job for another at will, would have to be denied and the sole authority of the state established in such matters as the assignment of tasks, the organization and direction of industry.

Writers like Yves Guyot, Eugene Richter, Herbert Spencer, Huxley, Goldwin Smith, and many others, have emphasized this criticism and assailed Socialism as the foe of individual freedom. Terrifying pictures have been drawn of the lot of the workers in such a society; their tasks assigned to them by some state authority, their hours of labor, and their remuneration similarly controlled, with no freedom of choice or right of change of occupation. Just as under the *adscriptio glebæ* of feudalism the worker was bound to the soil, so, these hostile critics of Socialism have argued, must the workers be bound to bureaucratically set tasks under Socialism. Just as, immediately prior to the breaking up of the Roman Empire, workers were thus bound to certain kinds of work and, moreover, to train their children to the same work, so, we have been told a thousand times, it must necessarily be in a Socialist state.

Of course all responsible Socialists have repudiated these fantastic caricatures of Socialism. They have uniformly insisted that Socialism is compatible with the highest individualism; that it affords the basis for a degree of personal freedom not otherwise obtainable. They have laughed to scorn the idea of a system which gave to the state the power to assign each man or woman his or her task. Every Socialist writer has insisted that the selection of occupation, for example, must be personal and free, and has assailed the idea of a regimentation or militarization of labor, pointing out that this would never be tolerated by a free democracy; that it was only possible in a despotic state, undemocratic, and not subject to the will and interest of the people. Many of the most brilliant and convincing pages of the great literature of modern international Socialism are devoted to its exoneration from this charge, particular attention being given to the anti-statist character of the Socialist movement and to the natural antagonism of democracy to centralization and bureaucracy.

It is a significant fact that from the middle of the nineteenth century right down to the present day the extreme radical left wing of the Socialist movement in every country has been bitter in its denunciation of those Socialists who assumed the continued existence of the state, rivaling the most extreme individualists in abuse of "the tyranny of the state." Without a single noteworthy exception the leaders of the radical left wing of the movement have been identified with those revolts against "statism" which have manifested themselves in the agitations for decentralized autonomy. They have been anti-parliamentarians and direct-actionists almost to a man.

By a strange irony of history it has remained for the self-styled Marxian Socialists of Russia, the Bolsheviki, who are so much more Marxist than Marx himself, to give to the criticism we are discussing the authority of history. They have lifted it from the shadowy regions of fantastic speculation to the almost impregnable and unassailable ground of established law and practice. The Code of Labor Laws of Soviet Russia, recently published in this country by the official bureau of the Russian Soviet Government, can henceforth be pointed to by the enemies of social democracy as evidence of the truth of the charge that Socialism aims to reduce mankind to a position of hopeless servitude. Certainly no freedom-loving man or woman would want to exchange life under capitalism, with all its drawbacks and disadvantages, for the despotic, bureaucratic régime clearly indicated in this most remarkable collection of laws.

As we have seen, Lenin and his followers were anti-statists. Once in the saddle they set up a powerful state machine and began to apotheosize the state. Not only did the term "Soviet State" come into quite general use in place of "Soviet Power"; what is still more significant is the special sanctity with which they endowed the state. In this they go as far as Hegel, though they do not use his spiritual terminology. The German philosopher saw the state as "the Divine Will embodied in the human will," as "Reason manifested," and as "the Eternal personified." Upon that conception the Prussian-German ideal of the state was based. That the state must be absolute, its authority unquestioned, is equally the basic conception upon which the Bolshevist régime rests. In no modern nation, not even the Germany of Bismarck and Wilhelm II, has the authority of the state been so comprehensive, so wholly dependent upon force or more completely independent of the popular will. Notwithstanding the revolutionary ferment of the time, so arrogantly confident have the self-constituted rulers become that we find Zinoviev boasting, "Were we to publish a decree ordering the entire population of Petrograd, under fifty years of age, to present themselves on the field of Mars to receive twenty-five birch rods, we are certain that 75 per cent. would obediently form a queue, and the remaining 25 per cent. would bring medical certificates exempting them from the flogging."

It is interesting to note in the writings of Lenin the Machiavellian manner in which, even before the *coup d'état* of

November, 1917, he began to prepare the minds of his followers for the abandonment of anti-statism. Shortly before that event he published a leaflet entitled, "Shall the Bolsheviki Remain in Power?" In this leaflet he pointed out that the Bolsheviki had preached the destruction of the state *only because, and so long as, the state was in the possession of the master class.* He asked why they should continue to do this after they themselves had taken the helm. The state, he argued, is the organized rule of a privileged minority class, and the Bolsheviki must use the enemy's machinery and substitute their minority. Here we have revealed the same vicious and unscrupulous duplicity, the same systematic, studied deception, as in such matters as freedom of speech and press, equal suffrage, and the convocation of the Constituent Assembly—a fundamental principle so long as the party was in revolt, anti-statism was to be abandoned the moment the power to give it effect was secured. Other Socialists had been derided and bitterly denounced by the Bolsheviki for preaching the "bourgeois doctrine" of controlling and using the machinery of the state; nothing but the complete destruction of the state and its machinery would satisfy their revolutionary minds. But with their first approach to power the tune is changed and possession and use of the machinery of the state are held to be desirable and even essential.

For what is this possession of the power and machinery of the state desired? For no constructive purpose of any sort or kind whatever, if we may believe Lenin, but only for destruction and oppression. In his little book, *The State and the Revolution*, written in September, 1917, he says: "As the state is only a transitional institution which we must use in the revolutionary struggle *in order forcibly to crush our opponents*, it is a pure absurdity to speak of a Free People's State. While the proletariat still needs the state, *it does not require it in the interests of freedom, but in the interests of crushing its antagonists.*"

Here, then, is the brutal doctrine of the state as an instrument of coercion and repression which the arch Bolshevist acknowledges; a doctrine differing from that of Treitschke and other Prussians only in its greater brutality. The much-discussed Code of Labor Laws of the Soviet Government, with its elaborate provisions for a permanent conscription of labor upon an essentially military basis, is the logical outcome of the Bolshevist conception of the state.

The statement has been made by many of the apologists of the Bolsheviki that the conscription of labor, which has been so unfavorably commented upon in the western nations, is a temporary measure only, introduced because of the extraordinary conditions prevailing. It has been stated, by Mr. Lincoln Eyre among others, that it was adopted on the suggestion of Mr. Royal C. Keely, an American engineer who was employed by Lenin to make an expert report upon Russia's economic position and outlook, and whose report, made in January of this year, is known to have been very unfavorable. A brief summary of the essential facts will show (1) that the Bolsheviki had this system in mind from the very first, and (2) that quite early they began to make tentative efforts to introduce it.

When the Bolsheviki appeared at the convocation of the Constituent Assembly and demanded that that body adopt a document which would virtually amount to a complete abdication of its functions, that document contained a clause—Article II, Paragraph 4—which read as follows: "To enforce general compulsory labor, in order to destroy the class of parasites, and to reorganize the economic life." In April, 1918, Lenin wrote:

> The delay in introducing obligatory labor service is another proof that the most urgent problem is precisely the preparatory organization work which, on one

hand, should definitely secure our gains, and which, on the other hand, is necessary to prepare the campaign to "surround capital" and to "compel its surrender." *The introduction of obligatory labor service should be started immediately, but it should be introduced gradually and with great caution, testing every step by practical experience, and, of course, introducing first of all obligatory labor service for the rich.* The introduction of a labor record-book and a consumption-budget record-book for every bourgeois, including the village bourgeois, would be a long step forward toward a complete "siege" of the enemy and toward the creation of a really *universal* accounting and control over production and distribution.[67]

[67] The Soviets at Work, p. 19

Some idea of the extent to which the principle of compulsory labor was applied to the bourgeoisie, as suggested by Lenin, can be gathered from the numerous references to the subject in the official Bolshevist press, especially in the late summer and early autumn of 1918. The extracts here cited are entirely typical: as early as April 17, 1918, *Izvestia* published a report by Larine, one of the People's Commissaries, on the government of Moscow, in which he said: "A redistribution of manual labor must be made by an organized autonomous government composed of workers; compulsory labor for workmen must be prohibited; it would subject the proletariat to the peasants and on the whole could be of no use, seeing the general stoppage of all labor. Compulsion can be used only for those who have no need to work for their living — members of heretofore ruling classes." *Bednota*, an official organ of the Communist Party, on September 20, 1918, published an interesting item from the Government of Smolensk, saying: "We shall soon have a very interesting community: we are bringing together all the landed proprietors of the district, are assigning them one property, supplying them with the necessary inventory, and making them work. Come and see this miracle! It is evident that this community is strictly guarded. The affair seems to promise well."

Here are seven typical news items from four issues of *Bednota*, the date of the paper being given after each item:

The mobilization of the bourgeoisie.—In the Government of Aaratov the bourgeoisie is mobilized. The women mend the sacks, the men clear the ruins from a big fire. In the Government of Samara the bourgeois from 18 to 50 years of age, not living from the results of their labor, are also called up. (September 19, 1918.)

Viatka, *24th September.*—The mobilization of the idlers (bourgeois) has been decided. (September 26, 1918.)

Nevel, *26th September.*—The executive committee has decreed the mobilization of the bourgeoisie in town and country. All the bourgeois in fit state to work are obliged to do forced labor without remuneration. (September 27, 1918.)

Kostroma, *26th September.*—The mobilized bourgeoisie is working at the paving of the streets. (September 27, 1918.)

The executive committee of the Soviet of the Government of Moscow has decided to introduce in all the districts the use of forced labor for all persons from 18 to 50 years of age, belonging to the non-working class. (September 27, 1918.)

Voronege, *28th September.*—The poverty committee has decided to call up all the wealthy class for communal work (ditch-making, draining the marshes, etc.). (September 29, 1918.)

Svotschevka, *28th September.*—The concentration of the bourgeoisie is being proceeded with and the transfer of the poor into commodious and healthy dwellings. The bourgeois is cleaning the streets. (September 29, 1918.)

From other Bolshevist journals a mass of similar information might be cited. Thus *Goloss Krestianstva*, October 1, 1918, said: "*Mobilization of the parasites.*—Odoeff, 28th September.—The Soviet of the district has mobilized the bourgeoisie, the priests, and other parasites for public works: repairing the pavements, cleaning the pools, and so on." On October 6, 1918, *Pravda* reported: "Chembar.—The bourgeoisie put to compulsory work is repairing the pavements and the roads." On October 11th the same paper reported Zinoviev as saying, in a speech: "If you come to Petrograd you will see scores of bourgeoisie laying the pavement in the courtyard of the Smolny.... I wish you could see how well they unload coal on the Neva and clean the barracks." *Izvestia*, October 19, 1918, published this: "Orel.—To-day the Orel bourgeoisie commenced compulsory work to which it was made liable. Parties of the bourgeoisie, thus made to work, are cleaning the streets and squares from rubbish and dirt." The *Krasnaya Gazeta*, October 16, 1918, said, "Large forces of mobilized bourgeoisie have been sent to the front to do trench work." Finally, the last-named journal on November 6, 1918, said: "The District Extraordinary Commission (Saransk) has organized a camp of concentration for the local bourgeoisie and *kulaki*.[68] The duties of the confined shall consist in keeping clean the town of Saransk. The existence of the camp will be maintained at the expense of the same bourgeoisie."

[68] *i.e., "close-fists."*

That a great and far-reaching social revolution should deny to the class overthrown the right to live in idleness is neither surprising nor wrong. A Socialist revolution could not do other than insist that no person able to work be entitled to eat without rendering some useful service to society. No Socialist will criticize the Bolsheviki for requiring work from the bourgeoisie. What is open to criticism and condemnation is the fact that compulsory labor for the bourgeoisie was not a measure of socialization, but of stupid vengeance. The bourgeois members of society were not placed upon an equality with other citizens and told that they must share the common lot and give service for bread. Instead of that, they were made a class apart and set to the performance of tasks selected only to degrade and humiliate them. In almost every reference to the subject appearing in the official Bolshevist press we observe that the bourgeoisie—the class comprising the organizers of industry and business and almost all the technical experts in the country—was set to menial tasks which the most illiterate and ignorant peasants could better do. Just as high military officers were set to digging trenches and cleaning latrines, so the civilian bourgeoisie were set to cleaning streets, removing night soil, and draining ditches, and not even given a chance to render the vastly greater services they were capable of, in many instances; services, moreover, of which the country was in dire need. A notable example of this stupidity was when the advocates of Saratov asked the local Soviet authorities to permit them to open up an idle soap-factory to make soap, of which there was a great scarcity. The reply given was that *"the bourgeoisie could not be suffered to be in competition with the working-class."* Not only was this a brutal policy, in view of the fact that the greater part of the bourgeoisie had been loyal to the March Revolution; it was as stupid and short-sighted as it was brutal, for it did not, and could not, secure the maximum services of which these elements were capable. It is quite clear that, instead of being dominated by the generous idealism of Socialism, they were mastered by hatred and a passion for revenge.

Of course the policy pursued toward the bourgeoisie paved the way, as Lenin intended it to do, for the introduction of the principle of compulsory labor in general. By pandering to the lowest instincts and motives of the unenlightened masses, causing them to rejoice at the enslavement of the formerly rich and powerful, as well as those only moderately well-to-do, Lenin and his satellites knew well that they were surely undermining the moral force of those who rejoiced, so that later they would be incapable of strong resistance against the application of the same tyranny to themselves. The publication of the Code of Labor Laws, in 1919, was the next step. This code contains 193 regulations with numerous explanatory notes, with all of which the ordinary workman, who is a conscript in the fullest sense of the word, is presumed to be familiar. Only a few of its outstanding features can be noted here. The principle of compulsion and the extent of its application are stated in the first article of the Code:

ARTICLE I

On Compulsory Labor

1. All citizens of the Russian Socialist Federated Soviet Republic, with the exceptions stated in Section 2 and 3, shall be subject to compulsory labor.

2. The following persons shall be exempt from compulsory labor:

(*a*) Persons under 16 years of age;

(*b*) All persons over 50 years;

(*c*) Persons who have become incapacitated by injury or illness.

3. Temporarily exempt from compulsory labor are:

(*a*) Persons who are temporarily incapacitated owing to illness or injury, for a period necessary for their recovery.

(*b*) Women, for a period of 8 weeks before and 8 weeks after confinement.

4. All students shall be subject to compulsory labor at the schools.

5. The fact of permanent or temporary disability shall be certified after a medical examination by the Bureau of Medical Survey in the city, district or province, by accident insurance office or agencies representing the former, according to the place of residence of the person whose disability is to be certified.

Note I. The rules on the method of examination of disabled workmen are appended hereto.

Note II. Persons who are subject to compulsory labor and are not engaged in useful public work may be summoned by the local Soviets for the execution of public work, on conditions determined by the Department of Labor in agreement with the local Soviets of trades-unions.

6. Labor may be performed in the form of:

(*a*) Organized co-operation;

(*b*) Individual personal service;

(*c*) Individual special jobs.

7. Labor conditions in government (Soviet) establishments shall be regulated by tariff rules approved by the Central Soviet authorities through the People's Commissariat of Labor.

8. Labor conditions in all establishments (Soviet, nationalized, public, and private) shall be regulated by tariff rules drafted by the trades-unions, in agreement with the directors or owners of establishments and enterprises, and approved by the People's Commissariat of Labor.

Note. In cases where it is impossible to arrive at an understanding with the directors or owners of establishments or enterprises, the tariff rules shall be drawn up by the trades-unions and submitted for approval to the People's Commissariat of Labor.

9. Labor in the form of individual personal service or in the form of individual special jobs shall be regulated by tariff rules drafted by the respective trades-unions and approved by the People's Commissariat of Labor.

It will be observed that this subjection to labor conscription applies to "all citizens" except for certain exempted classes. Women, therefore, are equally liable with men, except for a stated period before and after childbirth. It will also be observed that apparently a great deal of control is exercised by the trades-unions. We must bear in mind, however, at every point, that the trades-unions in Soviet Russia are not free and autonomous organs of the working-class. A free trades-union—that is, a trades-union wholly autonomous and independent of government control, *does not exist in Russia*. The actual status of Russian trades-unions is set forth in the resolution adopted at the ninth Congress of the Russian Communist Party, in March, 1920, which provides, that "All decisions of the All-Russian Central Soviet of Trades-Unions concerning the conditions and organization of labor are obligatory for all trades-unions and the members of the Communist Party who are employed in them, and *can be canceled only by the Central Committee of the Party.*" The hierarchy of the Communist Party is supreme, the trades-unions, the co-operatives, and the Soviet Government itself being subordinate to it.

Article II deals with the manner in which the compulsion to labor is to be enforced. Paragraph 16 of this article provides that "the assignment of wage-earners to work shall be carried out through the Departments of Labor Distribution." Paragraph 24 reads as follows: "*An unemployed person has no right to refuse an offer of work at his vocation,* provided the working conditions conform with the standards fixed by the respective tariff regulations, or in the absence of the same by the trades-unions." Paragraphs 27 to 30, inclusive, show the extraordinary power of the Departments of Labor Distribution over the workers:

27. Whenever workers are required for work outside of their district, a roll-call of the unemployed registered in the Department of Labor Distribution shall take place, to ascertain who are willing to go; if a sufficient number of such should not be found, *the Department of Labor Distribution shall assign the lacking number from among the unemployed in the order of their registration*, provided that those who have dependents must not be given preference before single persons.

28. If in the Departments of Labor Distribution, within the limits of the district, there be no workmen meeting the requirements, the District Exchange Bureau has the right, upon agreement with the respective trades-union, to send unemployed of another class approaching as nearly as possible the trade required.

29. An unemployed person who is offered work outside his vocation shall be obliged to accept it, on the understanding, if he so wishes, that this be only temporary, until he receives work at his vocation.

30. A wage-earner who is working outside his specialty, and who has stated his wish that this be only temporary, shall retain his place on the register on the Department of Labor Distribution until he gets work at his vocation.

It is quite clear from the foregoing that the Department of Labor Distribution can arbitrarily compel a worker to leave a job satisfying to him or her and to accept another job and remain at it until given permission to leave. The worker may be compelled by this power to leave a desirable job and take up a different line of work, or even to move to some other locality. It is hardly possible to imagine a device more effective in liquidating personal grudges or effecting political pressure. One has only to face the facts of life squarely in order to recognize the potentiality for evil embodied in this system. What is there to prevent the Soviet official removing the "agitator," the political opponent, for "the good of the party"? What man wants his sister or daughter to be subject to the menace of such power in the hands of unscrupulous officials? There is not the slightest evidence in the record of Bolshevism so far as it has been tried in Russia to warrant the assumption that only saints will ever hold office in the Departments of Labor Distribution.

Article V governs the withdrawal of wage-earners from jobs which do not satisfy them. Paragraph 51 of this article clearly provides that a worker can only be permitted to resign if his reasons are approved by what is described as the "respective organ of workmen's self-government." Paragraph 52 provides that if the resignation is not approved by this authority "the wage-earner must remain at work, but may appeal from the decision of the committee to the respective professional unions." Provision is made for fixing the remuneration of labor by governmental authority. Article VI, Paragraph 55, provides that "the remuneration of wage-earners for work in enterprises, establishments, and institutions employing paid labor ... shall be fixed by tariffs worked out for each kind of labor." Paragraph 57 provides that "in working out the tariff rates and determining the standard remuneration rates, all the wage-earners of a trade shall be divided into groups and categories and a definite standard of remuneration shall be fixed for each of them." Paragraph 58 provides that "the standard of remuneration fixed by the tariff rates must be at least sufficient to cover the minimum living expenses *as determined by the People's Commissariat of Labor* for each district of the Russian Socialist Federated Soviet Republic." Paragraph 60 provides that "the remuneration of each wage-earner shall be determined by his classification in a definite group and category." Paragraph 61, with an additional note, explains the method of thus classifying wage-earners. "Valuation commissions" are established by the "professional organizations" and their procedure is absolutely determined by the local Soviet official called the Commissariat of Labor. If a worker receives more than the standard remuneration fixed, "irrespective of the pretext and form under which it might be offered and whether it be paid in only one or in several places of employment"—Paragraph 65—the excess amount so received may be deducted from his next wages, according to Paragraph 68.

The amount of work to be performed each day is arbitrarily assigned. Thus, Article VIII, Paragraph 114, provides that "every wage-earner must during a normal working-day and under normal working conditions perform the standard amount of work fixed for the category and group in which he is enrolled." According to Paragraph 118 of the same article, "a wage-earner systematically producing less than the fixed standard may be transferred by decision of the proper valuation commission to other work in the same group and category, or to a lower group or category, with a corresponding reduction of wages." If it is judged that his failure to maintain the normal output is due to lack of good faith and to negligence, he may be discharged without notice.

An appendix to Section 80 provides that every wage-earner must carry a labor booklet. The following description of this booklet shows how thoroughly registered and controlled labor is in Sovdepia:

1. Every citizen of the Russian Socialist Federated Soviet Republic, upon assignment to a definite group and category (Section 62 of the present Code), shall receive, free of charge, a labor booklet.

Note. The form of the labor booklets shall be worked out by the People's Commissariat of Labor.

2. Each wage-earner, on entering the employment of an enterprise, establishment, or institution employing paid labor, shall present his labor booklet to the

management thereof, and on entering the employment of a private individual—to the latter.

Note. A copy of the labor booklet shall be kept by the management of the enterprise, establishment, institution, or private individual by whom the wage-earner is employed.

3. All work performed by a wage-earner during the normal working-day as well as piece-work or overtime work, and all payments received by him as a wage-earner (remuneration in money or in kind, subsidies from the unemployment and hospital funds), must be entered in his labor booklet.

Note. In the labor booklet must also be entered the leaves of absence and sick-leave of the wage-earner, as well as the fines imposed on him during and on account of his work.

4. Each entry in the labor booklet must be dated and signed by the person making the entry, and also by the wage-earner (if the latter is literate), who thereby certifies the correctness of the entry.

5. The labor booklet shall contain:

(*a*) The name, surname, and date of birth of the wage-earner;

(*b*) The name and address of the trades-union of which the wage-earner is a member;

(*c*) The group and category to which the wage-earner has been assigned by the valuation commission.

6. Upon the discharge of a wage-earner, his labor booklet shall under no circumstances be withheld from him. Whenever an old booklet is replaced by a new one, the former shall be left in possession of the wage-earner.

7. In case a wage-earner loses his labor booklet, he shall be provided with a new one into which shall be copied all the entries of the lost booklet; in such a

case a fee determined by the rules of internal management may be charged to the wage-earner for the new booklet.

8. A wage-earner must present his labor booklet upon the request:

(*a*) Of the managers of the enterprise, establishment, or institution where he is employed;

(*b*) Of the Department of Labor Distribution;

(*c*) Of the trades union;

(*d*) Of the officials of workmen's control and of labor protection;

(*e*) Of the insurance offices or institutions acting as such.

A wireless message from Moscow, dated February 11, 1920, referring to the actual introduction of these labor booklets, says:

The decree on the establishment of work-books is in course of realization at Moscow and Petrograd. The book has 32 pages in it, containing, besides particulars as to the holder's civil status, information on the following points:

Persons dependent on the holder, degree of capacity for work, place where employed, pay allowanced or pension, food-cards received, and so forth. One of these books should be handed over to all citizens not less than 16 years old. It constitutes the proof that the holder is doing his share of productive work. The introduction of the work-book will make it possible for us to ascertain whether the law as to work is being observed by citizens. This being the object, it will only be handed to workmen and employees in accordance with the lists of the business concerns in which they are working, to artisans who can produce a regular certificate of their registration as being sick or a certificate from the branches of the Public Welfare Administration, and to women who are engaged in keeping house, and who produce a certificate by the House Committee. When the distribution has been completed, all sick persons, not possessed of work-books, will be sent to their work by the branch of the Labor Distribution Administration.

We have summarized, in the exact language of the official English translation published by the Soviet Government Bureau in this country, the characteristic and noteworthy features of this remarkable scheme. Surely this is the ultimate madness of bureaucratism, the most complete subjection of the individual citizen to an all-powerful state since the days of Lycurgus. At the time of Edward III, by the Statute of Laborers of 1349, not only was labor enforced on the lower classes, but men were not free to work where they liked, nor were their employers permitted to pay them more than certain fixed rates of wages. In short, the laborer was a serf; and that is the condition to which this Bolshevist scheme would reduce all the people of Russia except the privileged bureaucracy. It is a rigid and ruthless rule that is here set up, making no allowance for individual likes or dislikes, leaving no opportunity for honest personal initiative. The only variations and modifications possible are those resulting from favoritism, political influence, and circumvention of the laws by corruption of official and other illicit methods.

We must bear in mind that what we are considering is not a body of facts relating to practical work under pressure of circumstance, but a carefully formulated plan giving concrete form to certain aims and intentions. It is not a record of which the Bolsheviki can say, "This we were compelled to do," but a prospectus of what they propose to do. As such the Bolsheviki have caused the wide-spread distribution of this remarkable Code of Labor Laws in this country and in England, believing, apparently, that the workers of the two countries must be attracted by this Communist Utopia. They have relied upon the potency of slogans and principles long held in honor by the militant and progressive portion of the working-class in every modern nation, such as the right to work and the right to assured living income and leisure, to win approval and support. But they have linked these things which enlightened workers believe in to a system of despotism abhorrent to them. After two full years of terrible experience the Bolsheviki propose, in the name of Socialism and freedom, a tyranny which goes far beyond anything which any modern nation has known.

It was obvious from the time when this scheme was first promulgated that it could only be established by strong military measures. No one who knew anything of Russia could believe that the great mass of the peasantry would willingly acquiesce in a scheme of government so much worse than the old serfdom. Nor was it possible to believe that the organized and enlightened workers of the cities would, as a whole, willingly and freely place themselves in such bondage. It was not at all surprising, therefore, to learn that it had been decided to take advantage of the military situation, and the existence of a vast organization of armed forces, to introduce compulsory labor as part of the military system. On December 11, 1919, *The Red Baltic Fleet*, a Bolshevist paper published for the sailors of the Baltic fleet, printed an abstract of Trotsky's report to the Seventh Congress of Soviets, from which the following significant paragraphs are quoted:

If one speaks of the conclusion of peace within the next months, such a peace cannot be called a permanent peace. So long as class states remain, as powerful centers of Imperialism in the Far East and in America, it is not impossible that the peace which we shall perhaps conclude in the near future will again be for us only a long and prolonged respite. So long as this possibility is not excluded, it is possible that it will be a matter *not of disarming, but of altering the form of the armed forces of the state.*

We must get the workmen back to the factories, and the peasants to the villages, re-establish industries and develop agriculture. Therefore, the troops must be brought nearer to the workers, and the regiments to the factories, villages, and cantons. We must pass to the introduction of the militia system of armed forces.

There is a scarcely veiled threat to the rest of the world in Trotsky's intimation that the peace they hope to conclude will perhaps be only a prolonged respite. As an isolated utterance, it might perhaps be disregarded, but it must be considered in the light of, and in connection with, a number of other utterances upon the same subject. In the instructions from the People's Commissar for Labor to the propagandists sent to create sympathy and support for the Labor Army scheme among the soldiers we find this striking passage: "The country must continue to remain armed for many years to come. *Until Socialist revolution triumphs throughout the world we must continue to be armed and prepared for eventualities.*" A Bolshevist message, dated Moscow, March 11, 1920, explains that: "The utilization of whole Labor Armies, retaining the army system of organization, may only be justified from the point of view of keeping the army intact for military purposes. As soon as the necessity for this ceases to exist the need to retain large staffs and administrations will also cease to exist." There is not the slightest doubt that the Bolsheviki contemplate the maintenance of a great army to be used as a labor force until the time arrives when it shall seem desirable to hurl it against the nations of central and western Europe in the interests of "world revolution."

On January 15, 1920, Lenin and Brichkina, president and secretary, respectively, of the Council of Defense, signed and issued the first decree for the formation of a Labor Army. The text of the decree follows:

Decree of the Workers' and Peasants' Council of Defense on the First Revolutionary Labor Army

1. The Third Workers' and Peasants' Red Army is to be utilized for labor purposes. This army is to be considered as a complete organization; its apparatus is neither to be disorganized nor split up, and it is to be known under the name of the First Revolutionary Labor Army.

2. The utilization of the Third Red Army for labor purposes is a temporary measure. The period is to be determined by a special regulation of the Council of Defense in accordance with the military situation as well as with the character of the work which the army will be able to carry out, and will especially depend on the practical productivity of the labor army.

3. The following are the principal tasks to which the forces and means of the third army are to be applied:

First:

(*a*) The preparation of food and forage in accordance with the regulation of the People's Commissariat for Food, and the concentration of these in certain depots:

(*b*) The preparation of wood and its delivery to factories and railway stations;

(*c*) The organization for this purpose of land transport as well as water transport;

(*d*) The mobilization of necessary labor power for work on a national scale;

(*e*) Constructive work within the above limits as well as on a wider scale, for the purpose of introducing, gradually, further works.

Second:

> (*f*) For repair of agricultural implements;

> (*g*) Agricultural work, etc.

4. The first duty of the Labor Army is to secure provisions, not below the Red Army ration, for the local workers in those regions where the army is stationed; this is to be brought about by means of the army organs of supply in all those cases where the President of the Food Commissariat of the Labor Army Council (No. 7) will find that no other means of securing the necessary provisions for the above-mentioned workers are to be had.

5. The utilization of the labor of the third army in a certain locality must take place in the locality in which the principal part of the army is stationed; this is to be determined exactly by the leading organs of the army (No. 6) with a subsequent confirmation by the Council of Defense.

6. The Revolutionary Council of the Labor Army is the organ in charge of work appointed, with the provision that the locality where the services of the Labor Army are to be applied is to be the same locality where the services of the Revolutionary Council of the Labor Army enjoys economic authority.

7. The Revolutionary Council of the Labor Army is to be composed of members of the Revolutionary War Council and of authorized representatives of the People's Commissariat for Food, the Supreme Council for Public Economy, the People's Commissariat for Agriculture, the People's Commissariat for Communication, and the People's Commissariat for Labor.

An especially authorized Council of Defense which is to enjoy the rights of presidency of the Council of the Labor Army is to be put at the head of the above Council.

8. All the questions concerning internal military organizations and defined by regulations of internal military service and other military regulations are to be finally settled upon by the Revolutionary War Council which introduces in

the internal life of the army all the necessary changes arising in consequence of the demands of the economic application of the army.

9. In every sphere of work (food, fuel, railway, etc.) the final decision in the matter of organizing this work is to be left with the representative of the corresponding sphere of the Labor Army Council.

10. In the event of radical disagreement the case is to be transferred to the Council of Defense.

11. All the local institutions, Councils of Public Economy, Food Committees, land departments, etc., are to carry out the special orders and instructions of the Labor Army Council through the latter's corresponding members either in its entirety or in that sphere of the work which is demanded by the application of the mass labor power.

12. All local institutions (councils of public economy, food committees, etc.) are to remain in their particular localities and carry out, through their ordinary apparatus, the work which falls to their share in the execution of the economic plans of the Labor Army Council; local institutions can be changed, either in structure or in their functions, on no other condition except with the consent of the corresponding departmental representatives who are members of the Labor Army Council, or, in the case of radical changes, with the consent of the corresponding central department.

13. In the case of work for which individual parts of the army can be utilized in a casual manner, as well as in the case of those parts of the army which are stationed outside the chief army, or which can be transferred beyond the limits of this locality, the Army Council must in each instance enter into an agreement with the permanent local institutions carrying out the corresponding work, and as far as that is practical and meets with no obstacles, the separate military detachments are to be transferred to their temporary economic disposal.

14. Skilled workers, in so far as they are not indispensable for the support of the life of the army itself, must be transferred by the army to the local factories and to the economic institutions generally under direction of the corresponding representatives of the Labor Army Council.

Note: Skilled labor can be sent to factories under no other condition except with the consent of those economic organs to which the factory in question is subject. Members of trades-unions are liable to be withdrawn from local enterprises for the economic needs in connection with the problems of the army only with the consent of the local organs.

15. The Labor Army Council must, through its corresponding members, take all the necessary measures toward inducing the local institutions of a given department to control, in the localities, the army detachments and their institutions in the carrying out of the latter's share of work without infringing upon the respective by-laws, regulations, and instructions of the Soviet Republic.

Note: It is particularly necessary to take care that the general state rate of pay is to be observed in the remuneration of peasants for the delivery of food, for the preparation of wood or other fuel.

16. The Central Statistical Department in agreement with the Supreme Council for Public Economy and the War Department is instructed to draw up an estimate defining the forms and period of registration.

17. The present regulation comes into force with the moment of its publication by telegraph.

President of the Council of Defense

V. Ulianov (Lenin).

S. Brichkina, SECRETARY.

Moscow, January 15, 1920.

On January 18, 1920, the *Krasnaya Gazeta* published the following order by Trotsky to the First Labor Army:

Order to the First Revolutionary Labor Army

1. The First Army has finished its war task, but the enemy is not completely dispersed. The rapacious imperialists are still menacing Siberia in the

extreme Orient. To the East the armies paid by the Entente are still menacing Soviet Russia. The bands of the White Guards are still at Archangel. The Caucasus is not yet liberated. For this reason the First Russian Army has not as yet been diverted, but retains its internal unity and its warlike ardor, in order that it may be ready in case the Socialist Fatherland should once more call it to new tasks.

2. The First Russian Army, which is, however, desirous of doing its duty, does not wish to lose any time. During the coming weeks and months of respite it will have to apply its strength and all its means to ameliorate the agricultural situation in this country.

3. The Revolutionary War Council of the First Army will come to an agreement with the Labor Council. The representatives of the agricultural institutions of the Red Republic of the Soviets will work side by side with the members of the Revolutionary Council.

4. Food-supplies are indispensable to the famished workmen of the commercial centers. The First Labor Army should make it its essential task to gather systematically in the region occupied by it such food-supplies as are there, as well as also to make an exact listing of what has been obtained, to rapidly and energetically forward them to the various factories and railway stations, and load them upon the freight-cars.

5. Wood is needed by commerce. It is the important task of the Revolutionary Labor Army to cut and saw the wood, and to transport it to the factories and to the railway stations.

6. Spring is coming; this is the season of agricultural work. As the productive force of our factories has lessened, the number of new farm implements which can be delivered has become insufficient. The peasants have, however, a tolerably large number of old implements which are in need of repair. The Revolutionary Labor Army will employ its workshops as well as its workmen in order to repair such tools and machinery as are needed. When the season arrives for work in the fields, the Red cavalry and infantry will prove that they know how to plow the earth.

7. All members of the army should enter into fraternal relations with the professional societies[69] of the local Soviets, remembering that such

organizations are those of the laboring people. All work should be done after having come to an understanding with them.

69 *i.e., trades-unions.*

8. Indefatigable energy should be shown during the work, as much as if it were a combat or a fight.

9. The necessary efforts, as well as the results to be obtained, should be carefully calculated. Every pound of Soviet bread, and every log of national wood should be tabulated. Everything should contribute to the foundation of the Socialist activities.

10. The Commandants and Commissars should be responsible for the work of their men while work is going on, as much as if it were a combat. Discipline should not be relaxed. The Communist Societies should during the work be models of perseverance and patience.

11. The Revolutionary Tribunals should punish the lazy and parasites and the thieves of national property.

12. Conscientious soldiers, workmen, and revolutionary peasants should be in the first rank. Their bravery and devotion should serve as an example to others and inspire them to act similarly.

13. The front should be contracted as much as possible. Those who are useless should be sent to the first ranks of the workers.

14. Start and finish your work, if the locality permits it, to the sound of revolutionary hymns and songs. Your task is not the work of a laborer, but a great service rendered the Socialist Fatherland.

15. Soldiers of the Third Army, called the First Revolutionary Army of Labor. Let your example prove a great one. All Russia will rise to your call. The Radio has already spread throughout the universe all that the Third Army intends in being transposed into the First Army of Labor. Soldier Workmen! Do not lower the red standard!

The President of the War Council of the Revolutionary Republic

[Signed] TROTSKY.

There is not the slightest doubt where Lenin and Trotsky found the model for the foregoing orders and the inspiration of the entire scheme. Almost exactly a century earlier, that is to say in the first quarter of the nineteenth century, Count Arakcheev, a favorite of Alexander I, introduced into Russia the militarization of agricultural labor. Peasant conscripts were sent to the "military settlements," formed into battalions under command of army officers, marched in proper military formation to their tasks, which they performed to martial music. The arable lands were divided among the owner-settlers according to the size of their families. Tasks were arbitrarily set for the workers by the officers; resignation or withdrawal was, of course, impossible; desertion was punished with great severity. Elaborate provisions were made by this monarchist autocrat for the housing of the conscript-settlers, for medical supervision, and for the education of the children. Everything seems to have been provided for the conscripts in these settlements except freedom.

Travelers gave most glowing accounts of Arakcheev's Utopia, just as later travelers did of the Russia of Nicholas II, and as the Ransomes, Goodes, Lansburys, and other travelers of to-day are giving of Bolshevist Russia. But the people themselves were discontented and unhappy, a fact evidenced by the many serious uprisings. Robbed of freedom, all initiative taken from them, so that they became abject and cowed and almost devoid of will power, like dumb beasts yet under the influence of desperate and daring leaders, they rose in revolt again and again with brutal fury. Arakcheev's Utopia was not intended to be oppressive or unjust, we may well believe. There are evidences that it was conceived in a noble and even generous spirit. It inevitably became cruel and oppressive, however, as every such scheme that attempts to disregard the variations in human beings, and to compel them to conform to a single pattern or plan, must do. At a meeting of the Central

Committee of the Communist Party in Petrograd Trotsky protested that only the "petty bourgeois intellectuals" could liken his system of militarized labor to Arakcheev's, but the facts speak for themselves. And in all Russia's tragic history there are no blacker pages than those which record her great experiments with militarized labor.

Addressing the joint meeting of the third Russian Congress of Soviets of National Economy, the Moscow Soviet of Deputies and the Administrative Boards of the Trades-Unions, on January 25, 1920, Trotsky made a report which required more than two hours for its delivery. Defining labor conscription, he said:

> We shall succeed if qualified and trained workers take part in productive labor. They must all be registered and provided with work registration books. Trades-unions must register qualified workmen in the villages. Only in those localities where trades-union methods are inadequate other methods must be introduced, in particular that of compulsion, because labor conscription gives the state the right to tell the qualified workman who is employed on some unimportant work in his villages, "You are obliged to leave your present employment and go to Sormova or Kolomna, because there your work is required."
>
> Labor conscription means that qualified workmen who leave the army must take their work registration books and proceed to places where they are required, where their presence is necessary to the economic system of the country. Labor conscription gives the Labor State the right to order a workman to leave the village industry in which he is engaged and to work in state enterprises which require his services. We must feed these workmen and guarantee them the minimum food ration. A short time ago we were confronted by the problem of defending the frontiers of the Soviet Republic, now our aim is to collect, load, and transport a sufficient quantity of bread, meat, fats, and fish to feed the working-class. We are not only confronted by the question of the industrial proletariat, but also by the question of utilizing unskilled labor.

There is still one way to the reorganization of national economy—the way of uniting the army and labor and changing the military detachments of the army into labor detachments of a labor army. Many in the army have already accomplished their military task, but they cannot be demobilized as yet. Now that they have been released from their military duties, they must fight against economic ruin and against hunger; they must work to obtain fuel, peat, and inflammable slate; they must take part in building, in clearing the lines of snow, in repairing roads, building sheds, grinding flour, and so on. We have already got several of these armies. These armies have already been allotted their tasks. One must obtain foodstuffs for the workmen of the district in which it was formerly stationed, and there also it will cut down wood, cart it to the railways, and repair engines. Another will help in the laying down of railway lines for the transport of crude oil. A third will be used for repairing agricultural implements and machines, and in the spring for taking part in working the land. At the present time among the working masses there must be the greatest exactitude and conscientiousness, together with responsibility to the end; there must be utter strictness and severity, both in small matters and in great. If the most advanced workmen in the country will devote all their thoughts, all their will, and all their revolutionary duty to the cause of regulating economic affairs, then I have no doubt that we shall lead Russia on a new free road, to the confounding of our enemies and the joy of our friends.

Going into further details concerning the scheme, Trotsky said, according to *Izvestia*, January 29, 1920:

Wherein lies the meaning of this transformation? We possess armies which have accomplished their military tasks. *Can we demobilize them? In no case whatever. If we have learned anything in the civil war it is certainly circumspection.* While keeping the army under arms, we may use it for economic purposes, with the *possibility of sending it to the front in case of need.*

Such is the present condition of the Third Soviet Army at Ekaterinburg, some units of which are quartered in the direction of Omsk. It numbers no less than *150,000 men, of whom 7,000 are Communists and 9,000 are sympathizers.* Such an army is class-conscious to a high degree. No wonder it has offered itself for employment for labor purposes. The labor army must perform definite and simple tasks requiring the application of mass force, such as lumbering operations, peat-cutting, collecting grain, etc. Trades-unions, political and Soviet organizations must, of course, establish the closest contact with the Labor Army. An experienced and competent workman is appointed as chief of staff of this army, and a former chief of staff, an officer of the general staff, is his assistant. The Operative Department is renamed the Labor-Operative Department, and controls requisitions and the execution of the labor-operative orders and the labor bulletins.

A great number of labor artels, with a well-ordered telegraph and telephone system, is thus at our disposal. They receive orders and report on their execution the same day. This is but the beginning of our work. There will be many drawbacks at first, much will have to be altered, but the basis itself cannot be unsound, as it is the same on which our entire Soviet structure is founded.

In this case we possess several thousand Ural workmen, who are placed at the head of the army, and a mass of men under the guidance of these advanced workmen. What is it? It is but a reflection on a small scale of Soviet Russia, founded upon millions upon millions of peasants, and the guiding apparatus is formed of more conscious peasants and an overwhelming majority of industrial workers. This first experiment is being made by the other armies likewise. It is intended to utilize the Seventh Army, quartered at the Esthonian frontier, for peat-cutting and slate-quarrying. If these labor armies are capable of extracting raw materials, of giving new life to our transport, of providing corn, fuel, etc., to our main economic centers, then our economic organism will revive.

This experiment is of the most vital moral and material importance. We cannot mobilize the peasants by means of trades-unions, and the trades-unions themselves do not possess any means of laying hold of millions of peasants. They can best be mobilized on a military footing. Their labor formations will have to be organized on a military model—labor platoons, labor companies, labor battalions, disciplined as required, for we shall have to deal with masses which have not passed through trades-union trading. This is a matter of the near future. We shall be compelled to create military organizations such as exist already in the form of our armies. It is therefore urgent to utilize them by adapting them to economic requirements. That is exactly what we are doing now.

At the ninth Congress of the Communist Party in March, according to *Izvestia* of March 21, 1920, Trotsky made another report on the militarization of labor, in which he said:

At the present time the militarization of labor is all the more needed in that we have now come to the mobilization of peasants as the means of solving the problems requiring mass action. We are mobilizing the peasants and forming them into labor detachments which very closely resemble military detachments. Some of our comrades say, however, that even though in the case of the working power of mobilized peasantry it is necessary to apply militarization, a military apparatus need not be created when the question involves skilled labor and industry because there we have professional unions performing the function of organizing labor. This opinion, however, is erroneous.

At present it is true that professional unions distribute labor power at the demand of social-economic organizations, but what means and methods do they possess for insuring that the workman who is sent to a given factory actually reports at that factory for work?

We have in the most important branches of our industry more than a million workmen on the lists, but not more than eight hundred thousand of them are actually working, and where are the remainder? They have gone to the villages, or to other divisions of industry, or into speculation. Among soldiers this is called desertion, and in one form or another the measures used to compel soldiers to do their duty should be applied in the field of labor.

Under a unified system of economy the masses of workmen should be moved about, ordered and sent from place to place in exactly the same manner as soldiers. This is the foundation of the militarization of labor, and without this we are unable to speak seriously of any organization of industry on a

> new basis in the conditions of starvation and disorganization existing today....

> In the period of transition in the organization of labor, compulsion plays a very important part. The statement that free labor—namely, freely employed labor—produces more than labor under compulsion is correct only when applied to feudalistic and bourgeois orders of society.

It is, of course, too soon to attempt anything in the nature of a final judgment upon this new form of industrial serfdom. In his report to the ninth Congress of the Communist Party, already quoted, Trotsky declared that the belief that free labor is more productive than forced labor is "correct only when applied to feudalistic and bourgeois orders of society." The implication is that it will be otherwise in the Communistic society of the future, but of that Trotsky can have no knowledge. His declaration springs from faith, not from knowledge. All that he or anybody else can know is that the whole history of mankind hitherto shows that free men work better than men who are not free. Arakcheev's militarized peasants were less productive than other peasants not subject to military rule. So far as the present writer's information goes, no modern army when engaged in productive work has equaled civilian labor in similar lines, judged on a per-capita basis. Slaves, convicts, and conscripts have everywhere been notoriously poor producers.

Will it be better if the conscription is done by the Bolsheviki, and if the workers sing revolutionary songs, instead of the hymns to the Czar sung by Arakcheev's conscript settlers, or the religious melodies sung by the negro slaves in our Southern States? Those whose only guide to the future is the history of the past will doubt it; those who, like Trotsky, see in the past no lesson for the future confidently believe that it will. The thoughtful and candid mind wonders whether the following paragraph, published by the *Krasnaya Gazeta* in

March, may not be regarded as a foreshadowing of Bolshevist disillusionment:

> The attempts of the Soviet power to utilize the Labor Army for cleansing Petrograd from mud, excretions, and rubbish have not met with success. In addition to the usual Labor Army rations, the men were given an increased allowance of bread, tobacco, etc. Nevertheless, it was found impossible to get not only any intensive work, but even, generally speaking, any real work at all out of the Labor Army men. Recourse, therefore, had to be had to the usual means—the men had to be paid a premium of 1,000 rubles for every tramway-truck of rubbish unloaded. Moreover, the tramway brigade had to be paid 300 rubles for every third trip.

In hundreds of statements by responsible Bolshevist officials and journals the wonderful morale of the Petrograd workers has been extolled and held up to the rest of Russia for emulation. If these things are possible in "Red Peter" at the beginning, what may we not expect elsewhere—and later? The *Novaya Russkaya Zhizn*, published at Helsingfors, is an anti-Bolshevist paper. The following quotation from its issue of March 6, 1920, is of interest and value only in so far as it directs attention to a Bolshevist official report:

> In the Soviet press we find a brilliant illustration (in figures) of the latest "new" tactics proclaimed by the Communists of the Third International on the subject of soldiers "stacking their rifles and taking to axes, saws, and spades."
>
> "The 56th Division of the Petrograd Labor Army, during the fortnight from 1st to 14th February, loaded 60 cars with wood-fuel, transported 225 sagenes,[70] stacked 43 cubic sagenes, and sawed up 39 cubic sagenes." Besides this, the division dug out "several locomotives" from under the snow.
>
> [70] *One sagene equals seven feet.*
>
> In Soviet Russia a regiment is about 1,000 strong, and a division is about 4,000. In the course of a fortnight the division worked twelve days. According to our

calculation this works out, on an average, at a fraction over one billet of wood per diem per Red Army man handled by him in one way or another.

Thus it took 4,000 men a fortnight to do what could, in former days, be easily performed by ten workmen.

Unfortunately, the Bolsheviks have not yet calculated the cost to the Workmen's and Peasants' Government of the wood-fuel which was loaded, transported, stacked, and sawn up by the 56th Division of the Labor Army in the course of a fortnight.

These quotations are not offered as proof of the uneconomical character of compulsory labor. It is useless to argue that question further than we have already done. But there is a question of vastly greater importance than the volume of production—namely, the effect upon the human elements involved, the producers themselves. It is quite clear that this universal conscription of the laborers cannot be carried out without a large measure of adscription to the jobs assigned them, however modified in individual cases. It is equally certain that under the conditions described by Lenin and Trotsky in the official utterances we have quoted, nothing worthy the name of personal freedom can by any possibility exist. The condition of the workers under such a system cannot be fundamentally different from that of the natives of Paraguay in the theocratic-communist régime established by the Jesuits in the seventeenth century, or from that of Arakcheev's militarized serfs. External and superficial differences there may be, but none of fundamental importance. The Bolshevist régime may be less brutal and more humane than Arakcheev's, but so was the Jesuit rule in Paraguay. Yet in the latter, as in the former, the workers were reduced to the condition of mere automatons until, led by daring spirits, they rose in terrible revolt of unparalleled brutality.

Such is the militarization of labor in the Bolshevist paradise, and such is the light that history throws upon it. We do not wonder that *Pravda* had to admit, on March 28, 1920, that mass-meetings to protest against the new system were being held in all parts of Soviet Russia. That the Russian workers will submit for long to the new tyranny is, happily, unthinkable.

XIV
LET THE VERDICT BE RENDERED

THE men and women of America are by the force of circumstance impaneled as a jury to judge the Bolshevist régime. The evidence submitted in these pages is before them. It is no mere chronicle of scandal; neither is it a cunningly wrought mosaic of rumors, prejudiced inferences, exaggerated statements by hostile witnesses, sensational incidents and utterances, selected because they are calculated to provoke resentment. On the contrary, the most scrupulous care has been taken to confine the case to the well-established and acknowledged characteristic features of the Bolshevist régime. The bulk of the evidence cited comes from Bolshevist sources of the highest possible authority and responsibility. The non-Bolshevist witnesses are, without exception, men of high character, identified with the international Socialist movement. There is not a reactionist or an apologist for the capitalist order of society among them. In each case special attention has been directed to their anti-Bolshevist views, so that the jury can make full allowance therefor. Moreover, in no instance has the testimony of witnesses of anti-Bolshevist views been cited without ample corroborative evidence from responsible and authoritative Bolshevist sources. The jury must now pass upon this evidence and render its verdict.

It is urged by the Bolsheviki and by their defenders that the time for passing judgment has not yet arrived; that we are not yet in possession of sufficient evidence to warrant a decision. Neither the Bolsheviki nor their defenders have the right to make this plea, for the simple reason that they themselves have long since demanded that, with less than a thousandth part of the testimony now before us, we pass judgment — and, of course, give our unqualified approval to Bolshevism and its works. It is a matter of record and of common knowledge that soon after the Bolshevist régime was instituted in Russia a vigorous, systematic propaganda in its favor and support was begun in all the western nations, including the United States. By voice and pen the makers of this propaganda called upon the people of the western nations to adopt Bolshevism. They presented glowing pictures of the Bolshevist Utopia, depicting it, not as an experiment of uncertain outcome, to be watched with sympathetic interest, but as an achievement so great, so successful and beneficent, that to refrain from copying it was both stupid and wrong. In this country, as in the other western nations, pamphlets extolling the merits of the Soviet régime were extensively circulated by well-organized groups, while certain "Liberal" weeklies devoted themselves to the task of presenting Bolshevism as a great advance in political and economic practice, a triumph of humanitarian idealism. Organizations were formed for the purpose of molding our public opinion in favor of Bolshevism.

It was not until this pro-Bolshevist propaganda was well under way that anything in the nature of a counter-propaganda was begun. For a considerable period of time this counter-propaganda in defense of existing democratic forms of government was relatively weak, and even now it has to be admitted that the pro-Bolshevist books and pamphlets in circulation in this country greatly outnumber those on the other side. In view of these facts, the defenders of Bolshevism have no moral right to demand suspension of judgment now. They themselves rushed to the bar of public opinion with a flimsy case, composed in its entirety of *ex parte* and misleading statements by interested witnesses, many of them perjured, and demanded an instant verdict of approval. Upon what intellectual or moral grounds, then, shall others be denied the right to appear before that same court of public opinion, with a much more complete case, composed mainly of unchallenged admissions and records of the Bolsheviki themselves, and to ask for a contrary verdict?

There is not the slightest merit in the claim that we do not possess sufficient evidence to warrant a conclusive verdict in the case. Whether the Soviet form of government, basing suffrage upon occupation and economic functioning, is better adapted for Russia than the types of representative parliamentary government familiar to us in the western nations, does not enter into the case at all. The issue is not Sovietism, but Bolshevism. It is the tragic failure of Bolshevism with which we are concerned. It has failed to give the people freedom and failed to give them bread. We know that there is no freedom in Russia, and, what is more, that freedom can never be had upon the basis of the Bolshevist philosophy. Whether in Russia or in this country, government must rest upon the consent of the governed in order to merit the designation of free government; upon any other basis it must be tyrannical. It is as certain now as it will be a generation or a century hence, as certain as that yesterday belongs to the past and is irrevocable, that Bolshevism is government by a minority imposed upon the majority by force; that its sanctions are not the free choice and consent of the governed.

We know as much now as our descendants will know a couple of centuries hence concerning the great fundamental issues involved in this controversy. More than seven centuries have elapsed since the signing of Magna Charta at Runnimede. Upon every page of the history of the Anglo-Saxon people, from that day in June, 1215, to the present, it is plainly written that government which does not rest upon the consent of the governed cannot satisfy free men. Throughout that long period the moral and intellectual energy of the race has been devoted to the attainment of the ideal of universal and equal suffrage as the basis of free government. There are many persons who do not believe in that ideal, and it is possible to bring against it arguments which do not lack plausibility or force. Czar Nicholas II did not believe in that ideal; George III did not believe in it; Nicolai Lenin does not believe in it. Lincoln did believe in it; Marx believed in it; the American people believe in it. At this late day it is not necessary to argue the merits of democratic government. The consensus of the opinion of mankind, based upon long experience, favors government resting upon the will of the majority, with proper safeguards for the rights of the minority, as against government by minorities however constituted. Bolshevism, admittedly based upon the theory of rule by a minority of the people, thus runs counter to the experience and judgment of civilized mankind in every nation. In Russia a democratic government conforming to the experience and judgment of civilized and free peoples was being set up when the Bolsheviki by violence destroyed the attempt.

More conclusive, however, is the moral judgment of the conduct of the Bolsheviki as exemplified by their attitude toward the Constituent Assembly: During the summer of 1917, the period immediately preceding the *coup d'état* of November, while the Provisional Government under

Kerensky was engaged in making preparations for the holding of the Constituent Assembly, the Bolsheviki professed to believe that the Provisional Government was not loyal to the Constituent Assembly, and that there was danger that this instrument of popular sovereignty would be crippled, if not wholly destroyed, unless Kerensky and his associates were replaced by men and women more thoroughly devoted to the Constituent Assembly than they. It was as champions and defenders of the Constituent Assembly that the Bolsheviki obtained the power which enabled them to overthrow the Provisional Government. As late as October 25th Trotsky denounced Kerensky, charging him with conspiring to prevent the convocation of the Constituent Assembly. He demanded that the powers of government be taken over by the Soviets, which would, he said, convoke the Assembly on December 12th, the date assigned for it. Immediately after the *coup d'état*, the triumphant Bolsheviki, at the All-Russian Congress of Soviets, announced that "pending the calling together of the Constituent Assembly, a Provisional Workers' and Peasants' Government is to be formed, which is to be called the Council of People's Commissaries." On the day following the *coup d'état*, November 8, 1917, Lenin made this very positive and explicit statement at the Soviet Congress:

> As a democratic government, we cannot disregard the will of the masses, even though we disagree with it. In the fires of life, applying the decree in practice, carrying it out on the spot, the peasants will themselves understand where the truth is. *And even if the peasants will continue to follow the Socialists-Revolutionists, and even if they will return a majority for that Party in the elections to the Constituent Assembly, we shall still say—let it be thus!* Life is the best teacher, and it will show who was right. And let the peasants from their end, and us from ours, solve this problem. Life will compel us to approach each other in the general current of revolutionary activity, in the working out of new forms of statehood. We should keep abreast of life; we must allow the masses of the people full freedom of creativeness.

On that same day the "land decree" was issued. It began with these words: "The land problem in its entirety can be solved only by the national Constituent Assembly." Three days after the revolt Lenin, as president of the People's Commissaries, published a decree, stating:

1. That the elections to the Constituent Assembly shall be held on November 25th, the day we set aside for this purpose.

2. All electoral committees, all local organizations, the Councils of Workmen's, Soldiers', and Peasants' Delegates and the soldiers' organizations at the front are to bend every effort toward safeguarding the freedom of the voters and fair play at the elections to the Constituent Assembly, which will be held on the appointed date.

If language has any meaning at all, by these declarations the Bolsheviki were pledged to recognize and uphold the Constituent Assembly.

As the electoral campaign proceeded and it became evident that the Bolsheviki would not receive the support of the great mass of the voters, their organs began to adopt a very critical attitude toward the Constituent Assembly. There was a thinly veiled menace in the following passages from an article published in *Pravda* on November 18, 1917, while the electoral campaign was in full swing:

To expect from the Constituent Assembly a painless solution of all our accursed problems not only savors of parliamentary imbecility, but is also dangerous politically.... The victory of the Petrograd proletariat and garrison in the November revolution furnishes the only possible guaranty of the convocation of the Constituent Assembly, and, what is not less important, assures success to such a solution of our political and social problems which the War and the Revolution have made the order of the day. The convocation of the Constituent Assembly stands or falls with the Soviet power.

The elections to the Constituent Assembly were held in a large majority of electoral districts on the 12th, 19th, and 26th of November, 1917—that is, after the *coup d'état*, in the full tide of Bolshevist enthusiasm. The Bolsheviki were in power, and there is abundant evidence that they resorted to almost every known method of coercion and intimidation to secure a result favorable to themselves. Of 703 deputies elected in 54 out of a total of 81 election districts, only 168 belonged to the Bolshevist Party. At the same time the Party of Socialists-Revolutionists proper, not reckoning the organizations of the same party among other nationalities of Russia, won twice that number of seats—namely, 338. Out of a total of 36,257,960 votes cast in 54 election districts the Bolshevist Party counted barely 25 per cent. The votes cast for their candidates amounted to 9,023,963, whereas the Socialists-Revolutionists polled 20,893,734—that is, 58 per cent. of all the votes cast.

When the election results were known *Pravda* and *Izvestia* both took the position that the victorious people did not need a Constituent Assembly; that a new instrument, greatly superior to the old and "obsolete" democratic instrument, had been created. On December 1, 1917, *Pravda* said: "If the lines of action of the Soviets and the Constituent Assembly should diverge, if there should arise between them any disagreements, the question will arise as to who expresses better the will of the masses. *We think it is the Soviets who through their peculiar organization express more clearly, more correctly, and more definitely the will of the workers, soldiers, and peasants....* This is why the Soviets will have to propose to the Constituent Assembly to adopt as the constitution of the Russian Republic, not that political system which forms the basis of its convocation (*i.e.*, Democracy), but the Soviet system, the constitution of the Republic of Workers', soldiers', and Peasants' Soviets." On December 7, 1917, the Executive Committee of the Soviet power published a resolution which indicated that this self-constituted authority, despite the most solemn pledges, was already tampering with the newly elected Constituent Assembly. The resolution asserted that the Soviet power had the right to issue writs for new elections where a majority of the voters expressed themselves as dissatisfied with the result of the elections already held. In other words, notwithstanding the fact that the elections for the Constituent Assembly had been held in November, while the Bolsheviki were in power, and the first meeting of that body was scheduled for December 12th, new elections might be ordered by the Soviet power in response to a request from the majority of the electorate. That the elections had gone so overwhelmingly against the Bolsheviki, most of their candidates being badly defeated, throws a sinister light upon this decision. *Pravda* demanded that the leading members of the Constitutional-Democratic Party be arrested, including those elected to the Constituent Assembly, and on December 13, 1917, it published this decree of the Council of People's Commissaries: "The leading members of the Constitutional-Democratic Party, as a party of enemies of the people, are to be arrested and brought to trial before the Revolutionary Tribunals."

On December 26, 1917, Lenin published in *Pravda* a series of nineteen "theses" concerning the Constituent Assembly. He therein set forth the doctrine that although the elections had taken place after the Bolshevist *coup d'état*, and under the authority and protection of the temporary Soviet power, yet the elections gave no clear indication of the real mind of the masses of the people, because, forsooth, the Socialists-Revolutionists Party, whose candidates had been elected in a majority of the constituencies, had divided into a Right Wing and a Left Wing subsequent to the elections. That the differences between these factions would be fully threshed out in the Constituent Assembly was obvious. Nevertheless, Lenin announced that the Constituent Assembly just elected was not suitable. Again we are compelled to connect this announcement with the fact that the Bolsheviki had not succeeded in winning the support of the electorate. In these tortuous logomachies we encounter the same immoral doctrine that we have noticed in Lenin's discussion of the demand for freedom of speech, publication, and assemblage. The demand for the convocation of the Constituent Assembly had been "an entirely just one in the program of revolutionary Social-Democracy" in the past, but now with the Bolsheviki in power it was a different matter! Whereas the Soviets had been declared to be the loyal protectors of the Constituent Assembly, Lenin's new declaration was, "The Soviet Republic represents not only a higher form of democratic institutions (in comparison with the middle-class republic and the Constituent Assembly as its consummation), it is also the sole form which renders possible the least painful transition to Socialism."

When the Constituent Assembly finally convened on January 18, 1918, there were sailors and Lettish troops in the hall armed with rifles, hand-grenades, and machine-guns, placed there to intimidate the elected representatives of the people. The Bolshevist delegates demanded the adoption of a declaration by the Assembly which was tantamount to a formal abdication. One of the paragraphs in this declaration read: "Supporting the Soviet rule and *accepting the orders of the Council of People's Commissaries*, the Constituent Assembly acknowledges its duty to outline a form for the reorganization of society." When the Constituent Assembly, which represented more than thirty-six million votes, declined to adopt this declaration, the Bolsheviki withdrew and later, by force of arms, dispersed the Assembly. It was subsequently promised that arrangements for the election of a new

Constituent Assembly would be made, but, as all the world knows, *no such elections have been held to this time.*

At the Congress of the Bolshevist Party—now Communist Party—held in February, 1918, Lenin set forth a brand-new set of principles for adoption as a program. He declared that the transition to Socialism necessarily presupposes that there can be "no liberty and democracy for all, but only for the exploited working-classes, for the sake of their liberation from exploitation"; that it requires "the automatic exclusion of the exploiting classes, and of the rich representatives of the petty bourgeoisie" and "the abolition of parliamentary government." On the basis of these principles the Constitution of the Russian Socialist Federated Soviet Republic was developed.

To say that we are not yet in a position to judge such a record as this is an insult to the intelligence. A century hence the record will stand precisely as it is and the base treachery and duplicity of the Bolsheviki will be neither more nor less obvious. The betrayal of the Constituent Assembly by the Bolsheviki constitutes one of the blackest crimes in the history of politics and is incapable of defense by any honest democrat. It is only necessary to imagine a constitutional convention representing the free choice of the electorate in any state of the Union thus dealt with by a political faction representing only a small minority of the population to arrive at a just estimate of its infamous character. As the evidence drawn from official Bolshevist sources shows, the Bolsheviki have not respected the integrity of the Soviet any more than they respected that of the Constituent Assembly. When Soviet elections have gone against them they have not hesitated to suppress the Soviets. Is there any room for rational doubt what the verdict of decent liberty-loving and law-respecting men and women ought to be? The Bolshevist régime was conceived in dishonor and born in infamy.

We are as fully competent to judge the Red Terror organized and maintained by the Bolsheviki as our descendants will be. The civilized world has long since made up its mind concerning the Reign of Terror in the French Revolution. Contemporary foreign opinion became the judgment of posterity. That it did not help the cause of freedom and democracy, which the Revolution as a whole served, is so plainly apparent and so universally admitted that it need not be argued. It rendered aid only to the reaction. When the leaders of the Bolsheviki proclaimed their intention of copying the methods of the Reign of Terror *it was already possible to form a just judgment of the spirit of their undertaking*. The civilized world had no difficulty in judging the conduct of the Germans in shooting innocent hostages during the war. Neither has it any difficulty in making up its mind concerning the wholesale shooting of innocent hostages by the Bolsheviki. From their own records we have read their admissions that hundreds and thousands of such hostages—men, women, and children—who were not even accused of crime, were shot down in cold blood. To say that we lack sufficient evidence to pronounce judgment upon such crimes is tantamount to a confession of lacking elemental moral sense.

It is sometimes said that these things are but the violent birth pangs which inevitably accompany the birth of a new social order. With such flimsy evasions it is difficult to have patience. This specious defense utterly lacks moral and intellectual sincerity. It is a craven coward's plea. If we are to use the facts and the language of obstetrics to illustrate the great Russian tragedy, at least let us be honest and use them with some regard to the essential realities. In terms of obstetrics, Russia in 1917 was like unto a woman in the agony of her travail. From March onward she labored to give birth to her child, the long-desired democratic freedom. She was carefully watched and tenderly cared for by the accoucheur, the Provisional Government. At the critical moment of her delivery a ruthless brute drove the accoucheur away from her side, brutally maltreated her, strangled her newly born infant, and in its place substituted a hideous monstrosity. That is the only true application of the obstetrical simile to the realities of the Russian tragedy. The sufferings of Russia under the Bolsheviki have nothing to do with the natural birth pains of the Russian Revolution. Nobody ever expected the Russian Revolution to be accomplished without suffering and hardship; revolutions do not come that way. For all the natural and necessary pains of such a profound event as the birth of a new social order every friend of Russian freedom was prepared. What was not foreseen or anticipated by anybody was that when the agony of parturition was practically at an end, and the birth of the new order an accomplished fact, such a brutal assault would be made upon the maternal body of Russia. It is upon this crime, infamous beyond infamy, that the great jury of civilized public opinion is asked to pronounce its condemnation.

There is absolutely no justification for the view that the evils of the Bolshevist régime, and especially its terroristic features, should be regarded as the inevitable incidental evil accompaniments of a great beneficent process. Neither is any useful purpose served by dragging in the French Revolution. The champions of Bolshevism cite that great event and assert that everybody now acknowledges that it was a great liberating force, a notable advance in the evolution of freedom and democracy, and that nobody now condemns it on account of the Reign of Terror.

This argument is the result of a lamentable misreading of history, where it is not a deliberate and carefully studied deception. No honest parallel can be drawn between the French Revolution and the Bolshevist Counter-Revolution. That there are certain similarities between the revolutionary movement of eighteenth-century France and that of twentieth-century Russia is fairly obvious. In both cases the revolutions were directed against corrupt, inefficient, and oppressive monarchical absolutism. In France in 1789 the peasantry formed about 75 per cent. of the population, the bourgeoisie about 20 per cent., the proletariat about 3 per cent., and the "privileged" class about 1 per cent. In Russia in 1917 the peasantry amounted to something over 85 per cent. of the population, the bourgeoisie—the merchants, manufacturers, tradesmen, and investors—to about 9 per cent., the proletariat to about 3 per cent., and the nobility and clergy to 1 per cent. Both in France and in Russia the peasantry was identified with the struggle against monarchical absolutism, being motivated by great agrarian demands.

Moreover, the similarities extend to the moral and psychological factors involved. In the French Revolution, precisely as in the Russian, we see a great mass of illiterate peasants led by a few intellectuals, abstract thinkers wholly without practical experience in government or economic organization. In both cases we find a naïve Utopianism, a conviction that a sudden transformation of the whole social order could be easily effected. What the shibboleths of Karl Marx are to the Bolsheviki the shibboleths of Rousseau were to many of the leaders of the French Revolution. And just as in 1789 there was a pathetic dependence upon *anarchie spontanée*, a conviction, wholly non-rational and exclusively mystical, that in the chaos and disorder creative powers latent in the masses would be discovered—itself an evidence of the purely abstract character of their thinking—so it was in Russia in

1917. The revolution which overthrew the absolutism of Nicholas II of Russia repeated many of the characteristic features of that which overthrew the absolutism of Louis XVI of France.

Yet the true parallel to the French Revolution is not the Bolshevist *coup d'état*, but the Revolution of March, 1917. It was not the Bolshevist revolution that overturned the throne of the Romanovs and destroyed czarism. That was done by the March Revolution. Whereas the French Revolution was a revolution against a corrupt and oppressive monarchy, the Bolshevist revolt was a counter-revolution against democracy. The Bolsheviki had played only a very insignificant part in the revolution against czarism. They rose against the Provisional Government of the triumphant people. This Provisional Government represented the forces that had overthrown czarism; it was not a reactionary body of aristocrats and monarchists, but was mainly composed of Socialists and radicals and was thoroughly devoted to republicanism and democracy. It had immediately adopted as its program all that the French Revolution attained, and more: it had placed suffrage upon an even more generous basis, and dealt much more thoroughly with the land problem. The Directory put Gracchus Babeuf to death for advocating the redistribution of the land in 1795, but the Provisional Government of Russia did not hesitate to declare for that in 1917 and to create the machinery for carrying it into effect. At the very moment when it was overthrown by the Bolsheviki it was engaged in bringing about the election of the Constituent Assembly, the most democratic body of its kind in history.

Finally, just as the French Revolution was characterized by a passionate national consciousness and pride, so that it is customary to speak of it as the birth of French nationalism, so the Provisional Government represented a newly awakened

Russian nationalism. Bolshevism, on the contrary, in its early stages, at any rate, represented the opposite, a violent antagonism to the ideology and institutions of nationalism. The French in 1793, and throughout the long struggle, were zealous for France and in her defense; the Bolsheviki cared nothing for Russia and would sacrifice her upon the altar of world revolution. In view of all these facts, it is simply absurd to liken the Bolshevist phase of the Russian Revolution, the counter-revolutionary phase of it, to the French Revolution.

There were phases of the French Revolution which can be fairly likened to the Bolshevist phase of the Russian Revolution. There is a striking analogy between the Reign of Terror instituted in 1793 and the Red Terror which began in Russia early in 1918. The Montagnards and the Bolsheviki are akin; the appeal of the former to the sansculottes and of the latter to the proletariat are alike. In both cases we see a brutal and desperate attempt to establish the dictatorial rule of a class comprising only 3 per cent. of the population. There is an equally striking analogy between the struggle of the Girondins against the Jacobins in France and the struggle of the Socialists-Revolutionists and Social Democrats against the Bolsheviki. In Russia at the beginning of 1920 the significant term "Thermidorians" began to be used. To compare Bolshevism to the Jacobin phase of the French Revolution is quite a different matter from comparing it to the Revolution as a whole.

The permanent achievements of the French Revolution afford no justification for the Reign of Terror. The Revolution succeeded in spite of the Terror, not because of it, and the success was attended by evils which might easily have been averted. To condemn the Terror is not to decry the Revolution. Similarly, the Russian Revolution will succeed, we may well believe, not because of the Red Terror or of the Bolsheviki, but in spite of them. The bitterest opponents of the Bolsheviki are the most stalwart defenders of the Revolution. No appeal to the history of the French Revolution can extenuate or palliate the crimes of the Bolsheviki. Perhaps their greatest crime, the one which history will regard as most heinous, is their wanton disregard of all the lessons of that great struggle. They could not have entertained any rational hope of making their terrorism more complete or more fearful than was the Reign of Terror, which utterly failed to maintain the power of the proletariat. They could not have been unaware of the fierce resistance the Terror provoked and evoked, the counter-terror and the reaction—the Ninth Thermidor, the Directory, the *coup d'état* of the Eighteenth Brumaire, the Empire. They could not have been ignorant of the fact that the Reign of Terror divided and weakened the revolutionary forces. That they embarked upon their mad and brutal adventure in the face of the plain lessons of the French Revolution is the unpardonable crime of the Bolsheviki.

Despite their copying of the vices of the worst elements in the French Revolution, the Bolsheviki are most closely connected in their ideals and their methods with those cruel and adventurous social rebels of the seventeenth and eighteenth centuries, whose exploits, familiar to every Russian, are practically unknown to the rest of the world. Upon every page of the record of the Bolshevist régime there are reminders of the revolt of Bogdan Khnielnitski (1644-53) and that of Stenka Razin (1669-71). These cruel and bloodthirsty men, and others of the same kind who followed them, appealed only to the savage hatred and envy of the serfs, encouraged them to wanton destruction and frightful terror. Quite justly does the Zionist organ, *Dos Yiddishce Volk*,[71] say:

_71_ *July 11, 1919.*

> The slogans of Bolshevist practice are, in fact, the old Russian slogans with which the Volga bands of Pubachev and Razin ambushed the merchant wagon-trains and the Boyars. It is very characteristic that the Central Committee of the Communist Party has seen fit to unveil, on May 1st, at Moscow, a monument to the Ataman Stenka Razin, the hero of the Volga robber raids in the seventeenth century. Razin, indeed, is the legitimate father of Bolshevist practice.

Here we may as well give attention to another appeal which the Bolsheviki and their champions make to French history. They are fond of citing the Paris Commune of 1871, and claiming it as the model for their tactics. This claim, which is thoroughly dishonest, has often been made by Lenin himself. In the "Theses on Bourgeois and Proletarian Democracies," published in *Pravda*, March 8, 1919, Lenin says: "Precisely at the present moment when the Soviet movement, covering the whole world, continues the work of the Paris Commune before the eyes of the whole world, the traitors to Socialism forget concrete experiences and the concrete lessons of the Paris Commune, repeating the old bourgeois rubbish about 'democracy in general.' The Commune was not a parliamentary institution." On many occasions Lenin has made similar references to the Commune of 1871. The official Bolshevist press constantly indulges in such statements. The *Krasnaya Gazeta*, for example, published an article on the subject on December 17, 1919, parrot-like repeating Lenin's sophistries.

The simple facts are that (1) the Paris Commune had nothing to do with Communism or any other social theory. It was an intensely nationalistic movement, inspired by resentment of a peace which it regarded as dangerous and humiliating to France. It was a movement for local independence; (2) it was not a class movement, but embraced the bourgeoisie as well as the proletariat; (3) it *was* a "parliamentary institution," based upon universal, equal suffrage; (4) the first act of the revolutionists in 1871 was to appeal to the will of the people, through popular elections, in which all parties were free and voting was, as stated, based on equal and universal suffrage; (5) within two weeks the elections were held, with the result that sixty-five revolutionists were chosen as against twenty-one elected by the opposition parties. The opposition included six radical Republicans of the Gambetta school and fifteen reactionaries of various shades. In the majority were representatives of every Socialist group and faction; (6) the Communards never attempted to set up a minority dictatorship, but remained true to the principles of democracy. This Karl Marx himself emphasized in his *The Civil War in France*. Bolshevist "history" is as grotesque as Bolshevist economics! No matter what we may think of the Commune of 1871, it cannot justly be compared to the cruel betrayal of Russian democracy by the Bolsheviki. The Communards were democrats in the fullest sense of the term and their brief rule had the sanction of a popular majority.

The Bolsheviki and their defenders are never tired of contending that most of the sufferings of the Russian people during the Bolshevist régime have been due, not to those responsible for that régime, but to the "blockade" imposed by the Allies upon Russian trade with foreign nations. Perhaps no single argument has won so much sympathy from sentimental and ill-informed people as this. Yet the falsity of the contention has been demonstrated many times, even by those Russians opposed to the blockade. A brief summary of the salient facts will show that this claim has been used as a peg upon which to hang a propaganda remarkable for its insincerity and its trickery.

The blockade was declared in November, 1917, shortly after the Bolsheviki seized the machinery of government. It was already quite apparent that they would make a separate peace with Germany, and that Germany would be the dictator of the peace. There was great danger that supplies furnished to Russia under these conditions would be used by the Germans. As a policy, therefore, the blockade was dictated by military considerations of the highest importance and was directed against the Central Empires, and not primarily against the Bolsheviki. It was, of course, inevitable that it would inflict hardship upon Russia, our former ally, and not merely upon the Bolsheviki. So long as the Central Empires were in a position to carry on the fight, however, and especially after the Brest-Litovsk Peace gave Germany such a command over the life of Russia, the maintenance of the blockade seemed to be of the highest importance from a military point of view. That it entailed hardship and suffering upon people who were our friends was one of the numerous tragedies of the war, not more terrible, perhaps—except as regards the number of people affected—than many of the measures taken in those parts of France occupied by the enemy or in the fighting-zone.

After the armistice and the cessation of actual fighting the question at once took on a new aspect. Many persons—the present writer among the number—believed and urged that the blockade should then be lifted entirely. The issue was blurred, however, by the fact that while this would certainly give aid to the Bolsheviki there was no assurance that it would in any degree benefit the people in Russia who were opposed to them. The discrimination in favor of the Bolsheviki practised in the distribution of food and everything else was responsible for this. It must be borne in mind that the blockade did not cut off from Russia any important source of food-supply. Russia had never depended upon other nations for staple foods. On the contrary, she was a food-exporting country. She practically fed the greater part of western Europe. Cutting off her *imports* did not lessen the grain she had; cutting off her *exports* certainly had the effect of *increasing* the stores available for home consumption. All this is as plain as the proverbial pikestaff.

The starvation of the Russian people was not caused by the blockade, which did not lessen the amount of staple foods available, but, on the contrary, increased it. The real causes were these: the breakdown of the transportation system, which made it impossible to transport the grain to the great centers of population; the stupid policy of the Bolsheviki toward the peasants and the warfare consequent thereon; the demoralization of industry and the resulting inability to give the peasants manufactured goods in exchange for their grain. It may be objected, in reply to this statement, that but for the blockade it would have been possible to import railway equipment, industrial machinery, and so on, and that therefore the blockade was an indirect cause of food shortage. The fallacy in this argument is transparent: as to the industrial machinery, Soviet Russia had, and according to Rykov still has, much more than could be used. As regards large importations of manufactured goods and railway equipment, what would have been exported in exchange for such imports? The available stocks of raw materials, especially flax and hides, were exceedingly small and would have exchanged for very little. We have the authority of Rykov for this statement also.

What, then, was there available for export? The answer is—*food grains*! In almost every statement issued by the Bolsheviki in their propaganda against the blockade wheat figured as the most important available exportable commodity. The question arises, therefore, *how could the export of wheat from Russia help to feed her starving people*? If there was wheat for export, hunger was surely an absurdity! Victor Kopp, representative of the Soviet Government in Berlin, in a special interview published in the London *Daily Chronicle,* February 28, 1920, made this quite clear, pointing out that the hope that Russia would be able to send food grains to central Europe in exchange for manufactured goods was entirely unfounded, because Russia sorely needed all her foodstuffs of every kind. Krassin, head of the department of Trade and Commerce in the Soviet Government, told Mr. Copping—that most useful of phonographs!—that the shattered condition of transportation "leaves us temporarily unable to get adequate supplies of food for our own cities, and puts entirely out of the question any possibility, at present, of assembling goods at our ports for sending abroad."[72] As a matter of fact, the raising of the blockade, if, and in so far as, it led to an export of wheat and other food grains in return for manufactured goods, *would have increased the hunger and underfeeding of the Russian people.*

[72] *Daily Chronicle,* London, February 26, 1920.

The Bolsheviki knew this quite well and did not want the blockade raised. They realized that the propaganda in other countries against the blockade was an enormous asset to them, whereas removal of the blockade would reveal their weakness. Support is given to this contention by the following passage from Rykov's report in January of this year:

> It is the greatest fallacy to imagine that the lifting of the blockade or conclusion of peace is able in any degree to solve our raw-material crisis. *On the contrary, the lifting of the blockade and conclusion of peace, if such should take place, will mean an increased demand for raw materials*, as these are the only articles which Russia can furnish to Europe and exchange for European commodities. The supplies of flax on hand are sufficient for a period of from eight months to a year. *But we shall not be able to export large quantities of flax abroad*, and the catastrophic decline in flax production as compared with

1919 raises the question whether the flax industry shall not experience in 1920 a flax shortage similar to the one experienced by the textile industry in cotton.

In the spring of 1919 Mr. Alexander Berkenheim, one of the managers of the "Centrosoyuz," with other well-known Russian co-operators, represented to the British Government that the blockade of Russia was inflicting hardship and famine only, or at least mainly, upon the innocent civil population. They argued that if the blockade were lifted the Bolsheviki would see to the feeding of the general population. Berkenheim and his friends applied for permission for their association to send a steamer to Odessa laden with foodstuffs, medicines, and other supplies, to be distributed exclusively among children and sick and convalescing civilians. Backed by influential British supporters, Berkenheim and his friends gave guaranties that not a single pound of such supplies would reach the Red Army. All was to be distributed by the co-operatives without any interference by the authorities. The Bolshevist Government gave a similar guaranty, stated in very definite and unequivocal terms. Accordingly, the British Government consented to allow the steamer to sail, and in June, 1919, the steamer, with a cargo of tea, coffee, cocoa, and rice, consigned to the "Centrosoyuz," arrived at Odessa. But no sooner had the steamer entered the port than the whole cargo was requisitioned by the Soviet authorities and handed over to the organization supplying the Red Army.

This treachery was the principal cause of the continuance of the blockade. That it was intended to have precisely that effect is not improbable. On January 16, 1920, the Supreme Council of the League of Nations, at its first meeting, upon the proposal of the British Government, decided to so greatly modify the blockade as to amount to its practical abandonment. Trade was to be opened up with Russia through the co-operatives, it was announced. The co-operatives were to act as importing and exporting agencies, receiving clothing, machinery, medicines, railroad equipment, and so on, and exporting the "surplus" grain, flax, hides, and so on, in return.

Immediately after that arrangement was announced the Bolsheviki adopted an entirely new attitude. They began to raise hitherto unheard-of objections. They could not permit trade with the co-operatives on the conditions laid down; the co-operatives were not independent organizations, but a part of the Soviet state machinery; trade must accompany recognition of the Soviet Government, and so on. Thus the "diplomatic" arguments went. In Russia itself the leaders took the position expressed by Rykov in the speech already quoted.

To sum up: the blockade was a natural military measure of precaution, rendered necessary by the actions of the Bolsheviki; it was directed primarily against the Germans; it was not at any time a primary cause of the food shortage in Russia. When efforts were made to ameliorate the condition of the civil population by raising the blockade the Bolsheviki treacherously defeated such efforts. The prolonged continuation of the blockade was mainly due to the policy of obstruction pursued by the Bolsheviki. No large volume of trade could have been had with Russia at any time during the Bolshevist régime. The Bolsheviki themselves did not want the blockade removed, and finally confessed that such removal would not help them. Certainly, the Allies and the United States made many mistakes in connection with the blockade; but, when that has been fully admitted, and when all that can fairly be said against that policy has been said, it remains the fact that the Bolsheviki were responsible for creating the conditions which made the blockade necessary and inevitable, and that their treachery forced its continuation long after the

Allies had shown themselves ready and even anxious to abandon it. At every step of their fatal progress in the devastation and spoliation of Russia the treachery of the Bolsheviki, their entire lack of honor and good faith, appear.

Herein lies the real reason why no civilized government can with safety to its own institutions—to say nothing of regard for its own dignity and honor—enter into any covenant with the Bolshevist Government of Russia or hold official relations with it. At the root of Bolshevism lies a negation of everything of fundamental importance to the friendly and co-operative relations of governments and peoples. When the leaders of a government that is set up and maintained by brute force, and does not, therefore, have behind it the sanction of the will of its citizens, being subject to no control other than its own ambitions, declare that they will sign agreements with foreign nations without feeling in the slightest degree obligated by such agreements, they outlaw themselves and their government.

Not only have the Bolsheviki boasted that this was their attitude, but they have gone farther. Their responsible leaders and spokesmen—Lenin, Trotsky, Zinoviev, Kamenev, Radek, and others—have openly declared that they are determined to use any and all means to bring about revolts in all other civilized countries, to upset their governments and institute Bolshevist rule. They have declared that only by such a universal spread of its rule can Bolshevism be maintained in Russia. "Soviet Russia by its very existence is a ferment and a propagator of the inevitable world revolution," wrote Radek in Maximilian Harden's *Zukunft*, in February, 1920. Referring to the Spartacist uprisings in Germany, he said: "You are afraid of Bolshevist propaganda penetrating into Germany with other goods. You recall an experiment already carried out by Germany. *Yes, I glory in the results of our work.*" "One does not demand a patent for immortality from the man to whom one sells a suit of underclothing ... and our only concern is trade," said Radek in the same article. When Radek wrote that he knew that he was lying. He knew that, far from being their "only concern," trade was the least of the concerns of the Bolsheviki. Upon this point the evidence leaves no room for doubt. In *The Program of the Communist Party*, Chapter XIX, Bucharin says, "The program of the Communist Party is not alone a program of liberating the proletariat of one country; it is the program of liberating the proletariat of the world." Lenin wrote in *The Chief Tasks of Our Times*: "Only a madman can imagine that the task of overthrowing international imperialism can be fulfilled by Russians alone. While in the west the revolution is maturing and is making appreciable progress, the task before us is as follows: We who in spite of our weakness are in the forefront must do all in our power to retain the occupied positions.... We must strain every nerve in order to remain in power as long as possible, *so as to give time for a development of the western revolution*, which is growing much more slowly than we expected and wished." Zinoviev wrote in *Pravda*, November 7, 1919, that "in a year, in two years, the Communist International will rule the world." Kalinin, president of the All-Russian Central Executive Committee of the Soviet Power, in his New-Year's greeting for 1920, published in the *Krasnaya Gazeta*, January 1, 1920, declared that, "Western European brothers in the coming year should overthrow the rule of their capitalists and should join with the Russian proletariat and establish the single authority of the Soviets through the entire world under the protection of the Third International." Many other statements of a similar character could be quoted to show that the Russian Bolsheviki's chief concern is not trade, but world-wide revolt on Bolshevist lines.

That the Bolsheviki would use the privileges and immunities accorded to diplomatic representatives to foster Bolshevist agitation and revolt is made manifest by their utterances and their performances alike. "We have no desire to interfere in the internal affairs of any country," said Kopp, in the interview already quoted, and the Soviet Government has repeatedly stated its willingness to give assurances of non-interference with the political or economic system of other countries. But of what use are assurances from men who boast that they are willing to sign agreements without the slightest intention of being bound by them? Take, for example, Trotsky's statement, published at Petrograd, in February, 1918: "If, in awaiting the imminent proletarian flood in Europe, Russia should be compelled to conclude peace with the present-day governments of the Central Powers, it would be a provisional, temporary, and transitory peace, with the revision of which the European Revolution will have to concern itself in the first instance. *Our whole policy is built upon the expectation of this revolution.*" Precisely the same attitude toward the Allies was more bluntly expressed by Zinoviev on February 2, 1919, regarding the proposed Prinkipo Conference: "We are willing to sign an unfavorable peace with the Allies.... *It would only mean that we should put no trust whatever in the bit of paper we should sign.* We should use the breathing-space so obtained in order to gather our strength in order that the mere continued existence of our government would keep up the world-wide propaganda which Soviet Russia has been carrying on for more than a year." Of the Third International, so closely allied with the Soviet Government, Zinoviev is reported by Mr. Lincoln Eyre as saying: "Our propaganda system is as strong and as far-reaching as ever. The Third International is primarily an instrument of revolution. This work will be continued, no matter what happens, legally or illegally. The Soviet

Government may pledge itself to refrain from propaganda abroad, but the Third International, never."[73]

[73] *New York World, February 26, 1920.*

Finally, there is the speech of Lenin before the Council of the People's Commissaries during the negotiations upon the ill-starred Prinkipo Conference proposal, in which he said:

> The successful development of the Bolshevist doctrine throughout the world can only be effected by means of periods of rest during which we may recuperate and gather new strength for further exertions. I have never hesitated to come to terms with bourgeois governments, when by so doing I thought I could weaken the bourgeoisie. It is sound strategy in war to postpone operations until the moral disintegration of the enemy renders the delivery of a mortal blow possible. This was the policy we adopted toward the German Empire, and it has proved successful. *The time has now come for us to conclude a second Brest-Litovsk*, this time with the Entente. We must make peace not only with the Entente, but also with Poland, Lithuania, and the Ukraine, and all the other forces which are opposing us in Russia. *We must be prepared to make every concession, promise, and sacrifice in order to entice our foes into the conclusion of this peace.* We shall know that we have but concluded a truce permitting us to complete our preparations for a decisive onslaught which will assure our triumph.

In view of these utterances, and scores of others like them, of what value are the "assurances of non-interference" — or any other assurances — offered by Chicherine, Lenin, and the rest? But we are not confined to mere utterances: there are deeds aplenty which fully bear out the inferences we have from the words of the Bolshevist leaders. In a London court, before Mr. Justice Neville, it was brought out that the Bolshevist envoy, Litvinov, had been guilty of using his position to promote revolutionary agitation. Not only had Litvinov committed a breach of agreement, said Mr. Justice Neville, but he had been guilty of a breach of public law. A circular letter to the British trades-unions was read by the justice, containing these words: *"Hence it is that the Russian revolutionaries are summoning the proletarians of all countries to a revolutionary fight against their government."* Even worse was the case of the Bolshevist ambassador, Joffe, who was expelled from Berlin for using his diplomatic position to wage a propaganda for the overthrow of the German Government, and this notwithstanding the fact that the Treaty of Brest-Litovsk in its second article specifically forbade "any agitation against the state and military institutions of Germany."

In an official note to the German Foreign Office, published in *Izvestia*, December 26, 1918, Chicherine boasted that millions of rubles had been sent to Berlin for the purpose of revolutionary propaganda. The duplicity revealed by this note was quite characteristic of the Bolshevist régime and in keeping with the record of Chicherine himself in his relations with the British Government during his stay in London, where he acted as one of the representatives of the Russians in London who were seeking repatriation. *Izvestia*, on January 1, 1919, contained an article by Joffe on "Revolutionary Methods," in which he said: "Having accepted this forcibly imposed treaty [Brest-Litovsk], revolutionary Russia of course had to accept its second article, which forbade 'any agitation against the state and military institutions of Germany.' But both the Russian Government as a whole and its accredited representative in Berlin *never concealed the fact that they were not observing this article and did not intend to do so.*" As a matter of fact, the agitation against the German Government by the Bolsheviki continued even after the so-called supplementary treaties of Brest-Litovsk, dated August 27, 1918, which, as pointed out by the United States Department of State, were not signed under duress, as was the original treaty, but were actively sought for and gladly signed by the Bolsheviki.

In view of these indisputable facts, is there any honest and worthy reason for suspending judgment upon the character of the Soviet Government? Surely it must be plainly evident to every candid and dispassionate mind that Bolshevism is practically a negation of every principle of honor and good faith essential to friendly and co-operative relations among governments in modern civilization. The Bolsheviki have outlawed themselves and placed themselves outside the pale of the community of nations.

The merits of Sovietism as a method of government do not here and now concern us. But we are entitled to demand that those who urge us to adopt it furnish some evidence of its superiority in practice. Up to the present time, no such evidence has been offered by those who advocate the change; on the other hand, all the available evidence tends to show that Soviet government, far from being superior to our own, is markedly inferior to it. We are entitled, surely, to call attention to the fact that, so far as it has been tried in Russia, Sovietism has resulted in an enormous increase in bureaucracy; that it has not done away with corruption and favoritism in government; that it has shown itself to be capable of every abuse of which other forms of government, whether despotic, oligarchic, or democratic, have been capable. It has not given Russia a government one whit more humane or just, one whit less oppressive or corrupt than czarism. It seems to be inherently bureaucratic and therefore inefficient. Be that how it may, it is impossible to deny that it has failed and failed utterly. Even the Bolsheviki, whose sole excuse for their assault upon the rapidly evolving democracy of Russia was their faith in the superiority of Sovietism over parliamentary government, have found it necessary to abandon it, not only in government, but in industry and in military organization.

In industry Sovietism, so far as it has been tried in Russia, has shown itself to be markedly inferior to the methods of industrial organization common to the great industrial nations, and the so-called Soviet Government itself, which is in reality an oligarchy, has had to abandon it and to revert to the essential principles and methods of capitalist industry. This is not the charge of a hostile critic: it is the confession of Lenin, of Trotsky, of Krassin, of Rykov, and practically every acknowledged Bolshevist authority. We do not say that the Soviet idea contains nothing of good; we do not deny that, under a democratic government, Soviets might have aided, and may yet aid, to democratize Russian industrial life. What we do say is that the Bolsheviki have failed to make them of the slightest service to the Russian people; that Bolshevism has completely failed to organize the industrial life of Russia, either on Soviet lines or any other, and has had to revert to capitalism and to call upon the capitalists of other lands to come and rescue them from utter destruction. After ruthlessly exterminating their own capitalists, they have been compelled to offer to give foreign capitalists, in the shape of vast economic concessions, a mortgage upon the great heritage of future generations of the Russian people and the right to exploit their toil.

So, too, with the military organization of the country: Starting out with Soviet management in the army, the present rulers of Russia soon discovered that the system would not work. As early as January, 1918, Krylenko, Commander-in-Chief of the military forces of the Bolsheviki, reported to the Central Executive Committee that the soldiers' committees were "the only remnant of the army." In May, 1919, Trotsky was preaching the necessity of "respect for military science" and of "a genuine army, properly organized and firmly ruled by a single hand." Conscription was introduced, not by law enacted by responsible elected representatives of the people, but by decree. It was enforced with a brutality and savagery unknown to this age in any other country. Just as in industry the "bourgeois specialists" were brought back and compelled to work under espionage and duress, so the officers of the old imperial army were brought back and held to their tasks by terror, their wives and children and other relatives being held as hostages for their conduct. *Izvestia* published, September 18, 1918, Trotsky's famous Order No. 903, which read: "Seeing the increasing number of deserters, especially among the commanders, orders are issued to *arrest as hostages* all the members of the family one can lay hands on: father, mother, brother, sister, wife, and children." Another order issued by Trotsky in the summer of 1919 said, "In case an officer goes over to the enemy, *his family should be made to feel the consequences of his betrayal.*"

Pravda[74] published an article giving an account of the formation of a Red cavalry regiment. From that article we learn that every officer mobilized in the Red Army had to sign the following statement:

[74] *No. 11, 1919.*

> I have received due notice that in the event of my being guilty of treason or betrayal in regard to the Soviet Government, my nearest relatives [names given] residing at [full address given] will be responsible for me.

What this meant is known from the many news items in the Bolshevist press relating to the arrest, imprisonment, and even shooting of the relatives of deserters. To cite only one example: the *Krasnaya Gazeta*, November 4, 1919, published a "preliminary list" of nine deserting Red Army officers whose relatives—including mothers, fathers, sisters, brothers, and wives—had been arrested. *Izvestia* printed a list of deserters' relatives condemned to be shot, *including children fourteen and sixteen years old.*

At the Joint Conference on National Economy in Moscow, January, 1920, Lenin summed up the experience of the Bolsheviki with Soviet direction of the army, saying, "In the organization of the army we have passed from the principle of commanding by committee to the direct command of the chiefs. We must do the same in the organization of government and industry." And again, "The experience of our army shows us that primitive organization based on the collectivist principle becomes transformed into an administration based upon the principle of individual power." In the *Program of the Communists* we read that "The demand that the military command should be elective ... has no significance with reference to the Red Army, composed of class-conscious workmen and peasants." In a pamphlet issued by the All-Russian Central Executive Committee in the latter part of 1918 we read that "Regimental Committees, acting as administrative organs, cannot exist in the Soviet Army." These quotations amply prove that Sovietism in the army was found undesirable and unworkable by the Bolsheviki themselves and by them abandoned.

We remember the glowing promises with which the first Red Army was launched: volunteers considering it an honor to be permitted to fight for the Communist Utopia; the "collective self-discipline"; the direction of the whole military organization by soldiers' committees, and all the rest of the wild vision. We compare it with the brutal reality, and the contrast between the hope and the reality is the measure of the ghastly failure of Bolshevism. The military system of the Bolsheviki is infinitely more brutal than the old Prussian system was. The Red Army is an army of slaves driven by terrorized slaves. Sovietism proved a fool's fantasy. The old military discipline came back harsher than ever; the death penalty was restored; conscription and mobilization at the point of the bayonet were carried out with a ferocity never equaled in any modern nation, not even in Russia under Czar Nicholas II. Was there ever a more complete failure?

The mass of evidence we have cited from Bolshevist authorities warrants the judgment that Sovietism, as exemplified during the Bolshevist régime, in every department of the national life, is at best an utterly impracticable Utopian scheme. Certainly every fair-minded person of normal intelligence must agree that there is nothing in the record of the experiment—a record, be it remembered, made by the Bolsheviki themselves—to rouse enthusiastic hopes or to justify any civilized nation in throwing aside the existing machinery of government and industrial organization and immediately substituting Sovietism therefor.

As for Bolshevism, in contradistinction from Sovietism, there can be no hesitation in reaching a verdict upon the evidence supplied by its own accredited spokesmen and official records. We have not massed the isolated crimes of individuals and mobs and presented the result as a picture of Russian life. That would be as unjust as to list all the accounts of race riots, lynchings, and murders in this country and offering the list as a fair picture of American life. Ignoring these things completely, we have taken the laws and decrees of Soviet Russia; its characteristic institutions; the things done by its government; the writings and speeches of its statesmen and recognized interpreters; the cold figures of its own reports of industry and agriculture. The result is a picture of Bolshevism, self-drawn, more ugly and repellent than the most malicious imagination could have drawn.

On the other side there is no single worthy creative achievement to be recorded. There are almost innumerable "decrees," some of them attractive enough, but there are no actual achievements of merit to be credited to the Bolsheviki.

Even in the matter of education, concerning which we have heard so much, there is not a scintilla of evidence that will bear examination which tends to show that they have actually accomplished anything which Russia will gratefully remember or cherish in the days that are to come. The much-vaunted "Proletcult" of Soviet Russia is in practice little more than a means of providing jobs for Communists. The Bolshevist publicist, Mizkevich, made this charge in *Izvestia*, March 22, 1919. "The Proletcult is using up our not very numerous forces, and spending public money, which it gets from ... the Commissariat for Public Instruction, on the same work that is done by the Public Instruction departments ... opposes its own work for the creation of proletarian culture to the same work of the agents of the proletarian authority, and thus creates confusion in the minds of the proletarian mass."

The Bolsheviki have published decrees and articles on education with great freedom, but they have done little else except harm. They have weakened the great universities and rudely interrupted the development of the great movement to improve and extend popular education initiated shortly before the Revolution by Count Ignatiev, the best friend of popular education that ever held office in Russia, compared to whom Lunacharsky is a cretin. They have imposed upon the universities and schools the bureaucratic rule of men most of whom know nothing of university requirements, are at best poorly educated and sometimes even illiterate.

Promising peace and freedom from militarism, they betrayed their Allies and played the game of their foes; they brought new wars upon the already war-weary nation and imposed upon it a militarism more brutal than the old. Promising freedom, they have developed a tyranny more brutal and oppressive than that of the Romanovs. Promising humane and just government, they instituted the *Chresvychaikas* and a vast, corrupt bureaucracy. Promising to so organize production that there should be plenty for all and poverty for none, they ruined industrial production, decreased agricultural production to a perilously low level and so that famine reigned in a land of plentiful resources, human and material. Promising to make the workers masters of the machines, free citizens in a great industrial democracy, they have destroyed the machines, forced the workers to take the places of beasts of burden, and made them bond-slaves.

The evidence is in: let the jury render its verdict.

FINIS

DOCUMENTS

[1]

Decree Regarding Grain Control

The disastrous undermining of the country's food-supply, the serious heritage of the four years' war, continues to extend more and more, and to be more and more acute. While the consuming provincial governments are starving, in the producing governments there are at the present moment, as before, large reserves of grain of the harvests of 1916 and 1917 not yet even threshed. This grain is in the hands of tight-fisted village dealers and profiteers, of the village bourgeoisie. Well fed and well provided for, having accumulated enormous sums of money obtained during the years of war, the village bourgeoisie remains stubbornly deaf and indifferent to the wailings of starving workmen and peasant poverty, and does not bring the grain to the collecting-points. The grain is held with the hope of compelling the government to raise repeatedly the prices of grain, at the same time that the holders sell their grain at home at fabulous prices to grain speculators.

An end must be put to this obstinacy of the greedy village grain-profiteers. The food experience of former years showed that the breaking of fixed prices and the denial of grain monopoly, while lessening the possibility of feasting for our group of capitalists, would make bread completely inaccessible to our many millions of workmen and would subject them to inevitable death from starvation.

The answer to the violence of grain-owners toward the starving poor must be violence toward the bourgeoisie.

Not a pood should remain in the hands of those holding the grain, except the quantity needed for sowing the fields and provisioning their families until the new harvest.

This policy must be put into force at once, especially since the German occupation of the Ukraine compels us to get along with grain resources which will hardly suffice for sowing and curtailed use.

Having considered the situation thus created, and taking into account that only with the most rigid calculation and equal distribution of all grain reserves can Russia pass through the food crisis, the Central Executive Committee of All Russia has decreed:

1. Confirming the fixity of the grain monopoly and fixed prices, and also the necessity of a merciless struggle with grain speculators, to compel each grain-owner to declare the surplus above what is needed to sow the fields and for personal use, according to established normal quantities, until the new harvest, and to surrender the same within a week after the publication of this decision in each village. The order of these declarations is to be determined by the People's Food Commissioner through the local food organizations.

2. To call upon workmen and poor peasants to unite at once for a merciless struggle with grain-hoarders.

3. To declare all those who have a surplus of grain and who do not bring it to the collecting-points, and likewise those who

waste grain reserves on illicit distillation of alcohol and do not bring them to the collecting-point, enemies of the people; to turn them over to the Revolutionary Tribunal, imprison them for not less than ten years, confiscate their entire property, and drive them out forever from the communes; while the distillers are, besides, to be condemned to compulsory communal work.

In case an excess of grain which was not declared for surrender, in compliance with Article I, is found in the possession of any one the grain is to be taken away from him without pay, while the sum, according to fixed prices, due for the undeclared surpluses is to be paid, one-half to the person who points out the concealed surpluses, after they have been placed at the collecting-points, and the other half to the village commune. Declarations concerning the concealed surpluses are made by the local food organizations.

Further, taking into consideration that the struggle with the food crisis demands the application of quick and decisive measures, that the more fruitful realization of these measures demands in its turn the centralization of all orders dealing with the food question in one organization, and that this organization appears to be the People's Food Commissioner, the Central Executive Committee of All Russia hereby orders, for the more successful struggle with the food crisis, that the People's Food Commissioner be given the following powers:

1. To publish obligatory regulations regarding the food situation, exceeding the usual limits of the People's Food Commissioner's competence.

2. To abrogate the orders of local food bodies and other organizations contravening the plans and actions of the People's Commissioner.

3. To demand from institutions and organizations of all departments the carrying out of the regulations of the People's Food Commissioner in connection with the food situation without evasions and at once.

4. To use the armed forces in case resistance is shown to the removal of food grains or other food products.

5. To dissolve or reorganize the food agencies in places where they might resist the orders of the People's Commissioner.

6. To discharge, transfer, turn over to the Revolutionary Tribunal, or subject to arrest officials and employees of all departments and public organizations in case of interference with the orders of the People's Commissioner.

7. To transfer the present powers, in addition to the right to subject to arrest, above, to other persons and institutions in various places, with the approval of the Council of the People's Commissioners.

8. All understandings of the People's Commissioner, related in character to the Department of Ways of Communication and the Supreme Council of National Economy, are to be carried through upon consultation with the corresponding departments.

9. The regulations and orders of the People's Commissioner, issued in accordance with the present powers, are verified by his college, which has the right, without suspending their operation, of referring them to the Council of Public Commissioners.

10. The present decree becomes effective from the date of its signature and is to be put into operation by telegraph.

Published May 14, 1918.

//
Regulation Concerning the Administration of National Undertakings

Part I

1. The Central Administration of Nationalized Undertakings, of whatever branch of industry, assigns for each large nationalized undertaking technical and administrative directors, in whose hands are placed the actual administration and direction of the entire activity of the undertaking. They are responsible to the Central Administration and the Commissioner appointed by it.

2. The technical director appoints technical employees and gives all orders regarding the technical administration of the undertaking. The factory committee may, however, complain regarding these appointments and orders to the Commissioner of the Central Administration, and then to the Central Administration itself; but only the Commissioner and Central Administration may stop the appointments and order of the technical director.

3. In connection with the Administrative Director there is an Economic Administrative Council, consisting of delegates from laborers, employees, and engineers of the undertaking. The Council examines the estimates of the undertaking, the plan of its works, the rules of internal distribution, complaints, the material and moral conditions of the work and life of the

workmen and employees, and likewise all questions regarding the progress of the undertaking.

4. On questions of a technical character relating to the enterprise the Council has only a consultative voice, but on other questions a decisive voice, on condition, however, that the Administrative Director appointed by the Central Administration has the right to appeal from the orders of the Council to the Commissioner of the Central Administration.

5. The duty of acting upon decisions of the Economic Administrative Council belongs to the Administrative Director.

6. The Council of the enterprise has the right to make representation to the Central Administration regarding a change of the directors of the enterprise, and to present its own candidates.

7. Depending on the size and importance of the enterprise, the Central Administration may appoint several technical and administrative directors.

8. The composition of the Economic Administrative Council of the enterprise consists of (*a*) a representative of the workmen of the undertaking; (*b*) a representative of the other employees; (*c*) a representative of the highest technical and commercial personnel; (*d*) the directors of the undertaking, appointed by the Central Administration; (*e*) representatives of the local or regional council of professional unions, of the people's economic council, of the council of workmen's deputies, and to the professional council of that branch of industry to which the given enterprise belongs; (*f*) a representative of the workmen's co-operative council; and (*g*)

a representative of the Soviet of peasants' deputies of the corresponding region.

9. In the composition of the Economic Administrative Council of the enterprise, representatives of workmen and other employees, as mentioned in points (*a*) and (*b*) of Article VIII, may furnish only half of the number of members.

10. The workmen's control of nationalized undertakings is realized by leaving all declarations and orders of the factory committee, or of the controlling commission, to the judgment and decision of the Economic Administrative Council of the enterprise.

11. The workmen, employees, and highest technical and commercial personnel of nationalized undertakings are in duty bound before the Russian Soviet Republic to observe industrial discipline and to carry out conscientiously and accurately the work assigned to them. To the Economic Administrative Council are given judicial rights, including that of dismissal without notice for longer or shorter periods, together with the declaration of a boycott for non-proletariat recognition of their rights and duties.

12. In the case of those industrial branches for which Central Administrations have not yet been formed, all their rights are vested in provincial councils of the national economy, and in corresponding industrial sections of the Supreme Council of the National Economy.

13. The estimates and plan of work of a nationalized undertaking must be presented by its Economic Administrative Council to the Central Administration of a given industrial branch at least as often as once in three

months, through the provincial organizations, where such have been established.

14. The management of nationalized undertakings, where such management has heretofore been organized on other principles because of the absence of a general plan and general orders for the whole of Russia, must now be reorganized, in accordance with the present regulation, within the next three months (*i.e.*, by the end of May, new style).

15. For the consideration of the declarations of the Economic Administrative Council concerning the activity of the directors of the undertaking at the Central Administration of a given branch of industry, a special section is established, composed one-third of representatives of general governmental, political, and economic institutions of the proletariat, one-third of representatives of workmen and other employees of the given industrial branch, and one-third of representatives of the directing, technical, and commercial personnel and its professional organizations.

16. The present order must be posted on the premises of each nationalized undertaking.

Note.—Small nationalized enterprises are managed on similar principles, with the proviso that the duties of technical and administrative directors may be combined in one person, and the numerical strength of the Economic Administrative Council may be cut down by the omission of representatives of one or another institution or organization.

Part II

17. A Central Administration [Principal Committee] for each nationalized branch of industry is to be established in connection with the Supreme Council of the National Economy, to be composed one-third of representatives of workmen and employees of a given industrial branch; one-third of representatives of the general proletariat, general governmental, political, and economic organizations and institutions (Supreme Council of National Economy, the People's Commissioners, All-Russian Council of Professional Unions, All-Russian Council of Workmen's Co-operative Unions, Central Executive Committee of the Councils of Workmen's Delegates) and one-third of representatives of scientific bodies, of the supreme technical and commercial personnel, and of democratic organizations of All Russia (Council of the Congresses of All Russia, co-operative unions of consumers, councils of peasants' deputies).

18. The Central Administration selects its bureau, for which all orders of the Central Administration are obligatory, which conducts the current work and carries into effect the general plans for the undertaking.

19. The Central Administration organizes provincial and local administrations of a given industrial branch, on principles similar to those on which its own organization is based.

20. The rights and duties of each Central Administration are indicated in the order concerning the establishment of each of them, but in each case each Central Administration unites, in its own hands (*a*) the management of the enterprises of a given industrial branch, (*b*) their financing, (*c*) their technical unification or reconstruction, (*d*) standardization of the working conditions of the given industrial branch.

21. All orders of the Supreme Council of National Economy are obligatory for each Central Administration; the Central Administration comes in contact with the Supreme Council in the person of the bureau of productive organization of the Supreme Council of National Economy through the corresponding productive sections.

22. When the Central Administration for any industrial branch which has not yet been nationalized is organized, it has the right to sequestrate the enterprises of the given branch, and equally, without sequestration, to prevent its managers completely or in part from engaging in its administration, appoint commissioners, give orders, which are obligatory, to the owners of non-nationalized enterprises, and incur expenses on account of these enterprises for measures which the Central Administration may consider necessary; and likewise to combine into a technical whole separate enterprises or parts of the same, to transfer from some enterprises to others fuel and customers' orders, and establish prices upon articles of production and commerce.

23. The Central Administration controls imports and exports of corresponding goods for a period which it determines, for which purpose it forms a part of the general governmental organizations of external commerce.

24. The Central Administration has the right to concentrate, in its hands and in institutions established by it, both the entire preparation of articles necessary for a given branch of industry (raw material, machinery, etc.) and the disposal to enterprises subject to it of all products and acceptances of orders for them.

Part III

25. Upon the introduction of nationalization into any industrial branch, or into any individual enterprise, the corresponding Central Administration (or the temporary Central Administration appointed with its rights) takes under its management the nationalized enterprises, each separately, and preserves the large ones as separate administrative units, annexing to them the smaller ones.

26. Until the nationalized enterprises have been taken over by the Central Administration (or principal commissioner) all former managers or directorates must continue their work in its entirety in the usual manner, and under the supervision of the corresponding commissioner (if one has been appointed), taking all measures necessary for the preservation of the national property and for the continuous course of operations.

27. The Central Administration and its organs establish new managements and technical administrative directorates of enterprises.

28. Technical administrative directorates of nationalized enterprises are organized according to Part I of this Regulation.

29. The management of a large undertaking, treated as a separate administrative unit, is organized with a view to securing, in as large a measure as possible, the utilization of the technical and commercial experience accumulated by the undertaking; for which purpose there are included in the composition of the new management not only representatives of the laborers and employees of the enterprise (to the number of one-third of the general numerical strength of the management) and of the Central Administration itself (to the

number of one-third or less, as the Central Administration shall see fit), but also, as far as possible, members of former managements, excepting persons specially removed by the Central Administration and, upon their refusal, representatives of any special competent organizations, even if they are not proletariat (to a number not exceeding one-third of the general membership of the management).

30. When nationalization is introduced, whether of the entire branch of the industry or of separate enterprises, the Central Administrations are permitted, in order to facilitate the change, to pay to the highest technical and commercial personnel their present salaries, and even, in case of refusal on their part to work and the impossibility of filling their places with other persons, to introduce for their benefit obligatory work and to bring suit against them.

31. The former management of each nationalized undertaking must prepare a report for the last year of operation and an inventory of the undertaking, in accordance with which inventory the new management verifies the properties taken over. The actual taking over of the enterprise is done by the new management immediately upon its confirmation by the principal committee, without waiting for the presentation of the inventory and report.

32. Upon receipt in their locality of notice of the nationalization of some enterprise, and until the organization of the management and its administration by the Central Administration (or the principal commissioner, or institution having the rights of the principal commissioner) the workmen and employees of the given enterprise, and, if possible, also the Council of Workmen's Deputies, the Council of National Economy, and Council of Professional Unions, select temporary commissioners, under whose supervision and

observation (and, if necessary, under whose management) the activity of the undertaking continues. The workmen and employees of the given enterprise, and the regional councils of national economy, of professional unions, and of workmen's delegates have the right also to organize temporary managements and directorates of nationalized enterprises until the same are completely established by the Central Administration.

33. If the initiative for the nationalization of a given enterprise comes, not from the general governmental and proletariat organs authorized for that purpose, but from the workmen of a given enterprise or from some local or regional organization, then they propose to the Supreme Council of National Economy, in the bureau of organization of production, that the necessary steps be undertaken through the proper production sections, according to the decree of 28th February regarding the method of confiscating enterprises.

34. In exceptional cases local labor organizations are given the right to take temporarily under their management the given enterprise, if circumstances do not permit of awaiting the decision of the question in the regular order, but on condition that such action be immediately brought to the notice of the nearest provincial council of national economy, which then puts a temporary sequestration upon the enterprise pending the complete solution of the question of nationalization by the Supreme Council of National Economy; or, if it shall consider the reasons insufficient, or nationalization clearly inexpedient, or a prolonged sequestration unnecessary, it directs a temporary sequestration or even directly re-establishes the former management of the enterprise under its supervision, or introduces into the composition of the management representatives of labor organizations.

35. The present order must be furnished by the professional unions of All Russia to all their local divisions, and by the councils of factory committees to all factory committees, and must be published in full in the *Izvestia* of all provincial councils of workmen's and peasants' deputies.

Published March 7, 1918.

III

Instructions on Workers' Control

(Official Text)

I. Agencies of Workers' Control in Each Enterprise.

I. Control in each enterprise is organized either by the Shop or Factory Committee, or by the General Assembly of workers and employees of the enterprise, who elect a Special Commission of Control.

II. The Shop or Factory Committee may be included in its entirety in the Control Commission, to which may be elected also technical experts and other employees of the enterprise. In large-scale enterprises, participation of the employees in the Control Commission is compulsory. In large-scale enterprises a portion of the members of the Control Commission is elected by trade sections and classes, at the rate of one to each trade section or class.

III. The workers and employees not members of the Control Commission may not enter into relations with the management of the enterprise on the subject of control except upon the direct order and with the previous authorization of the Commission.

IV. The Control Commission is responsible for its activity to the General Assembly of employees and workers of the enterprise, as well as to the agency of workers' control upon which it is dependent and under the direction of which it functions. It makes a report of its activity at least twice a month to these two bodies.

II. Duties and Privileges of the Control Commission.

V. The Control Commission of each enterprise is required:

1. To determine the stock of goods and fuel possessed by the plant, and the amount of these needed respectively for the machinery of production, the technical personnel, and the laborers by specialties.
2. To determine to what extent the plant is provided with everything that is necessary to insure its normal operation.
3. To forecast whether there is danger of the plant closing down or lowering production, and what the causes are.
4. To determine the number of workers by specialties likely to be unemployed, basing the estimate upon the reserve supply and the expected receipt of fuel and materials.
5. TO DETERMINE THE MEASURES TO BE TAKEN TO MAINTAIN DISCIPLINE IN WORK AMONG THE WORKERS AND EMPLOYEES.
6. To superintend the execution of the decisions of governmental agencies regulating the buying and selling of goods.
7. (A) TO PREVENT THE ARBITRARY REMOVAL OF MACHINES, MATERIALS, FUEL, ETC., FROM THE PLANT WITHOUT AUTHORIZATION FROM THE AGENCIES WHICH REGULATE ECONOMIC AFFAIRS, AND TO SEE THAT INVENTORIES ARE NOT TAMPERED WITH.

(b) To assist in explaining the causes of the lowering of production and to take measures for raising it.

8. To assist in elucidating the possibility of a complete or partial utilization of the plant for some kind of production (especially how to pass from a war to a peace footing, and what kind of production should be undertaken), to determine what changes should be made in the equipment of the plant and in the number of its personnel to accomplish this purpose; to determine in what period of time these changes can be effected; to determine what is necessary in order to make them, and the probable amount of production after the change is made to another kind of manufacture.

9. To aid in the study of the possibility of developing the kinds of labor required by the necessities of peace-times, such as the method of using three shifts of workmen, or any other method, by furnishing information on the possibilities of housing the additional number of laborers and their families.

10. TO SEE THAT THE PRODUCTION OF THE PLANT IS MAINTAINED AT THE FIGURES TO BE FIXED BY THE GOVERNMENTAL REGULATING AGENCIES, AND, UNTIL SUCH TIME AS THESE FIGURES SHALL HAVE BEEN FIXED, TO SEE THAT THE PRODUCTION REACHES THE NORMAL AVERAGE FOR THE PLANT, JUDGED BY A STANDARD OF CONSCIENTIOUS LABOR.

11. To co-operate in estimating costs of production of the plant upon the demand of the higher agency of workers' control or upon the demand of the governmental regulating institutions.

VI. Upon the owner of the plant, the decisions of the Control Commission, which are intended to assure him the possibility of accomplishing the objects stated in the preceding articles, are binding. In particular the Commission may, of itself or through its delegates:

1. Inspect the business correspondence of the plant, all the books and all the accounts pertaining to its past or present operation.

2. Inspect all the divisions of the plant—shops, stores, offices, etc.

3. Be present at meetings of the representatives of the directing agencies; make statements and address interpellations to them on all questions relating to control.

VII. The right to give orders to the directors of the plant, and the management and operation of the plant are reserved to the owner. The Control Commission does not participate in the management of the plant and has no responsibility for its development and operation. This responsibility rests upon the owner.

VIII. The Control Commission is not concerned with financial questions of the plant. If such questions arise they are forwarded to the governmental regulating institutions.

IX. The Control Commission of each enterprise may, through the higher organ of workers' control, recommend for the consideration of the governmental regulating institutions the question of the sequestration of the plant or other measures of constraint upon the plant, but it has not the right to seize and direct the enterprise.

III. Resources of the Control Commission of each Plant.

X. To cover the expenses of the Control Commission, the owner is bound to place at its disposal not more than two per cent. of the amount paid out by the plant in wages. The wages lost by the members of the Factory or Shop Committee and by the members of the Control Commission as a result of performing their duties during working hours when they cannot be performed otherwise, are paid out of this two-per-cent. account. Control over expenditures from the above-mentioned fund is exercised by the Commission of Control and Distribution of the trades-unions of the industrial branch concerned.

IV. Higher Agencies of Workers' Control.

XI. The organ immediately superior to the Control Commission of each enterprise consists of the Commission of Control and Distribution of the trades-union of the industrial branch to which the plant in question belongs.

All decisions of the Control Commissions of each enterprise may be appealed to the Commission of Control and Distribution of the trades-union exercising jurisdiction.

XII. At least half of the members of the Commission of Control and Distribution are elected by the Control Commissions (or their delegates) of all plants belonging to the same branch of industry. These are convened by the directors of the trades-union. The other members are elected by the directors, or by delegates, or else by the General Assembly of the trades-union. Engineers, statisticians, and other persons who may be of use, are eligible to election to membership in the Commission of Control and Distribution.

XIII. The executive directorate of the union is authorized to direct and review the activity of the Commission of Control and Distribution and of the Control Commission of each plant under its jurisdiction.

XIV. The Control Commission of each plant constitutes the executive agency of the Commission of Control and Distribution for its branch of industry, and is bound to make its activity conform to the decisions of the latter.

XV. The Commission of Control and Distribution of the trades-union has the authority of its own accord to convene the General Assembly of workers and employees of each enterprise, to require new elections of Control Commissions of each plant, and likewise to propose to the governmental regulating agencies the temporary closing down of plants or the dismissal of all the personnel or of a part of it, in case the workers employed in the plant will not submit to its decisions.

XVI. The Commission of Control and Distribution has entire control over all branches of industry within its district, and according to the needs of any one plant in fuel, materials, equipment, etc., assists that plant in obtaining supplies from the reserve of other plants of the same kind either in active operation or idle. If other means cannot be found, it proposes to the Governmental Regulating Commissions to close down particular plants so that others may be sustained, or to place the workmen and employees of plants which have been closed down, either temporarily or definitively, in other plants engaged in the same kind of manufacture, or to take any other measures which are likely to prevent the closing down of plants or an interruption in their operation, or which are thought capable of insuring the regular operation of said plants in conformity with the plans and decisions of the governmental regulating agencies.

Remark.—The Commissions of Control and Distribution issue technical instructions for the Control Commissions of each plant of their branch of industry and according to their technical specialties. These instructions must not in any respect be inconsistent with these regulations.

XVII. Appeal may be made against all decisions and all acts of the Commission of Control and Distribution to the regional Council of Workers' Control.

XVIII. The operating expenses of the Commission of Control and Distribution for each branch of industry are covered by the balances in the treasury of each plant (Art. 17) and by equal assessments on the state and the trades-union exercising jurisdiction.

XIX. The Local Council of Workers' Control considers and decides all questions of a general nature for all or for any of the Commissions of Control and Distribution of a given locality and co-ordinates their activity to conform with advices received from the All-Russian Council of Control by the Workers.

XX. Each Council of Workers' Control should enact compulsory regulations to govern the working discipline of the workmen and employees of the plants under its jurisdiction.

XXI. The Local Council of Workers' Control may establish within it a council of experts, economists, statisticians, engineers, or other persons who may be useful.

XXII. The All-Russian Council of Workers' Control may charge the All-Russian Trades-Union or the regional trades-union of any branch of industry with the duty of forming an All-Russian Commission or a Regional Commission of Control and Distribution, for the given branch of industry. The regulations for such an All-Russian or Regional Commission of Control and Distribution, drafted by the Union, must be approved by the All-Russian Council of Workers' Control.

XXIII. All decisions of the All-Russian Soviet of Workers' Control and all decisions of other governmental regulating agencies in the realm of economic regularization are binding upon all the agencies of the institution of workers' control.

XXIV. These regulations are binding upon all institutions of workers' control, and apply *in toto* to plants which employ one hundred or more workmen and employees. Control over plants employing a smaller personnel will be effected as far as possible on the basis of these instructions as a model.

THE END

www.ingramcontent.com/pod-product-compliance
Lightning Source LLC
Chambersburg PA
CBHW062121280526
45788CB00001B/11